Towards a Varieties Grammar of English

Urs Dürmüller

Towards a Varieties Grammar of English

PETER LANG
Berne, Frankfurt/M.

CIP-Kurztitelaufnahme der Deutschen Bibliothek

Dürmüller, Urs:
Towards a Varieties Grammar of English / Urs Dürmüller. – Berne; Frankfurt/M.: Lang, 1983.
ISBN 3-261-05027-6

Published with support of the Swiss National Science Foundation.
800 copies

Table of Contents

Acknowledgments

I wish to express my gratitude to the Swiss National Science Foundation, which, through a generous grant made it possible for me to take leave from my everyday duties in Berne, Switzerland, and pursue my research interests abroad.

While being affiliated with the Department of Linguistics, University of California at Berkeley (October 1978 to June 1980) and the Summer Institute of the Linguistic Society of America, Department of Linguistics, University of New Mexico at Albuquerque (June 1980 to August 1980) I greatly profited from the erudition and expertise of a great number of truly outstanding scholars. My thanks are due in particular to Alan DUNDES, Susan ERVIN-TRIPP, Charles FILLMORE, John GUMPERZ, Paul KAY, George LAKOFF, John SEARLE (Berkeley) and to Derek BICKERTON, Allan HUDSON-EDWARDS, Garland BILLS, Joshua FISHMAN and Michael SILVERSTEIN (Summer Institute of the Linguistic Society of America 1980); they all gave generously of their time to answer my questions and discuss my queries, to listen to or read my manuscripts and comment on them.

I am also grateful to John SPENCER (Leeds) for good counsel concerning the scope of my project in its initial stage; to Burton RAFFEL (Denver) for advice on chapter 1; to Riley SMITH (Bloomsbury) and John ALGEO (Georgia) for commentary on chapter 2; to Peter TRUDGILL (Reading), Karana HATTERSLY-DRAYTON (Berkeley), Catherine DAVIES (Berkeley) and Allan METCALF (Linguistic Atlas of California) for their remarks on materials contained in chapter 3; to Elizabeth TRAUGOTT (Stanford) and Svenka SAVIC (Novi Sad) for illuminating comments and suggestions concerning various aspects of chapter 4.

I was also fortunate enough to have several papers connected with this study accepted by various conference selection committees. In particular I should like to mention «An Outside View of American English Language Varieties», invited by the American Dialect Society, Pacific Coast Regional Meeting, California State University Sacramento, May 5, 1979; «English Language Varieties in the San Francisco Bay Area», invited by the 1980 Summer Meeting of the American Dialect Society, University of New Mexico, Albuquerque, July 17, 1980; «Anathema: Holistic Grammar», Seminar, invited by the 1980 Linguistic Society of America Summer Institute, University of New Mexico, Albuquerque, July 31, 1980; «Towards a Varieties Grammar of English», British Association for Applied Linguistics, Annual Meeting, University of Sussex, September 18–20, 1981; and «Problems in the Writing of Varieties Grammars», Xth World Congress of Sociology, UNAM, Mexico City, August 16–21, 1982. These papers contain substantial parts of chapters 2, 3, and 4 of the present study. I still appreciate the opportunities I had to present my ideas on these fora.

My thanks are also due to Professors R. Fricker, H. Utz and G. Redard of Berne University who encouraged me to pursue my interests in the United States.

Finally, my thanks are due to my family, my wife and my children, who accompanied me to the Far West and provided me not only with a true home but also with a relativizing perspective on linguistics.

General Introduction

Towards a Varieties Grammar of English attempts to investigate and discuss some of the implications and possibilities of a manual written to bring together various varieties of the English language. The study does not actually present such a varieties grammar of English, but it prepares the ground for such future work. This is done by concentrating on three separate approach areas, which are each focussed on in one of the three parts of the study.

Part I is concerned with the impact of language variation on communication in society. It proceeds from the outsider's observations on the status and functions of language varieties in English speaking countries – a perspective so far not yet adopted in comparable studies – and then extends this view to overlap with that of the native speaker's. The only position available to the outsider, i.e. to accept all the varieties of English, including dialects, as registers, is the position also taken by the native speaker once he is confronted with the selection mechanism of a varieties grammar. A varieties grammar, it is suggested, must be written as a grammar of choice, a grammar with a functional dimension.

In Part II, the question of competence in a varieties grammar is investigated through an account of a number of English language varieties.

It is one of the by-products of this study that it offers, in chapter 3, a first social dialectology of the English language in the San Francisco Bay Area and thus also a first approach to a description of California English that goes beyond Anglo English. This part of the study reveals that competence in a varieties grammar based on a selection mechanism cannot be limited to a narrowly conceived linguistic competence, but must include cultural aspects of language. Since it is concluded that a varieties grammar would have to account for considerably more than only phonology and syntax, the discussion on language varieties and notions of grammar in Part III (chapter 4) makes holism an important issue and redefines grammar in holistic terms. Throughout the study, varieties are defined as typolects. Although there are a number of 'lectal' terms available already, I introduce 'typolect' as a new term. It is proposed as a useful tool for descriptive linguistics since it contrasts with idiolect and covers various types of language varieties. It is shown that typolects can be defined in terms of folklore, in terms of stylistics, and in terms of various sociolinguistic models.

As the title of the study indicates, no varieties grammar of English is presented here. The difficulties suspected in chapter 1 as awaiting any linguist attempting to write a varieties grammar are indeed there, and in formidable proportions. The present study concludes that the idea of producing a formal varieties grammar for all the varieties of English must be given up, but it indicates nevertheless that at least the writing of less formalized ad hoc varieties grammars might be possible. Such a varieties grammar would be set up for a preferably small repertoire of English language varieties within the taxonomic system of the potential-selection model sketched at the end of Part III. The simplest case would involve typolectal varieties taken from existing corpora and fed into a computer according to the principles of unit classification and rule ordering required by a holistic varieties grammar.

Towards a Varieties Grammar of English – the title of the study has a tentative ring because there are still so many points to be debated; because the problems to be solved are still enormous. Nevertheless, the concept of a varieties grammar remains a challenge, a topic to be tackled, even if the contribution of a single scholar is relatively small and can only be tentative. It is as a modest contribution towards the still evasive goal of a varieties grammar that this study should be read, stimulating discussion, I hope, because of the novel and probably unorthodox positions it takes. As such it is much more open to attack than if it had been conceived within the safe home of a well-established theoretical framework. I do hope, however, that even linguists who will have to take issue with me will share my conviction that advances in linguistics today seem most promising if canonical theories are questioned and if the raw linguistic data are again allowed to have some impact.

URS DÜRMÜLLER University of Bern
English Seminar March 1982

Part I: Introduction

Part I contains two chapters. Chapter 1 explores the notion and the implications of a varieties grammar from the Babel myth to considerations in present-day educational politics. While chapter 1 also serves some general introductory function in that it sounds most of the topics that are later on taken up in more detail, chapter 2 establishes the outside point of view from which the functional status of varieties in a varieties grammar is deduced. Speaker (mainly EFL) attitudes towards English language varieties are discussed, and, along the line begun in chapter 1, some reasons are given why an approach towards a varieties grammar of English is undertaken at all. It is argued that a varieties grammar might be a means to bridge gaps in communication not only in the case of EFL speakers encountering speakers of diverse English language varieties, but also in the case of native speakers of English belonging to different groups. A varieties grammar should not aim at comprising the whole of English, but at a few varieties only, such as those represented in speech repertoires.

CHAPTER 1

1 Exploring the Notion of a Varieties Grammar

1.1 The After Babel Dilemma

> First, the whole earth was of one language and of one speech. Then pride filled the hearts of men so that they started to build a city and a tower whose top was to reach unto heaven. However, the Lord Jehova came down to earth to punish this presumption. He confounded the language of men so that they might no longer understand one another's speech. They were no longer able to cooperate in the building of their tower and were scattered abroad upon the face of all the earth.
>
> (*Genesis* 11:1–9)

This is the story of the tower of Babylon as it is reported to us in *Genesis*. The sins and prides of Babylon were punished, and mankind was cursed with sharing not one, but speaking many different tongues.[1] In his highly intriguing book, *After Babel*, George STEINER takes up the myth in order to deal with one of its legacies: the need for translation. Although he devotes much space and argumentation to the topic of translating from one language into another, he is also aware that translation is frequently necessary even within one such language. Like many linguists today, STEINER considers language as something heterogenous, having a number of language varieties. For example, he evokes «the phonetician's parlour-trick to locate, often to within a few dozen miles, the place of origin of an American from the border states or a north-country Englishman» (1976:31); he also comments lucidly on upper-class English diction, which «with its sharpened vowels, elisions, and modish slurs, is both a code for mutual recognition – accent is worn like a coat of arms – and an instrument of ironic exclusion. (. . .) The ornamental irrelevancies and elided insinuations are not addressed so much to the tradesman or visitor as to one's fellow

1 By far the best account of the myth and its many ramifications can be found in BORST 1957–63.

officer or clubman who will recognize in them signals of complicity» (32); he has noticed that «the privileged speak to the world at large as they do to themselves, in a conspicuous consumption of syllables, clauses, prepositions, concomitant with their economic resources and the spacious quarters they inhabit» and that «men and women of the lower class do not speak to their masters and enemies as they do to one another, hoarding what expressive wealth they have for internal use. (. . .) Very often the seeming inarticulateness of the labourer, the thick twilight of Cockney speech, or the obeisant drag of Negro response are a well-judged feint.» (33) Between dialectal and sociolectal varieties like these as well as between other varieties correlated with various types of situations, STEINER finds a «self-evident» need for translation. (32) Yet – and this is what I want to argue here – in order to make translation from one language variety into another possible, a key to the different uses of inflection, syntactical structures, choices and meanings of words and phrases, text types and discourse conventions must be found.

George STEINER, who is so perfectly at home in so many languages, is not only an expert in language translation, but also, which goes along with it, a sharp observer of language forms. Since he has three mother-tongues which he speaks and writes with indistinguishable ease[2], he can adopt a uniquely advantageous stance towards any of them: at once intuitive (from the inside) and critical (from the outside). I cannot adopt this double view-point; when dealing with English, I have no choice but to approach that language and its varieties from an outside point of view. English is not my mother-tongue, and my knowledge of it not an intimate one. However, it seems to me that the outsider is in a more advantageous, because more objective, position vis-a-vis the varieties of a language than the average insider. For what should be obvious to native speakers (but not always is) is strikingly evident to the

2 «Tests made of my ability to perform rapid routine calculations in them have shown no significant variations of speech or accuracy. I dream with equal verbal density and linguistic-symbolic provocation in all three. (. . .) Attempts to locate a 'first language' under hypnosis have failed.» (1976:115) STEINER's three mother-tongues are English, French, and German.

outsider: English is not English: There are several and distinct varieties of English. The curse of Babel is felt even in clearly delimited areas where ethnic groups, social classes, different generations and professions use kinds of English deviant from the standard set by educational institutions and distinct from each other. In order to understand varieties which are not part of their own speech repertoires insiders and outsiders alike are faced with the necessity to translate; but in order to be able to translate, they have to know the linguistic characteristics of the varieties in question. Since learning is the obvious key to a language problem like that, a student would want to turn to a grammar (a pedagogical grammar, i.e.). Yet, there are no grammars that build easy bridges between the varieties of a language. Although there are several accounts of single varieties (mostly dialects) and some contrastive studies of a certain dialect or sociolect versus the standard language, a grammar for several varieties of English does not exist yet. To date, no one has compiled the storehouse of information about the individual varieties of English to which a student or teacher (whether insider or outsider) might turn in order to explain one variety in terms of another or with reference to a wider frame. Having such a varieties grammar at hand might be a means to remove some of the effects of the curse of Babel, at least within one language.

Einar HAUGEN, in his essay «The Curse of Babel», lists some other efforts made by man to remove the obstacle of language diversity: «The economic disadvantages of having more than one language in a country or in the world are so patent as to make an almost irresistible argument for homogenization to be used by administrators who are congenitally and professionally hostile to language minorities. Such people argue for (1) assimilation by force; (2) assimilation by precept; (3) assimilation by teaching. In any case assimilation. Groups that refuse to assimilate must either be (1) repatriated or (2) segregated. Repatriation can be brutal and may be impossible. Segregation is contrary to the spirit of an open society. Yet it is the policy practiced by most religious communities and the ultimate justification for the existence of nations. Within a nation it is enforced by geographical separation, by economic necessity, by class differences, and by caste distinctions.» (1973:55) It becomes clear that HAUGEN cannot back any of these solutions. Instead he pleads for two «humanistic solutions» that «suggest themselves immediately to men of good will». These are: «(1) deliberately to inculcate and to promote by means of education a spirit in the general population of interest and understanding of minority peoples, and (2) to make sure that people who speak differently understand and are understood, if necessary by making them bilingual.» (55) HAUGEN thus does not want to go back to the *status quo ante*, the «Before Babel», but to accept the situation «After Babel» with its diversification of languages and language varieties and educate people to become polyglot (49), not necessarily to the degree George STEINER has achieved, but at least to the extent that makes understanding between the groups of one society unproblematic. Such groups should be guided to speak to rather than at each other – to paraphrase a happy formulation of STEINER's (1976:32).

In order to find a way, out of the After Babel situation of language diversity, *koinés, lingua francas* and standard languages were developed in many places of the world. In this study I am not concerned with English as the *lingua franca* of the modern world nor with Standard English as the means of establishing some degree of communication in any speech community of the English speaking world. (In fact, there are reasons to doubt that Standard English as treasured by educators is an adequate means of communication – whatever its other values may be; cp. chapter 3.8.) I am concerned much more with a multilingual or multivarietal repertoire of English as it might be in use in a given speech community. In what appears to be a political issue, too, I follow HAUGEN and consider the education of polyglot speakers a more humane solution to the Babel dilemma than the enforcement of one variety at the cost of other varieties. As a linguist, I value language heterogeneity higher than language homogeneity, richness of forms more than poverty in variation (but see chapter 4.2). Examining the implications which the notion of a varieties grammar has is not just a political or ideological act; it is a genuine task for linguists for the challenge it poses, and even more so because the question seems to have been largely suppressed in recent years. I do not have in mind here the work of comparative-historical linguistics although the Babel story may have stimulated some of the efforts of 19th century linguists to relate languages in terms of an original unity. I am thinking here, of course, of the views held by Noam CHOMSKY and the great influence they have had and still are having on American and European linguistics. CHOMSKY's effort to establish a conceptual unity of human languages may have been a necessary reaction against a certain superficiality of an earlier generation of US linguists; however, it should never have blinded linguists to the extent of not acknowledging differences any more or of abstracting language from its socio-cultural context. Indeed, to quote Dell HYMES, «the more one emphasizes universals, in association with a developing, powerful faculty of language within persons themselves, the more mysterious actual languages become. Why are there more than one, or two, or three? If the internal faculty of language is so constraining, must not social, historical, adaptive forces have been even more constraining, to produce the specific plenitude of languages actually used? (. . .) The many differences do not disappear, and the likenesses, indeed, are far from all Chomskyan universals. (. . .) Most of language begins where abstract universals leave off.» (1973:63) Or to speak with STEINER: «the ripened humanity of language, its indispensable conservative and creative force lie in the extraordinary diversity of actual tongues, in the bewildering profusion and eccentricity (though there is no centre) of their modes. The psychic need for particularity, for «in-clusion» and invention is so intense that it has, during the whole of man's history until very lately, outweighed the spectacular, obvious material advantages of mutual comprehension and linguistic unity. In that sense, the Babel myth is once again a case of symbolic inversion: mankind was not destroyed but on the contrary kept vital and creative by being scattered among tongues.» (1976:232f.)

1.2 Sociolinguistic Remedies

Relief of the «After Babel Effect» within the realm of one language may be achieved through the study of language variation and the socio-cultural groups represented by different speakers of that language. Work in this field is carried out separately by groups of sociolinguists dealing with variation in language or with the sociology of language. So far, these traditions have not found together, although adherents of both camps could probably agree on the five points of motivation for the study of language variation listed by Walt WOLFRAM (1976) as valid for the USA:

(1) sociopolitical considerations
(2) considerations for an historical perspective of American life
(3) considerations for the differences between spoken and written language forms
(4) utilitarian or applicational considerations focussing mainly on the teaching of basic educational skills
(5) theoretical considerations

As hinted already, the study of language variation in the USA must be understood as a reaction against a linguistic tradition which tended to ignore variation in language. In BLOOMFIELDian structural linguistics and then again in CHOMSKYan transformational-generative grammar language variation was treated, if at all, as an interesting anomaly; at best non-random variation in language was seen as part of SAUSSURE's external linguistics (1916) and therefore put outside the study of linguistics proper. BLOOMFIELD (1933) seems to have considered variation in language as something unpredictable and random, whereas any variation in language occurring in the language of CHOMSKY's ideal speaker-hearer (1965) were simply performance errors. Neither DE SAUSSURE nor CHOMSKY were ignorant of the many outside factors that might influence language use, but both deemed it more profitable not to consider so-called extralinguistic matters. And, in a way, they were right: With an «ideal speaker-listener in a perfectly homogenous speech community» (CHOMSKY 1965:3), linguistics became a well-bounded field for which it was relatively easy to develop models and theories. Both, DE SAUSSURE's definition of *langue* and CHOMSKY's definition of *competence* did not encourage work on language variation. In SAUSSURE's term *langue*, it was implied that every member of a language community has internalized the collectively validated code; similarly, CHOMSKY's notion of *competence* bases on the idea that a single individual has internalized the speech of a larger community. With the emergence of sociolinguistics as a new and increasingly powerful discipline, language was no longer assumed to be a homogenous entity, but a heterogenous one; the study of language varieties and variation patterns in language became possible and was looked upon as highly desirable. William LABOV and his pioneering work (1966), in which it was established that language variation can nonrandomly be correlated with extralinguistic factors,[3] were greeted as liberating American linguists from their imprisonment in the homogeneity hypothesis. More than ten years later, there is no pressure any more to separate 'extralinguistic matters' from 'linguistics proper'. The removal of the self-imposed and somewhat artificial boundaries may have made the object of study less accessible; but, at the same time, language itself, being no longer divested of context, became richer again. The field of linguistics has expanded again to do greater justice to its object of study and analysis: language.

Pre-structuralist schools of linguistics had been aware of language diversity and language variability in their own way. To the philologists of comparative-historical linguistics, e.g., it became clear that language does not only change in time, but also due to population migration and settlement history. Allowing for language expansion in time and place, they were able to develop the notion of language families and to specify linguistic correspondences between individual family members. Family trees were drawn to show how contemporary languages or dialects were related to each other and ultimately descended from the same parent tongue. This conception, which has frequently been attacked, but never fundamentally weakened, must also be taken into account when language varieties are discussed today. Indeed, KANNGIESSER (1972) and WÄCHTLER (1977) have used the term 'family' with explicit reference to intralanguage variation (see 4.1.3). From historical-comparative linguistics the study of language dialects could develop quite naturally. Dialectologists first worked within the tribal hypothesis, but then came to replace this with the wave

3 The results of LABOV's research showed that the variety concept must be extended so as to include more types of variation than found within traditional dialectology. He demonstrated that the variability in the speech of over 100 randomly selected New York City residents was positively correlated with such factors as the social class of a group of speakers and the style-shifting of a particular speaker.

theory. It was discovered that language diversity is also a function of social factors: «Work in attempting to establish dialect boundaries showed conclusively that language change is not a question merely of 'genetic' development whereby so-called sound laws determine how the daughter languages will differ from their common parent, but is largely a result of a dynamic social process of diffusion whereby a linguistic form spreads to other areas because it has taken on an important social function of one kind or another.» (GUMPERZ and BENNETT, 1979:24) This does not mean that the family assumption for language varieties must be given up, but that the differences between the individual varieties are to be explained in socio-cultural terms primarily. By 1925, when Otto JESPERSEN published his essay «Mankind, Nation, and Individual from a Linguistic Point of View», linguists had become aware of language diversity and the social conditions of language use. JESPERSEN, basing himself on Malinowski, stated that language is essentially characterized by «the context, the circumstances, the whole situation and relation between two interlocutors.» (1925:10) He saw language variation not only represented in «dialects as determined by facts of geography» (41), but also in speech communities like «the family, the clan, the tribe, the people or nation and (. . .) the supernation.» (41) Although JESPERSEN here had gained modern-looking insights, he did not proceed to exploit them. Equally, the many structuralists who were working on the early segments of the *Linguistic Atlas of the United States and Canada* never brought their training to their studies in dialectology. As is well-known today, it was only Uriel WEINREICH who raised the question «Is a Structural Dialectology Possible?» (1954) and thus opened the way for new ways of language description also including variation and varieties. Structuralist views then led to the proposal of diasystems (MOULTON, 1960); generative views led to the discussion of models of grammar that were expected to include not only one, but various styles of an individual speaker (KLIMA, 1964), the styles used in particular speech communities (LABOV, 1972d) or even the whole of a language (BAILEY, 1973). The way these or similar proposals can be used to write a varieties grammar and thus to remedy the «After Babel Situation» is discussed in chapter 4.2.

1.3 Implications of a Varieties Grammar

Most of the linguists working on models of language variation have found themselves battling with the question of how far the notion of grammar can be stretched. Clearly, restricting oneself to idiolect is just as wrong as widening the outlook to include every single variety (as in BAILEY's polylectal grammar) is impossible. Nevertheless, the notion of a varieties grammar should not simply be discarded. It indicates that a grammar of a language like English should not be restricted to the «innocent» speaker-hearer (FILLMORE, 1979a), but include what CHOMSKY called «grammatically irrelevant conditions». Thus, a varieties grammar would reflect the fact that language systems are the product of outside factors. Whatever statements are made about the levels of language organization like phonology, morphology, syntax, lexicon, semantics, discourse conventions, they are affected by statements about other factors like time, place, topic chosen, channel used, and participants involved. Such a grammar would not only deal with a speaker's ability to formulate grammatically acceptable sentences, but also with the appropriateness of verbal messages in the context of their acceptability in a broader sense. (cp. GUMPERZ, 1972) In addition, the term 'varieties grammar' wants to preserve the notion that in spite of all these factors, some rules about the varieties in question should be formulated in a somewhat systematic way. To many grammarians – especially in the USA – it would probably appear that a varieties grammar should be built on a kind of deep structure which would be the same for all the language varieties. Differences between individual varieties would be seen as differences between their surface structures, whereas the system of propositions expressing meaning would be kept stable. Within this basic model, every variety would be treated as equal to the others; i.e., a varieties grammar would not make a difference between an accepted form of language standard and various corruptions of or deviations from it; it would much more view the interrelationship of varieties according to the model suggested by BARATZ (1969) and consider varieties as self-contained (surface) systems, neither deficient nor superior; it would assume that the data always reveal regular and systematic correspondences between the different surface structures (cf. WOLFRAM, 1972:35). This view is in line with current generative positions in dialectology. HALLE (1962) and KEYSER (1963) argued that there are indeed abstract underlying structures to the dialects of a language; and CHOMSKY and HALLE (1968:49) claimed that «very different dialects may have the same or very similar systems of underlying representations». Although the Identity Hypothesis defended by them has recently come under attack – HAUSMANN (1975), among others, rejected it on empirical and theoretical grounds – it remains attractive by virtue of its simplicity. In fact, even LABOV remained within the framework of transformational-generative grammar. Whereas CHOMSKY's speaker-hearer represented an idealization of an idiolect, LABOV created an equally idealized construct: the statistically idealized member of a speech community, a speaker-hearer now of a typolect (defined 4.1.2). The rules that say that a certain language feature is applied (or not applied) x % of the time, does not predict the behavior of any real individual; instead, such figures represent an average found in a given group of speakers. Since each individual is said to fit into a regular pattern of social and stylistic stratification, LABOV thinks it unnecessary to resolve the community into as many separate grammars as there are speakers. (1971:457)

Yet, in spite of the fact that the assumptions of transformational-generative grammar are accepted by variationists, I consider it more cautious not to subscribe to a strict generative position when working towards a varieties grammar. It seems to me that the so-called extralinguistic matters are an essential part of a varieties grammar; and these are more satisfactorily retained in an anthropological approach to linguistics. This discussion is also touched upon in chapter two, especially 2.4, and taken up more fully and with more detail in chapter four.

Whatever the approach, writing a varieties grammar for a language like English is certainly a most formidable task. Yet, it seems to me that this is the direction (socio)linguists ought to explore, even if, for the time being, only tentative and suggestive results can be expected. Since the notion of a 'varieties grammar' seems to have so many ramifications, it is necessary to delimit its field of application. It cannot possibly enumerate all the networks of social relationships in which individuals interact or the communicative tasks which these relationships entail although they may be decisive in the creation of particular language varieties. But it can hint as to how linguistic behavior is to be shaped in a clearly defined setting or with regard to some specified speech event. It cannot be bothered with factors of communicative competence that are transferable or can be assumed to be so, like selection of topic or readiness to assume a role in social interaction. It cannot deal with the perceptual or cognitive mechanisms which assign actors to certain social categories and invest them with the rights and duties implied therein. It is also doubtful to what degree statements about background expectations other than those associated with typolects can be made because these are difficult to formulate even for anthropologists (GUMPERZ, 1970). Although it is true, as GUMPERZ has observed, that two speakers who «may speak closely related and, on the surface, mutually intelligible varieties of the same language, (. . .) may nevertheless misunderstand each other because of the differences in usage rules resulting from differences in background» (1970:12), a varieties grammar cannot go so far as to indicate individual usage rules. A varieties grammar, by necessity, must aim at rules that are group or situation or genre specific. Formulating rules about individual speech behavior would lead to a grammar of idiolects instead of a grammar or typolects, i.e., of varieties showing what is typical and more generally acceptable in either a group, a situation or a text type. But there are limitations even within this broader frame. As Susan ERVIN-TRIPP has noted (1968:25f.), «forms which allow specific exceptions, or which have options so that too great or too little frequency might be conspicuous, cannot be taught deliberately so easily. Such rules can be acquired by newcomers only by long and intense exposure rather than formal teaching.» The greatest obstacles, however, seem to lie in the domain of formalization. Although it seems quite certain that statements about the relation of the internal organization of language and external factors like time, location, participants, channel and topic can be made, it is doubtful to what degree these can be formalized to satisfy the requirements of a grammar. When working on the Hindi teaching materials, GUMPERZ (1966) found: «To make formal statements of the relationship between social norms and language choice would, in view of the present limited knowledge, be a formidable task. (. . .) For the purpose of language instruction, however, the anthropologist's experience (. . .) can at least provide a useful approximation.»

Indeed, there seem to be areas for which a varieties grammar might be useful and in which it might work. Since a varieties grammar would contain statements about what kind of language to use when, where and how, it might be read less as a far-ranging description of language organization, language function and language use than as a codification of rules and strategies to be followed in a given (typical) situation. It would probably work best if it were restricted to a particular kind of speakers with a particular speech repertoire in a particular area. Although it is theoretically possible to conceive a varieties grammar that would cover, e.g., the whole of English, practical considerations would suggest that the scope of a varieties grammar be radically delimited. The research reported in chapter 2.3 on the communicative competence of EFL speakers in the San Francisco Bay Area seems to indicate that for a certain group of speakers a variety repertoire could indeed be expressed in sets of grammatical (if holistic, cp. 4.1.1) statements.

Ultimately, a varieties grammar of that kind would not simply be another theoretical balloon produced by the anti-CHOMSKY factory, but also do justice to some of the other considerations mentioned by WOLFRAM as motivating the study of language variation (see p. 19): It would reflect sociopolitical issues by making accessible to classes of speakers the speech repertoire of the whole community to which they belong. It would make explicit the differences between spoken and written language forms (since channel decides on the variety to be used), and through its awareness of different styles employed by speakers would surely also serve general educational purposes. And by also including culture-specific information, it should indeed be a means to remove at least some of the effects created by the collapse of the tower of Babel and the ensuing curse put on intergroup communication.

1.4 Summary

Work towards a varieties grammar, I have argued, is based on a view of language as heterogenous, not homogenous. The aim of such work is to provide a key to different varieties from a unifying perspective and within an integrative model. This model should not simply contrast the inventories of two varieties (as in Contrastive Linguistics), but establish the interrelationship of any number of varieties from the angle of a commonly shared base or an all-embracing superstructure (see chapter 4). Thus, the exploration of the notion of a varieties grammar is of theoretical interest to linguists. In my view, however, to provide such a key should also yield practical results. To come up with suggestions about how the interrelationship of varieties can be demonstrated is politically advisable. And to make any such proposals applicable to situations of language translation and language teaching seems to be a basic requirement in the time after Babel.

Although the base component of a TG grammar appears to be a tempting starting point for an integrative approach, Chomskyan linguistics seem to be less hospitable to the notion of a varieties grammar than proposals within sociolinguistics. In any case, the possibility of re-defining linguistics in a more holistic sense (see chapter 4.1) must be kept open.

2 An Outside View of English Language Varieties

2.1 Language Diversity

> Constance Goddard has a mission in life. Call it a vendetta. It's not aimed against any person or a group of people. It's not a fight against wrong thought or some killer disease.
>
> Constance Goddard's enemy is the sound of a New Yorker talking.
>
> She doesn't mind a New York accent per se, as long as it is kept in the general vicinity of the Hudson river. But when New Yorkers began moving into her native Marin County, bringing their energetic speech patterns with them, Constance rankled.
>
> «It's really a drag listening to people from New York talk,» she says, her breathy voice untainted by regional color. «It upsets me when I hear a New York accent, or anything that grates my ears the way that does.»
>
> So she decided to do something about it. In the spirit of enlightened benevolence, she established California Diction, a sort of accent therapy center, which, at 25 bucks a throw ($ 35 for house calls) will teach willing New Yorkers how to talk Californian.
>
> «We're here to offer a service to newcomers to this area, especially to New Yorkers,» she says. «They come here and find themselves OK as far as dress and looks and mannerisms. But when they open their mouths, they alienate everyone. We're here to help them, help them adjust to life in Marin County.» (. . .)

What Peter J. Boyer reported here in the *Oakland Tribune* (February 4, 1979, p. 6-E) illustrates very nicely that Americans are still very much dialect conscious. According to Halliday (1978:185), a dialect is «what you speak»; this being determined by «who you are». Dialect gives away your regional and/or social place of origin and/or adoption. The newspaper clipping shows that there are a number of occasions in which the self-identification through one's dialect causes some problems. Not every American seems to be proud of his dialect; and not every American is ready to respect the dialect of his fellow citizens. That is why in some areas – like California – dialect speakers find themselves under pressure to give up their native speech habits and speech pathologists are doing flourishing business.

The outsider, of course, never finds himself in such a situation. His is no single dialect of English. He speaks English as a foreign language. Where he comes from, what his social status is, how much education he has received, cannot be told from his way of speaking English. Of course, if he is able to speak Standard English fluently, this will allow native speakers of English to conclude that he is educated; however, if he were also able to speak a non-standard variety of English and a native speaker of English were overhearing him just using that, he would be wrong in inferring lack of education on the EFL speaker's part; on the contrary, he would have to conclude that this EFL speaker's education is much higher: In addition to mastering Standard English – which is common food everywhere abroad – he may have learnt everyday folk speech as well – which abroad is reserved for the chosen few and presupposes a high degree of sophistication. His accent as an EFL speaker may betray his native language as non-English, but that would not allow an American or Englishman to draw any conclusions about his social and educational status. And even if it did, it is not clear what relevance such inferences should have for the evaluation of a foreigner in the USA.[1]

In the case of American English – to discuss only this segment of English – dialectological information is therefore more valuable to Americans than to outsiders. Americans can make inferences from each other's dialects about their respective backgrounds, and apparently they do so quite frequently. When decoding American speech, non-native speakers of English, too, may have an interest

1 Within HALLIDAY's terminology, saying that the outsider does not share any dialect of American English also means that he doesn't have any sociolect. He does not belong to a group of speakers which regards itself as a social unit within American culture and life (e.g.). There is, therefore, no immediate need for him to express group solidarity by favoring those linguistic features that set the group apart from other speakers of English. Of course, there are certain considerations on the part of the outsider that make it desirable for him to share a certain code. If he wants to express solidarity with a group, his adoption of the group specific speech patterns will be of some help, no doubt; it should be restricted, however, to the realms of the lexicon, of semantics, and pragmatics, mainly; for as much as imitation in these areas might indeed be a means to remove distance, attempts to imitate accents might have effects disastrous to the building-up of a relationship.

to get background information that can be gleaned from dialect. It is doubtful, however, whether the outsider will ever make further distinctions than those made customarily since the publication of KURATH's *A Word Geography of the Eastern United States* (1949). He might be able to hear the differences between northern, midland, and southern speech; but dialects of a smaller order – like those identified in the collections of WILLIAMSON and BURKE (1971) or ALLEN and UNDERWOOD (1971) – will probably escape him. In spite of the apparent richness of dialects,[2] the outsider does not experience the American language as characterized by dialect variation mainly. As an EFL speaker he has been trained to believe that English is a fairly homogenous language anyway; and when he notices – as he inevitably will – that this hypothesis is wrong, he does not interpret the recognizable differences as dialectal in the first place. What he notices are ways of speaking that differ markedly from the standard he has learnt; ways of speaking that seem to be correlated with ethnicity, social class, and occupation.

That language differences might be significant if measured against parameters of that kind was seen by American dialectologists themselves. The distinction made most often was that between cultivated and folk usage or educated and uneducated speech. As much as this broad classification may be a highly political and much politicized issue in American life, it is surely not a difference observed by the outsider. With regard to such society internal struggles, he is prone to adopt a position of neutrality. WOLFRAM (1972:35) has noted that «it is quite common for a socially dominant culture to view a socially subordinate one as having an inadequate means of communication.» This attitude, however, cannot be shared by someone who does not belong to the social group in question. A foreigner coming to an English-speaking country or using English anywhere else in the world should not be

2 To the outsider, the range of dialectal variation would, on all counts, seem smaller than suggested in the work of the dialectologists; he would be impressed by the social mobility in the USA, by the fluid social class system there, and the highly developed mass media. Considering these factors, he would conclude that dialectal differences, in the USA, can't be too great.

made or expected to share the manifestations of linguistic ethnocentrism of the dominant classes in Great Britain or the USA; on the contrary, his attitude toward the different varieties spoken in these countries should be class-neutral. Even within the English-speaking countries one has become aware of the fact that the one-sided favoring of one social variety is essentially undemocratic. When Ossie DAVIES (1972) said that the English language was his enemy, he had in mind not only the linguistic differences in vocabulary, grammar, and pronunciation, but even more so the social and political clash between Standard English and Black Vernacular English. Indeed, if social pressure is to be relieved, the different varieties must be given equal respect. If communication between social and ethnic groups is to be bettered, mutual understanding must be created in a way characterized by efforts on more than one side. This means that majority group members speaking Standard English should be taught to understand different varieties, just as speakers of non-standard varieties are being taught their dialect (cp. chapter 1.1).

In the USA and Great Britain, Standard English is still the prestige variety. Other varieties, however, are at least theoretically being acknowledged. To quote from the *US Conference of Composition and Communication* (1974): «We affirm the students' right to their own patterns and varieties of language – the dialects of their nurture, or whatever dialects in which they find their own identity and style.»

In the Caribbean, this tendency has already led to a redefinition of the relationship between standard and non-standard. There, «the movement towards independence of the territories in the region has been accompanied by the rejection of external symbols of formal colonial status. Together with the hemisphere-wide consciousness shift towards 'people power', regionally expressed as 'black power', this has affected the orderliness with which attitudes towards the official languages and the Creoles can be stated. Indeed, it is now prestigious and fashionable to use Creole for purposes which might otherwise have called for the official language.» (CARRINGTON, 1976:27). School authorities in Trinidad and Tobago are aware of this new language situation; they expect teachers «to adopt a commonsense and humane attitude to what is acceptable in the local society» and they warn them that «it is pedantic to insist on a particular British-English structure when it is clear that such a structure is rarely or never employed by educated Jamaicans» (quoted from CARRINGTON, 1976:34). CARRINGTON's findings are corroborated by research done by Donald WINFORD (1976) on teacher attitudes towards language varieties in a Creole community. The cases he discusses show most impressively that the social values attached to non-standard varieties in the Caribbean are no longer interpreted as negative. He concludes that «the emphasis for creole situations is not so much on the replacement of 'stigmatized' features, as on the acquisition of a secondary system in addition to native patterns of speech.» (1976:74)

Language diversity in the English-speaking world, it appears, is increasingly taken as what it is: a mirror in linguistic terms of culturally and socially different population groups. Varieties of English are no longer of interest only if they can be placed on the diachronic axis, but also if found on a synchronic (mostly the contemporary) axis.

2.2 English Language Varieties and the Teaching of English

Looking at English as a world language and from the outside, such observations strongly suggest that the English language (as a corpus) should be made accessible to those who want to learn it in more than only one variety form. Although textbooks of Standard English try to put their 'grammar' into some situational context, they do not reflect the heterogenous nature of the English language accurately. This has to do with the fact that authors of textbooks have copied one another assiduously rather than included the data made availabe by linguistic research, and that teachers of English are generally uninformed about other dialects than the standard (HESS, 1973). This point can be illustrated by an examination of the requirements of a college admission test like TOEFL.

According to the Preface of *Barron's How to Prepare For The Test of English as a Foreign Language* (compiled by Pamela J. SHARPE, 1977), seventy thousand students from 120 countries take the Test of English as a Foreign Language (TOEFL) every year at test centers in the United States and in their home countries. Passing TOEFL grants the foreign student admission to US universities and colleges; the test is also used by scholarship selection committees and other institutions to measure the English proficiency of candidates.

TOEFL tests language skills in three sections: Listening Comprehension, Structure and Written Expression, Reading Comprehension and Vocabulary. The requirements appear in more detailed form in the *English Proficiency Chart* issued by the National Association for Foreign Students Affairs (nafsa), jointly produced by The Consortium on Intensive English Programs (CIEP), The Association of Teachers as a Second Language (ATESL), and The Admission Section (ADSEC). These boards specify the conditions under which a foreign student is admitted to a minimal, partial, or the full academic program. Admission to full academic programs, e.g., is granted if the foreign student's proficiency level can be described as follows:

- writes with occasional errors in idiom at somewhat below native speed; demonstrates good understanding and control of organization of expository/argumentative essay
- reads and understands general academic material; displays ability to extract salient elements, sometimes with the use of dictionary, at somewhat below native speed
- understand academic and colloquial conversation, and most lectures with no difficulty
- speaks fluently with only occasional idiomatic imprecision.

If the foreign student is up to this level, no additional EFL course work is required; he is admitted to academic programs without any restrictions. If not, restrictions will be imposed.

Obviously, EFL courses devise their programs so as to meet the standards set by the *English Proficiency Chart* and to prepare their students for the TOEFL test. They mostly do not and cannot have any other goals in mind. This means that a student learning English abroad or one enrolled in an English language program for foreigners in the USA (or Britain) will get a good training in Academic Standard English (cp. 3.8) and acquire those language skills that make it possible for him to read books, write a paper, understand a lecture, and converse with fellow students and teachers.

What TOEFL does not test and what therefore is not or hardly ever trained by such preparatory English courses is communicative competence in a broader sense. Recent work by linguists, above all sociolinguists, has established for good that linguistic description must do justice to language being something heterogeneous (WEINREICH, HERZOG and LABOV, 1968). Apart from interesting discussions on the theoretical level, more practically oriented endeavors were made to show that the idea of language uniformity is a dead-end hypothesis. After the work done and inspired by LABOV (1966), variation in language can no longer be considered an unpredictable and random phenomenon (BLOOMFIELD, 1933) or as the output of performance errors (CHOMSKY, 1965); variation is now seen as part of linguistic competence, quite definitely correlated with both external and internal linguistic factors. Of even greater interest to English language teachers and EFL students, however, might be the broad concept of the *ethnography of speaking*. As developed by Dell HYMES (1962), it was set up to examine the ways in which language is actually used in different cultures. It makes statements about all kinds of language varieties («ways of speaking») and their interpretation in and by various language communities.(cp. 4.3.3.3)

Since much work in this area was done with regard to language communities of alien cultures, results about the acquisition of language skills by outsiders were gained as well. It became obvious that foreigners or non-native speakers cannot be satisfied with learning language structures; they must learn to use the language which they have acquired from textbooks in real contexts. What they need is more than a grammatical competence in CHOMSKY's sense; they need what Hymes termed *communicative competence;* they have to learn when to use which variety where and how.

These new insights of linguistics, however, are not yet shared by educators. In EFL teaching especially, the post-Bloomfieldian and post-Chomskyan awareness of 'extralinguistic' matters and of general language diversity has not had any noticeable effect yet. This is quite surprising in view of the fact that from the outside the English language field does not present itself any longer as a circular one (with England in its center), but as an elliptical one (with Britain and the USA as the two focal points) or even a multicentred one (showing the stratification of English all over the world). Indeed, whoever approaches English from the outside must be struck by the great amount of language variation he encounters, not only on a global level, but even within a single English-speaking country. He is taken by surprise because EFL courses, as they are taught abroad, have not prepared him for other varieties than what is commonly called standard. Charles-James N. BAILEY (1978) noted this shortcoming of EFL teaching abroad when observing English language teaching at German pre-university schools in Berlin. He detected a lack of style sensitivity among the students and attributed this to the almost exclusive emphasis put by their teachers on Standard English. «The style that is generally taught is the most formal one, the most archaic of all, the least appropriate for students of school and university ages – if the most congenial to pedants and older teachers.» As a corrective measure he urges «that as more and more is known about the variation patterns of English and other languages, such patterns should be taught to language learners with the object of developing in them the ability to employ the variants of a language in the same pattern and to progress from one style to another as nearly like a native-speaker as possible.» (1978:238)

The English language, then, cannot be equated with Standard English, which traditionally is intimately related to the style of formal writing. On the contrary, what should be studied first and foremost is everyday speech (LABOV, 1972a:xiii). It would even be said that studying the kind of English required by TOEFL is wrong. Charles-James N. BAILEY put it quite emphatically: «Certainly, the aim of having foreign students emulate an age (and class) which they could never authentically represent strikes me as wrong-headed.» (1978:239) What he meant is that the kind of English taught at Berlin Gymnasiums and required by TOEFL in the USA (and the Cambridge exams in Britain) does not give the student the possibility to familiarize with other, socially more adequate varieties of English.

Indeed, Standard English is only one among many different varieties of English. If it is spoken at all (cp. 3.8), then only by intellectuals and members of the upper classes; it is not used by younger people and not by members of the lower classes. LABOV also maintains that Standard English is not the «best» (i.e., most logical and precise) variety either: «All too often, 'standard English' is represented by a style that is simultaneously overparticular and vague. The accumulating flow of words buries rather than strikes the target. It is this verbosity which is most easily taught and most easily learned, so that words take the place of thought, and nothing can be found behind them.» (1972d:202) I have no intention here to examine this criticism of Standard English and how this bears on the teaching of English. I certainly see the importance of students acquiring proficiency in Standard English for academic and other purposes, but I consider it equally vital for them to be introduced to other varieties of English as well. Yet, teachers of English as a foreign language make the experience that their efforts of teaching Standard to their students are frequently frustrated by interference phenomena due to other varieties of English. If they are oriented towards British Standard, many of their students will inevitably be exposed to forms of American English in out-of-school situations. More importantly, they will also find out that for their students the prestige dialect is not identical with Standard, but rather with some «lower» variety of English. Indeed, the recognition of the fact that in the USA adolescents model their language behavior after that of their peers (LABOV, 1970) also holds true – *mutandis mutandum* – for the foreign language learning situation. Here the peers appear in comic strips, in movies, on records, etc. And surely, the language of such idols is not Textbook Standard, though English nevertheless.

Simon HERMAN (1961) has pointed out that the success of acquiring competence in a second language depends on a psychological factor of group reference: «the readiness of a person to learn and use a second language may depend in part on the measure of his willingness to identify with the group with which the language is associated.» (1961:162f.) If this is true of adults trying to learn Hebrew in Israel (as in the case discussed by HERMAN), then this is probably even more so with regard to young people learning English, which for them is the language of fashionable – and sometimes underground – culture and certainly not of the middle and upper class establishment.

Until recently, teachers might have been willing to refer to a catalog of specific teaching devices with which to avoid the traps of substandard forms in English. Today, however, this is no longer only a question of how to cope with transfer in foreign language teaching, but one of recognizing and doing justice to the different varieties of English.

2.3 On the Communicative Competence of EFL Students

The small-scale research reported in this section was carried out by me in the winter of 1978/1979 in close collaboration with the English Language Program, University Extension, University of California, Berkeley.[3] It was drawn up so as to measure the range of the communicative competence in English of students ready to take the TOEFL exam. The basic hypothesis was that finishing students of such English language programs would have only insufficient command of language varieties other than Standard. E.g., they would not be able to express themselves adequately on a low-class level, they would lack the appropriate verbal strategies for many everyday communications, and they would not be able to understand non-standard varieties. According to these assumptions a questionnaire was drawn up containing questions about the subjects' language background and their language expectations in the first part and a number of test questions in the second part. In these tests, Standard English was contrasted with non-standard, Standard American with Standard British; examples of Californian and Black Vernacular English were given, and subjects were exposed to taped conversations of a group of white and a group of black inhabitants of the San Francisco Bay Area belonging to the same age-group as the subjects interviewed. Twelve different speech situations were made up requiring the subjects to

3 I should like to thank Judy HOYEM, then at the English Language Program, University Extension, University of California, Berkeley, for giving me much help, and the students interviewed for having co-operated so willingly. The project was carried out by me in my capacity of Research Associate, Dept. of Linguistics, University of California, Berkeley, and approved by the Graduate Division (Faculty Research Permit).

complete dialogs on the appropriate formal or informal level of speech. Thus, the students had to show whether they understood dialect or sociolect specific language (passively), whether they could express themselves on the appropriate stylistic levels, and whether they were able to translate the contextualized discourse of one variety into that of another (actively).[4]

To the question «What is English to you?» the subjects unanimously gave predictable answers of the kind

> a means of communication
> a means to meet other people
> an international language
> the most important language in the world

One interviewee was more specific in saying

> the language of the American people and of
> American culture

All these answers are interpretable as expressing the subjects' wish to actually communicate with the population of English speaking countries.[5] They all, indeed, stated that communication with Eng-

4 The tests were administered in interview form to half a dozen volunteers who had just completed an intensive 10-weeks' course in Advanced English (December 1978). The material of the test questions, in some instances, goes back to available sources. For the part on British English/American English, Peter STREVEN's *British and American English* (Collier-Macmillan, 1972) was used; the examples of California English were taken from *The Daily Californian* (UC Berkeley campus daily) and Cyra MCFADDEN's Marin County Novel *The Serial* (New York: The American Library 1978) and checked against the speech habits of native Bay Area speakers; examples of Black English were taken from Walter W. WOLFRAM and Ralph W. FASOLD, *The Study of Social Dialects in American English* (Englewood Cliffs, N.J.: Prentice Hall 1974); two of the test situations for language in context were adapted from John J. GUMPERZ and Celia ROBERTS, *Developing Awareness Skills for Interethnic Communication* (National Centre for Industrial Language Training, Southill, Middlesex, 1978); the taped conversations, both black and white speech, were borrowed from the Berkeley Language Behavior Research Laboratory (courtesy John J. GUMPERZ).

5 In answer to the Direct Attitude Questions asked by CHIHARA and OLLER (1978), EFL students indicated the following reasons: They wanted to learn

lish speaking people for them included members of all social classes (upper, middle, lower), all ethnic groups (White, Black, Chicano, Chinese, . . .), speakers of Standard and Non-Standard English and of all ages. In spite of this tolerant, outgoing and world-embracing attitude, most of them (84%) mentioned more narrowly professional goals as having motivated them into learning English; specific mention was made of the usefulness of English for business, law, technology, and entertainment.

There was a certain awareness among the subjects interviewed of the existence of several varieties of English. Those who had been trained in British English before entering the University of California Extension Language Program (66%) thought this (or the «Oxford accent») to be the «most correct» variety; once slang was mentioned as being more useful than standard; but in general the subjects were hesitant to identify varieties as either more correct, more proper, or more beautiful than other varieties.

As «good» former students, they were all able to tell Standard English from Non-Standard; Non-Standard was recognized as deviating from the norm in examples like these:

> I saw the man who did it, but I never told anybody.
> I seen the bloke what done it, but I never told nobody.
>
> He says you are and I say you are not.
> He says you be and I says you ben't.

Telling one variety from another, however, was already a very difficult task. All the subjects showed great insecurity in applying even such sweeping labels like American or British Standard. It appeared that although they had been taught what is standard and what not, they had not been trained to observe the differences between British and American English systematically. Only 50%, e.g., were able to identify such an obvious case as «I wish I could

English so as to be able to visit an English-speaking country in whose language, literature and culture they had taken an interest; they would travel to an English-speaking country (like the USA) «to get to know many different kinds of people», «to find out how people live there», and «to have new experiences.»

have gotten here» as American. Subjects felt safer with lexical items, as in

There's a bad wreck on the freeway.	(AmE)
There's a bad crash on the motorway.	(BrE)
Did you have your vacation yet?	(AmE)
Have you had your holidays yet?	(BrE)
I work nights as a bar-tender.	(AmE)
I work at night as a barman.	(BrE)

Correctness was 100% for example 1, 66% for example 2, 50% for example 3. Out of a possible 22 points in the American/British test, subjects scored an average of 10 points, with no one over 15, and no one below 2.

Since all the subjects had expressed their wish to talk to and understand all the members of the English speech community, they were tested on their comprehension of two varieties. One was the informal Californian White English of the San Francisco Bay Area to which all the subjects had been exposed for at least the three months previous to the test. Although the test examples had been taken mostly from student speech and *Daily Californian* advertisements, the subjects did not do too well. None of them was able to explain the meanings of all the expressions asked. Results:

Item asked		Correct answers (%)
hanging out	«I was hanging out at Lake Temescal»	84%
mellow	«He is mellow»	50%
laid-back	«She is a laid-back person»	33%
boogie	«Let's go boogie down the street»	33%
going bananas	«I am going bananas»	33%
bummed out	«Ms. Murphy was feeling bummed out»	33%
tab	«Harvey paid his tab»	33%
rapping	«We were just sitting together and rapping» ..	16%
hash	«Help needed: Women to hash for fraternity»	16%
uppity	«Harvey tipped the uppity waitress»	0%
rap	«Rap for lesbian mothers»	0%
scoping in on	«I was scoping in on that child»	0%

The subject with the longest experience in the San Francisco Bay Area (four years and married to a native Californian) knew 4 out of 12 items, and the Japanese who previously had qualified slang as useful, 6 out of 12. All the others were below 4, even down to 0. Yet, in their personal comments on this part of the test, they all showed lively interest in this variety of English; they also mentioned that they had heard some of the expressions in the street and elsewhere, but had not been prepared to ask about their meanings. Apparently, overcoming language barriers all by yourself needs a lot of courage and energy; one wonders whether EFL programs should not extend their services so as to give the students some introduction to the local vernacular varieties as well.

The second non-standard variety of English with which the subjects were confronted was Vernacular Black English. The written examples were fully understood only by the subject who had sought and found contacts with black musicians. The others were correct only about «He don't know nothin'», the double negation being quite easily equated with a simple negation and not with non-negation (as some Anglo educators would have it), while the remaining examples were mostly left to guessing. Again it became obvious that the students had never been taught any rules about Black English.

Although quaint vocabulary items were much less frequent, the test on listening comprehension did not yield better results. The subjects were asked to listen to two taped conversations, one of White Berkeley students, the other of Black Bay Area highschoolers. Only the Japanese student who had indicated a disc jockey as his favorite speaker of English and the Chinese girl married to an American were able to make out the contents and the verbal interaction of those conversations without any outside help. The others, whether European (French, Italian) or Asiatic (Japanese, Chinese) had predictable difficulties in understanding. Free moving, informal Californian white speech was not found to be much easier to follow than the differently accented black speech.

The last part of the test dealt with active use of language in context. The subjects were confronted with given situations and asked for appropriate verbal reactions. For instance, they were asked what kind of expressions they might use to end a conversation (a) with a close friend, (b) with someone they didn't know so well, and (c) with someone they had just seen for the first time. Their answers were:

Subject	situation a	situation b	situation c
1	See you	Good bye	Good bye
2	See you later	It was nice talking to you	Nice to meet you
3	Okay, see you	I hope to see you again, bye bye	It was a pleasure to see you
4	Okay, see you, take it easy	See you again	I am very glad to have seen you, it was nice talking to you
5	Bye, see you next time	I think I have to go now	It was nice to meet you, hope to see you again
6	I think I have to leave now, bye, see you later	I have to leave you now, see you later	I have to leave now, see you later

All these expressions succeed in signalling that the speaker wants to break off, but quite often they are somewhat outside the formulaic phrasing which idiomatic usage would show. That there is still a certain limitation in communicative competence is best seen where a speaker does not express gradation between the levels of formality (1bc, 6), or where – often due to lacking fluency in Standard English – the formula chosen is not quite fitting (2c, 5b, 6c) or extended beyond what seems necessary (4c, 6a). The subjects were also tested on the way in which they would address different people in different situations. One case was addressing a physician (nameplate: John D. FISHER, M.D.), the other addressing any fellow student. The answers given were the following:

Subject	Physician	Fellow student
1	Hello	Hi
2	Hi	Hi, how are you
3	Doctor	Hey, you
4	How do you do	Hi, how are you doing
5	Good morning	Hi, how are you
6	Good morning, Doctor Fisher	Hi, you guy

In this second set of formulas, the subjects – with the exception of 2 – were apparently able to make a distinction between a more formal address system (for the doctor) and an informal one (for the student).

A third test situation dealt with sending one's good wishes to a third party. The subjects were asked to phrase this for a situation in which they knew both the transmitter and the receiver of the wishes very well (a), and for a situation in which there was a clear difference in social status between them and the transmitter (b). The following answers were given:

Subject	situation a	situation b
1	Would you say hello to ...	Would you say hello to ...
2	Say hi to ... for me	Give my regards to ...
3	Lots of love to ...	Say to ... all my love
4	Please tell hello for me	Would you please give my best regards to ...
5	(wouldn't know)	
6	If you see ..., can you address to ... my best wishes	If you see ..., can you address to ... my best wishes

Here, in a speech act which is less frequent than greeting, only two subjects (2, 4) found appropriate wording for both situations. (The identical phrasing of 1 might also be considered acceptable, while that of 6 would certainly not.)

More interesting than the results gained from further similar situations (asking permission to smoke, inviting someone for supper, accepting or refusing an invitation) were those of a translation exercise. The subjects were asked to translate the following piece of written information into everyday speech (as if complaining about it to a close friend): «Students are required to submit their assignment work by the end of the term.» Solutions:

Subject	Answer
1	We are required to submit our assignment work by the end of the term.
2	We are required to submit our work by the end of the term.
3	We have to give our work to the teachers.
4	We have to hand in our work.
5	We have to give our work at the end of class.
6	We are required to give back our assignments by the end of the term.

Obviously, half of the students did not see the point of translation, i.e. of making the contents of the written sentence fit a different situation. And only one subject (4) gave a satisfactory translation, the others were entirely or partially unable to do so. This part of the test made it clear that EFL students might have greater difficulty in finding appropriate wording where they cannot resort to everyday formulas. Even if it is true that they can pick up rules about well-bounded speech events like addressing people, asking permission etc., they cannot be expected to detect the rules that govern variety specific language in less ritualized episodes. This, then, appears to be an area in which they need help.

Although results gained from interviews of six subjects only cannot be said to be fully representative, the findings of this small-scale research can nevertheless be stated with some force. This is so because these results by and large confirm the impressions of many EFL teachers.

In commenting on the findings I refer to the three levels of communicative competence identified by HYMES (1968). He distinguishes

Minimal communicative competence
Average communicative competence
Maximal communicative competence

In minimal communicative competence, the speaker is characterized by a single speech habit in a single social sphere without any shifting of repertoire or code; in average communicative competence, he has a command of a set of speech habits which is neither large nor small and is able to use these in a limited range of different social spheres and to shift his verbal repertoire accordingly; and in maximal communicative competence, he has command of versatile speech habits in many social spheres and is able to shift his verbal repertoire with ease.

Traditional training of EFL students (as in English language programs preparing for TOEFL) leads to a kind of communicative competence that can be termed minimal. Both, the explicit statements of the *English Proficiency Chart* and an analysis of the TOEFL tests, make it clear that the goal of such courses must be (written) Standard English for academic purposes. The social sphere can be defined as upper or upper-middle class and academic, the repertoire as including the kind of English used in lectures and in college papers. But although the *English Proficiency Chart* (more so than TOEFL) also allows some functional varieties and common colloqualisms within Academic English, the student is not expected to master a second repertoire for another social sphere.

EFL teachers have come to see these limitations and have been trying to widen their students' communicative competence so as to include everyday speech habits as well. The University Extension, University of California, Berkeley, e.g., has developed a program which they call *Experiences in the American Language*. Its function is «to bridge the gap between formal 'classroom' English and the more idiomatic English encountered day to day in the United States.» (HOEPPNER and ROSENFELD, 1977:vii). It recognizes that foreign students following their courses do not only have educational and/or economic goals in mind, but often seek a broadening (and maybe adventurous) cultural experience in different surroundings and life-styles. Accordingly, the authors deal with various speech events, use role-play and give «contact assignments» (out-of-class activities designed to give students opportunities to speak to Americans out of class). A similar program developed by Marilyn MARTIN-JONES at Stanford intends «to illustrate how different aspects of speech events, such as the identity, status and number of participants, the channel, the setting, the topic, the motives and goals of the participants, effect the way in which people choose to talk to each other.» (1978:2) If enough time is allowed in working with such materials, the communicative competence of EFL students will indeed be widened. It might be developed to become what HYMES termed average competence. This, as it seems to me, is the goal which all EFL teaching should try to reach. It will be necessary for teachers and students to step outside the speech community of the college/university campus and the social, bureaucratic and commercial networks typically associated with it (within which Marilyn MARTIN-JONES still remains). Students are ready to take this step, some are even prepared to take it without guiding help. They show interest in all kinds of English language varieties and would like to understand these, if not to speak them. Again, a varieties grammar might be a welcome means to fulfil the necessary guiding and helping function.

2.4 Classification of Varieties

Before the foreigner can be taught the variation patterns of English, it ought to be determined which of these patterns are identifiable to the outsider and which he needs to know for efficient communication. I am therefore attempting now to develop a model of English language varieties that reflect the views and needs of the outsider.[6] To him English, if at all, shows variation both diachronically and synchronically. These differences do not appear on the level of idiolects, but on the level of typolects; i.e. the outsider sees and hears not the individual, but the typical; he makes abstractions and idealizations directed at practical classification. English thus is presented to him in nice chunks: this is British, that is Am-

6 The outsider I have in mind is an EFL speaker with a pragmatic-practical interest in English. He approaches English for various reasons, though mainly professional or touristic. I do not assume a world diglossic situation, in which English assumes the position of an H language and the outsider's mother-tongue that of L; I simply figure a non-native speaker of English, who, induced by the prestige enjoyed by the English language and its *lingua franca* function, has been eager to learn this language and now wants to use it.

erican; or: this is Old English, that is Middle English; this is the English of the British upper classes, that is the English used by New York taxi drivers; this is polite formal English, that is slang. Along this line, the outsider will classify English language varieties like this:[7]

(1) Historical varieties of English

These refer to the English language on its various stages within the historical development. Such stages can be distinguished from one another by observing changes through time on any level of language organization (textual, lexical, syntactical, morphological, phonological, graphemic). There are more historical varieties of English than just Old English, Middle English, and Modern English, as was successfully illustrated by Barbara STRANG's (1970) bicentennical cuts; it is probably a fair guess to say that there emerged a new historical variety of English with every new generation of speakers in the language.

(2) Regional varieties of English

This label captures the notion that at a given point in time, English is/was not structured identically in all the areas it is/was in use. Dialectal differences could be observed in Old and Middle English already and have not been lost in the later history of English nor in the spread of English all over the world in modern times.

(3) Social varieties of English

Occasionally called sociolects, social varieties are not defined as region specific, but as class or group specific. Differences show up in the comparison of the speech of upper, middle, and lower-class speakers. Although the study of social varieties is of more recent date and has centred almost exclusively on data from Present-Day

7 Research conducted by me in Berne, Switzerland, in 1977/78, showed that highschoolers (Gymnasiasten) after four years of EFL course work make these distinctions without hesitation.

English, social varieties have existed on earlier stages of English as well, as a reading of Dickens or Middle English prose, e.g., will illustrate.

(4) Situational varieties of English

Apparently, a three-dimensional model for the classification of the varieties of English is insufficient. Even if time, place and class are indicated, speakers may still use more than one variety, the differences being determined by the factors that characterize the communicative situation entered by the speaker.

Although still crude, this kind of classification reflects some of the question currently asked in the course of definition of language varieties by linguists. WÄCHTLER (whom I quote here as an outside authority) formulates these questions (1977:19):

> Variation als geographisch bedingte Differenzierung?
> Variation als sozial bedingte Differenzierung?
> Variation als Bedingung des Sprechakts, des Kontexts, des Mediums?
> Sprachliche Variation als Teil der (sozialen) (Rollen-)Interaktion?
> Sprachliche Variation im Rahmen von Diglossie und Bilingualismus, auf mikro- oder makrolinguistischer bzw. sprachsoziologischer Ebene?

From an interdisciplinary point of view, there is certainly no uniform theory of language diversity. Since variation in language can be viewed from so many angles, difficulties are bound to arise at the level of definition already. It appears that a complete explanation and determination of the occurrences of variants is impossible; there are simply too many contributive factors; and individual speakers always have space and freedom for role-play and their own interpretations of variables. In spite of all these complexities, it is necessary for our purposes to define more accurately what we have in mind when speaking about language varieties of English.

At the basis of definition there is the notion that language is a means of communication developed by human beings; that it facilitates understanding between speaker(s) and hearer(s). Language is not seen as a random series of symbols, but as systematically structured. There are rules operating on all the levels of language organization: phonology, morphology, syntax, lexicology, text types and discourse conventions. In addition languages have developed means for the distinction of different functions and occasions; variation is shown according to dialects, sociolects, registers or styles.[8]

Even a brief review of the contribution to the study of language varieties from different linguistic traditions (comparative-historical, dialectological, structural, generative, pragmatic) suggests that a classification of varieties would be more complex than the one sketched above (pp. 46–47). The number of subgroups can be increased by the number of parameters used. It was this great number of critical parameters (a «mixed bag», as he called it) which induced Raven Mc David, Jr. (1970) to finally dismiss the term 'dialect' in favor of the more neutral term 'variety'. So far, there does not seem to exist any single theoretical model which could accomodate the range of English language varieties envisaged here. Indeed, there are almost as many models and taxonomic systems as there are variationists. I shall pick out, therefore, in a somewhat arbitrary way, a few models developed in British work of recent years, discuss them briefly and try to combine them into a new model illustrating what I consider the main variety classes.[9]

My starting point is the model proposed by Rona in 1970. It reflects the multidimensionality of language in that it accounts for

8 Dialect is commonly understood to refer to a specialized selection from among all the levels of language organization distinctive of geographical areas. Sociolect is also a specialized selection from among all the levels of language organization, distinctive of social group, however. Since dialects and sociolects frequently overlap, modern dialectology comprises both (Weinreich, 1953:54). Hartman and Stork (1973) would also include the diachronic dimension here: «A regional, temporal, or social variety of language differing in pronunciation, grammar and vocabulary from the standard language, which in itself is a socially favored dialect.» Registers are commonly understood to be selections associated with particular functions or professions; they would include what is often referred to as jargon or cant (argot, lingo); cp. however the extension of the definition of register to cover all kinds of language varieties which is offered in the course of the present discussion for the case of the EFL speaker.

9 Wächtler (1977) also discusses Rona, Gregory and Quirk; his aim, however, is different from mine: He does not attempt to set up his own system of varieties classification, nor does he propose to link this well-known British work to results gained in recent American sociolinguistic research.

(a) diatopic (local-regional), (b) diastratic (social-cultural), (c) diachronic (historical), and (d) diatypic (functional-stylistic) language variation. This makes it possible to house (a) apparent areal differences, (b) socially and culturally motivated differences, (c) differences due to language change in the course of time, and (d) differences according to style or register.

Figure 1 RONA 1970. Multidimensionality of varieties

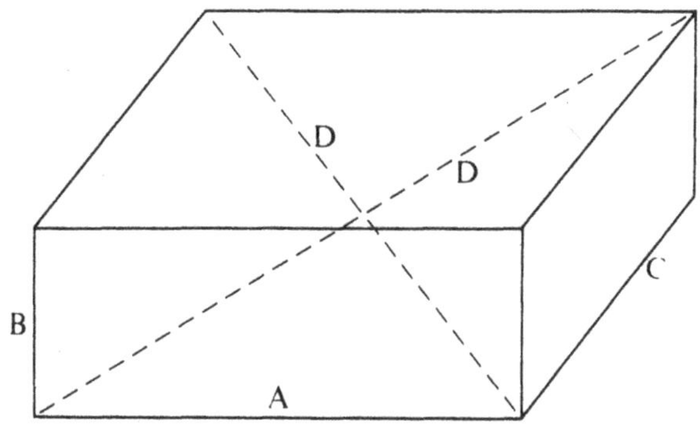

RONA's classification of varieties as diatopic, diastratic, diachronic, or diatypic corresponds to the tentative grouping of varieties given from the outsider's point of view (above, pp. 46 to 47). It seems to be basically useful. However, it lacks the elaboration of the diatypic dimension which is necessary for the needs of the EFL speaker. Here, GREGORY's suggestions (1967) can be helpful:

Figure 2 GREGORY 1967. Classification of varieties

1 Dialectal

	situational categories	*contextual categories*	*examples of English varieties (descriptive contextual categories)*	
user's	individuality	idiolect	Mr. X's English, Miss Y's English	*dialectal varieties:* the linguistic reflection of reasonably permanent characteristics of the *user* in language situations
	temporal provenance	temporal dialect	Old English, Modern English	
	geographical provenance	geographical dialect	British English, American English	
	social provenance	social dialect	Upper Class English, Middle Class English	
	range of intelligibility	standard/non standard dialect	Standard English, Non Standard English	

2 Diatypic

	situational categories	*contextual categories*	*examples of English varieties (descriptive contextual categories)*	
user's	purposive role	field of discourse	Technical English, Non-Technical English	*diatypic varieties:* the linguistic reflection of recurrent characteristics of user's *use* of language in situations
	medium relationship	mode of discourse	Spoken English, Written English	
	addressee relationship	tenor of discourse		
	(a) personal	personal tenor	Formal English, Informal English	
	(b) functional	functional tenor	Didactic English, Non-Didactic-English	

GREGORY establishes a fundamental difference between varieties that reflect reasonably permanent characteristics of the user in language situations (idiolect, temporal dialect, geographical dialect, standard/nonstandard) and varieties that reflect the recurrent characteristics of the user's use of language in situations (field, mode and tenor of discourse). This is the crucial distinction also made by HALLIDAY, a distinction, I have already said, that does not apply to the outside speaker of English who does not share any dialect of English. Dialectal variation – to elaborate on this point – is variation between speech communities, to some extent also within speech communities; it is determined not only geographically, but socially as well; it is determined, in HALLIDAY's words (1978:185) «by 'who you are', your regional and/or social place of origin and/or adoption.» Diatypic variation, on the other hand, is determined «by 'what you are doing', the nature of the ongoing activity.» When speaking about the various kinds of diatypic variation, HALLIDAY uses the term 'register'. He subgroups diatypic varieties by means of the labels 'field,' 'tenor', and 'mode', exactly like GREGORY.

The field of discourse largely determines the content of what is being said; the tenor of discourse refers to the participants in the speech situation; the mode of discourse covers the channel of communication, written or spoken, and the particular rhetorical mode selected (1978:223). With the inclusion of rhetorical genre under mode, HALLIDAY can simplify GREGORY's system: «functional tenor» is no longer needed (cp. Figure 2). HALLIDAY claims that if a situation is characterized with the help of these three variables, prediction of the kind of language to be used is possible (226). This last point is of importance to the outsider as an EFL speaker. We will have to come back to it.

Looking back on GREGORY's tabulation now (Figure 2), a word must still be said about the class he calls 'idiolect'. As hinted before, idiolects might of course be discernible from the point of view of the outsider, too; but they cannot be important to him. I stress again that as an EFL speaker he is mainly interested in typical varieties, varieties that are group or situation specific. That is why idiolects won't be considered in this study; what is emphasized is the notion of 'typolect'.

In an attempt to combine GREGORY's classification with RONA's broader one, we might bring together GREGORY's 'temporal dialect' with RONA's 'diachronic'; GREGORY's 'geographical' with RONA's 'diatopic', and his 'social' and 'standard/nonstandard' varieties with RONA's 'diastratic' ones. The diatypic varieties mentioned by RONA need the further subdivision according to GREGO-

RY's and HALLIDAY's concepts of 'field', 'tenor' and 'mode'. When quoting HALLIDAY above I mentioned some of these concepts: content, participants and channel.

The model developed by QUIRK et al. (1972) gives further suggestions. They distinguish between six variety classes:

Figure 3 QUIRK, LEECH, GREENBAUM and SVARTVIK, 1972: Variety classes

Variety Classes	*Varieties within each Class*
Region:	$R_1, R_2, R_3, R_4, \ldots$
Education and social standing:	$E_1, E_2, E_3, E_4, \ldots$
Subject matter:	$S_1, S_2, S_3, S_4, \ldots$
Medium:	$M_1, M_2, \ldots$
Attitude:	$A_1, A_2, A_3, A_4, \ldots$
Interference:	$I_1, I_2, I_3, I_4, \ldots$

In this classification, 'region' seems to go with RONA's 'diatopic'; 'education' and 'social standing' with 'diastratic'; 'subject matter', 'medium' and 'attitude' might be subgroups of RONA's 'diatypic' dimension. Labels for the diachronic dimension QUIRK et al. do not have. A strange class, found only in this model is 'Interference'. The authors themselves agree that this «should be seen as being on a very different basis from the other types of variety» (1973:7). They refer to «the trace left by someone's native (non-English) language upon the foreign (English) language he has acquired.» Of course, there are varieties of English characterized by admixtures of other languages; but it is simpler to treat these, too, as either regional or social. For our purpose, 'Interference' is not considered. It is more important to note the correspondences between the other variety classes: When speaking about varieties according to subject matter, QUIRK et al. have in mind GREGORY's 'field of discourse'; when referring to varieties according to medium, GREGORY's 'mode of discourse'; when speaking of varieties according to attitude, GREGORY's 'tenor of discourse', subgroup (a).

For this last class, which, according to Halliday, is the only one to be considered under the heading of 'tenor', Quirk et al. propose a further subdivision (1973:7):

(rigid) – formal – (neutral) – informal – (familiar)

'Tenor' thus becomes a label also comprising a class of varieties elsewhere called 'styles'. Actually, Quirk et al.'s subdivision meets very well with Martin Joos' well-known classification of styles (1962):

Frozen – formal – consultative – casual – intimate

If the models proposed by Rona, Gregory, Halliday and Quirk et al. are brought together in accordance with the combinations and simplifications suggested above, the varieties of a language like English could be represented in terms of the following chart:

Figure 4 Summary chart of varieties classification

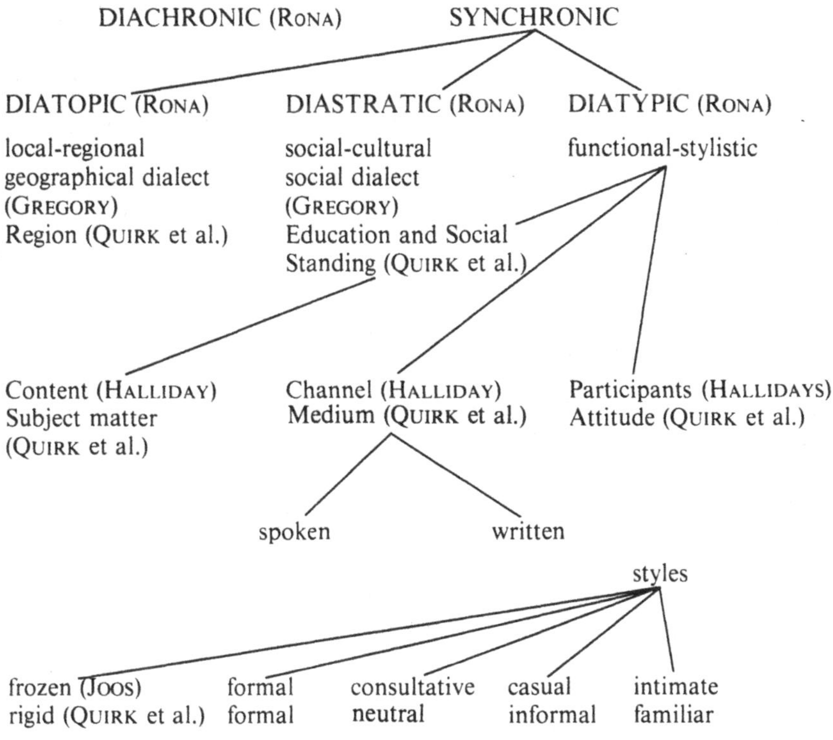

To the outsider English shows two main kinds of variation: diachronic variation and synchronic variation. Both appear in this chart. Although he is again and again reminded of diachronic variation – when reading Thomas JEFFERSON, e.g., or when coming across archaisms in a dictionary – the EFL speaker is more concerned with synchronic variation. He first experiences synchronic variation in its form of grammatical variation – as in the marking of tense in the verb system –, and phonological variation – as when comparing the pronunciation habits of his teacher to those of his favorite rock singer –, as well as lexical variation – as in innumerable exercises on synonyms; only later does he become aware of the existence of large bundles of language elements that together appear as local-regional, social-cultural or stylistic-functional varieties of a language like English.

As pointed out before, this model, through its acceptance of GREGORY and HALLIDAY, is still based on the fundamental distinction between dialect (language of user) and register (language of use). It does not live up, therefore, to the claim that the outsider does not share any dialect of English. The classification of language varieties it suggests, however, seems to be a sound one. We will therefore go on discussing language varieties in these terms, while at the same time attempt to exclude the notion of dialect completely.[10]

In order to achieve this goal I will have to review linguistic work of another tradition. It seems significant to me that many of the categories of variety classification identified so far meet with categories set up in the work of sociolinguists. In the work of American sociolinguists – on some of which I shall now concentrate – there is indeed a certain overlap in terminology with that used in our chart (Figure 4), especially when the determining factors in communication are discussed.

Susan ERVIN-TRIPP, in her important article on the interaction of language, topic and listener (1964), found that language differs be-

10 Another reason why a varieties grammar rather than a dialects grammar is envisaged in this study is the conviction on my part that there seems to be a need for an integrative approach not only with regard to regional varieties of English, but even more so to social and functional-stylistic varieties.

tween one situation and another. Variety labels of the kind noted above could be related to specific speech situations or speech events. People were noticed to switch between varieties even within discourse. ERVIN-TRIPP was able to identify two marked styles, formal and informal, both contrasting with an unmarked colloquial style. In her model for speech events, which she characterized as interaction of variables, she isolated variables like 'setting' (physical locale and situation in a more general sense), 'topic' (manifest content of what is being talked about), 'channel' (whether oral, written, or broadcast), 'participants' (mainly their social status and their level of education), and 'function' (goal, comprising, as it seems, both illocutionary force and perlocutionary effect).

Of these variables, some find direct parallels in our classification of language varieties (Figure 4): The styles mentioned by ERVIN-TRIPP correspond to those named by QUIRK et al. ('formal'/'formal' – 'colloquial'/'neutral' – 'informal'/'informal'); ERVIN-TRIPP's 'channel' and 'participants' are also listed by HALLIDAY, and her 'topic' refers to HALLIDAY's 'content' and QUIRK et al.'s 'subject matter'. 'Setting' appears to be a more complex notion: it is related to local-regional varieties, but goes much beyond the diatopic into the realm of milieu and even atmosphere; 'function' finally is a category not found in the chart.

In her second highly influential article, «On sociolinguistic rules» (1972), ERVIN-TRIPP even more definitely tried to relate speech styles to contexts of discourse. She found that these speech styles draw on the linguistic varieties present in a speech community, an insight closely linked up with work done by John J. GUMPERZ.[11] GUMPERZ' interpretation of varieties is derived from his notion of the speech community. He defines a speech community

11 ERVIN-TRIPP's contribution to language description is considered by Dell HYMES (1974:202) as «a culmination of the quest in linguistics through this century for adequate descriptive concepts.» The decisive step taken by ERVIN-TRIPP was, according to HYMES, «to recognize speech styles themselves as the elements of a further system of rules. (. . .) The study of the structure of relationships among speech styles might also open up the possibility of a generative approach; and its makes the study of social meaning as embodied in roles, activities, and situations integral to the explanation of the meanings of the speech styles themselves.»

as «any human aggregate characterized by regular and frequent interaction by means of a shared body of verbal signs and set off from similar aggregates by significant differences in language use.» (1971b:114) People living together in a speech community are said to have a speech repertoire consisting of several varieties. Thus, GUMPERZ defines 'repertoire' as follows: «The totality of dialectal and superposed variants regularly employed within a community make up the verbal repertoire of that community.» (1971b:125) When giving examples of what an individual's choice from the speech repertoire might indicate, GUMPERZ (1971b:115) makes use of labels that again parallel, to some degree at least, the terminology used in our classification of varieties (Figure 4). He mentions variables like 'family background', 'rustic', 'educated or uneducated classes', 'urbanite', some of which seem to fit in with the diastratic group; 'Southerner', 'Northerner', which reflect the diatopic classification; and 'friendly', 'distant', 'familiar', 'deferential', 'superior', 'inferior', which go well with the diatypic. Indeed, GUMPERZ agrees that speech varieties within a speech community «can be classified according to their usage, their origins, and the relationship between speech and social action that they reflect.» (1971b:116) Although GUMPERZ is not interested in a formalistic varieties classification of the kind proposed above, he does make one distinction: He distinguishes between dialectal and superposed varieties. «Dialectal variation relates to distinctions in geographical origin and social background», «superposed variation refers to distinctions between different types of activities carried on within the same group.» (1971:120f.) This clearly parallels HALLIDAY's distinction between dialectal and diatypic variation.[12]

By looking at the work done by ERVIN-TRIPP and GUMPERZ, it becomes quite obvious that even interactional sociolinguists cannot do without certain variety labels.[13] However, by emphasizing

12 Although the term 'dialect' occurs again with GUMPERZ here, I have adduced these statements to my discussion. The main point, after all, is to demonstrate the similarity between the work of the British linguists and that of some American sociolinguists in the process of varieties labelling.

13 Cp. also LUCKMANN (1969), who, from the point of view of sociology, distinguishes: ecologically determined communication; communication

discourse situations and interaction in conversation rather than the diversification of language into different systems, their approach to language variation is more dynamic than the one taken by the British linguists.

For our purpose of presenting the outsider's view of English language varieties, it seems useful to explore some of the notions forwarded by ERVIN-TRIPP and GUMPERZ and try to link them up with the classification of varieties reached above. These notions are: speech event and situation (ERVIN-TRIPP) and repertoire and speech community (GUMPERZ).

At least from an outside point of view, variety labels like 'Middle English', 'General American' or 'Black English' are not informative and accurate enough. Such a classification overlooks the fact that not only within Middle English, but also within General American or Black English (or any other similar class) speech and texts may vary considerably. They need definition not only in terms of either historical segment, dialect, sociolect, or style, but through a combination of such labels. Thus, the branching classification of varieties suggested in Figure 4 cannot be the ultimate goal. Another step has to be taken so that a text or a portion of speech can be defined in a way that reflects RONA's multidimensionality more accurately.

ERVIN-TRIPP (1972:233–234) discusses hypothetical utterances which are the result of variety mixture; e.g.:

> How's it going, Your Eminence? Centrifuging OK? Also have you been analyzin' whatch'unnertook t'achieve?

This result, of course, is not what I expect when saying that varieties should be defined through a combination of labels. What I mean is that language varieties must be characterized by their components, components that have often been individualized and stressed so much as to become variety labels themselves. Speech is never only temporal, local, or occupational; it is all of that and more in combination. (see chapter 2.5)

ordered to institutional spheres (like kinship, politics, religion, economy); occupational jargons and codes evolving in social classes.

ERVIN-TRIPP's point in the example adduced was the working of co-occurrence rules. «Once a selection has been made, . . . later occurrences within the same utterance, conversation, or even between the same dyad may be predictable.» (1972:233) In her example, the inconsistent selections are made by pairing an informal phrase with formal morphological form, by combining a formal address with an informal greeting, etc. «Co-occurrence rules refer to the selection of alternates within the repertoire of a speaker in terms of previous or concomitant selections.» (1972:240) These co-occurrence restrictions affect all the levels of language organization (prosody, grammar, discourse). The existence of evidence for such co-occurrence rules was forwarded by various scholars: for grammatical morphemes and phonology by LABOV, 1966, for lexicon and morphology by FISHER, 1964, for style by ERVIN-TRIPP, 1972; a generalization was then made by John J. GUMPERZ. Co-occurrence rules became an important aspect of GUMPERZ' concept of the speech repertoire. GUMPERZ has summed up his views in his Language and Society Lectures (Berkeley, 1979), where he speaks of co-occurrence expectations which are culturally determined; the individual speaker has a range of stylistic variants which he uses according to context and speech event; variation in language is thus no longer simply a matter of grammatical rules but of conversational maxims (GRICE, 1975) working for the moment.[14] The fact that such co-occurrence rules have been worked out is highly important for our purpose here: It makes it possible to state and predict what kind of language – which variety – should be used in a given situation. A speaker can be given hints regarding which language elements to draw out of the whole stock of language at his disposal.

Situation, speech event, context – these sociolinguistic units become decisive for the kind of language to be used. In the view now proposed, the speaker has a repertoire of varieties at his disposal which he can use according to the occasion. LABOV is one of the sociolinguists who do not share this viewpoint. As he sees it, vari-

14 In 1972, GUMPERZ had spoken of «co-occurrence clusters» (21) and, like ERVIN-TRIPP, he had stated that «the speaker's choice of a particular value of a variable is always constrained by previous selections of variables.»

ation is inherent to the system; it occurs at regular intervals and can be expressed in variable rules (see 4.2.3). He thus opposes the possibility of variety mixture in special codes. However, he would agree that speech situations and other social factors largely determine variation. LABOV sees a problem in the fact that variation might occur in individual speech even in one particular situation. Such idiolectal variation, it seems to me, does not show to the same degree if attention is given to groups of speakers instead of to individuals. And it is group specific speech patterns or typolects that are central to this study.

2.5 Speech Repertoires

We can now try to show how varieties of English may constitute a speech repertoire of the EFL speaker. Taking up the earlier discussion on dialect and register, we can now state that all language varieties of English are diatypic varieties or registers in HALLIDAY's sense. No single variety is the outsider's dialect; no English dialect expresses who he is. On the contrary, whatever variety he uses is determined – in HALLIDAY's words – by the ongoing activity. The way varieties are handled by the outsider confirms HALLIDAY's own observation that dialects may come to be an aspect of register even for native speakers (1978:34), as in the case of dialect switching according to context.

For the outsider and EFL speaker, then, language varieties of English are first of all registers. Registers here should be defined in a way that goes beyond HALLIDAY to include clearly sociolinguistic features. Thus register can be defined as a language variety distinguished by circumstances of use, sensitive to such factors as the context and topic of discourse, as well as the relative status (age, sex, occupation) and familiarity (closeness, distance) of the people speaking. That registers of this kind are very much a reality in, say, American English was proved by case studies on baby talk, classroom teaching language, doctor talk, religious language, etc. Elaine ANDERSEN (1977) stressed the importance of register talk when demonstrating that even four year old children know the difference between registers and exploit them for play. Our notion of register, however, allows us to include varieties of less specific and less bounded kinds as well. Registers come to be identified with the speech varieties or the speech styles GUMPERZ mentions as making up a speech repertoire. Instead of the classification of varieties proposed above (Figure 4), I suggest now that a classification inspired by GUMPERZ' notion of speech repertoire can reflect the views and needs of the outsider much better.

Although most EFL teaching materials might suggest the contrary, knowledge of language varieties is advisory to the outside speaker of English, though probably less so for actual language production than for language comprehension. Although imitating accents of so-called non-standard speakers is never a good idea – unless the outsider also shares the whole cultural and social background with his partner in conversation, accurate imitation of a native speaker's accent might actually terminate the conversation – the outsider should nevertheless be able to understand the kind of English used by his partner in conversation. Active production is necessary in those varieties that are used in connection with particular situations and/or subject-matters. The outsider must not only be able to understand technical English, e.g., but, if he wants to participate in a discussion, on, say, electro-dynamics, he must also be able to produce the special variety required in this context. Equally, it is not sufficient if he recognizes certain forms of American English as polite, he must also be able to produce polite language himself. This, then, means that the outsider – almost as much as the insider – must know which variety is appropriately used where, when, and how.

Such considerations suggest a working model for language varieties that is speaker-oriented. In the following, the speaker is characterized by his own cultural background: his family, his education, his knowledge about the world, his experiences and his expectations. All this decides in part on how he is to use the language available to him. Equally or even more important are the other factors he has to take into consideration: speech act, topic, channel; social status, sex, age, ethnicity, occupation of himself and his partner(s) in conversation; location and time. According to these factors he selects those language items that fit his momentary communicative purpose and the given situation. Language items thus selected make up one register out of his speech repertoire. In order to picture the idealized selectional process, we might want to see language arranged in circles around the speaker. Figure 5 may illustrate this:

Figure 5 Variety selection process

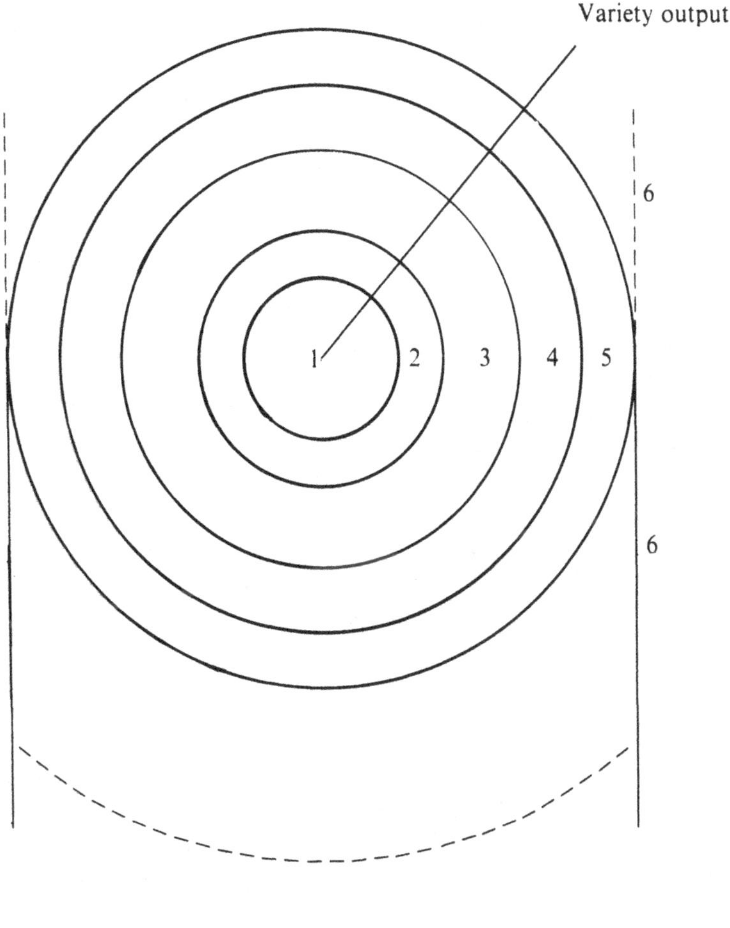

Factors

1 Speaker background, incl. expectations
2 Topic
3 Channel
4 Participants: their social status, sex, age, ethnicity, occupation
5 Location
6 Time

In order to get the appropriate language variety (register) the speaker has to twist these circles (as it were) until the spots containing the language items required for a particular occasion are all arranged in the output line. The speaker (1) is in the center; this center also contains the experience and the knowledge particular to him. Around the speaker are arranged the layers of language from which he is drawing the linguistic material relevant for the topic chosen (2), the channel chosen (3), for interaction with partners in conversation and geared towards their social status, sex, age, ethnicity, and occupation (4), and for a particular area of the English-speaking world (5) at a given point of time (6). In a particular case, (1) might be identified as a male UCB student (undergraduate), (2) as last night's CAL movie, (3) as oral, (4) as close friends and fellow students of (1), and (5) as the Berkeley campus. If, in this model, the circular field is enlarged into a cylinder, the diachronic dimension can be housed, too. Any varieties can now be defined from the speaker's point of view by cutting up the cylinder at some point of time. Time being, say, June 22, 1980, topic the preceding night's CAL movie, channel oral, participants close friends of the speaker, location UC Berkeley campus, a rather well-defined variety of American English emerges whose linguistic characteristics should be listable to the degree necessary for an outside speaker of English. According to this model, the outsider is expected to assess a situation with regard to topic, channel, participants and setting in order to select the appropriate kind of English from his EFL repertoire. Sometimes the register used will be one of the diatopic, diastratic or diatypic varieties identified before (Figure 4); more often, however, it will be a combination of some of these, e.g. a conversational film review (diatypic) in student jargon (diastratic) in California English (diatopic). Ideally, the repertoire of the outsider should come close in its potential to the repertoire of the native speaker. We know, however, that there is an attitudinal difference, in that the outsider's English language repertoire does not include any dialect, but registers exclusively (above, p. 59). And the number of these registers or the range of his repertoire is determined by where in the USA he is living, what the ongoing activity is, and who the persons participating are –

much more so than in the case of the native speaker whose varieties repertoire is subject to certain practical limitations as well.

If the outsider is a foreign student learning English as a second or foreign language and he is made to see English as more than a uniform *lingua franca,* special attention should be given to the building up of his varieties repertoire. It would seem advisable to instruct him (1) in one of the two varieties of English used for international communication: American or British English. (2) The one not used in his schooling should be pointed out to him through contrastive analysis. (3) Within the standard language chosen the formal as well the informal varieties must be made available to him, one serving academic (mainly written) purposes, the other everyday speech. (4) In addition, he should be given instruction in those non-standard varieties he is bound to encounter in that area of the English-speaking world he has come to or plans to go to. For the San Francisco Bay Area, and assuming a white EFL student, all this might lead to a speech repertoire consisting of varieties like

Standard Academic English
American Network English

in which he would have active competence, and varieties like

Black Vernacular English
Chicano English
Mellowspeak etc.

in which he would have passive competence only.[15] To delimit his speech repertoire further, one would have to include a catalog of his fields of study and further interests as well as a list of the social groups of which the native speakers he meets in social interaction are members. With such knowledge at hand, one would then be

15 The labels of the varieties are identical with those used in chapter 3 if the varieties in question are mentioned in both places. In chapter 3, American Network English is not included among the varieties of English in the San Francisco Bay Area presented; it is mentioned here because the foreigner will be greatly impressed by the speech style of the mass media. Mellowspeak, Black (Vernacular) English, Chicano English and Standard Academic English are all described in chapter 3.

able to say which varieties of (American) English he needs to know (actively or passively) and which should be part of his repertoire of English as a foreign language.

2.6 Summary

Throughout this chapter it has been suggested that a manual of the kind offered by a varieties grammar might be a means to relieve some of the needs of the outsider, the EFL speaker of English. It has been claimed that the outsider, too, is aware of the real-world existence of several language varieties beside the artificial Textbook Standard English in which he is commonly instructed. The attitude of the outsider towards the various varieties is neutral, although, of course, it may be influenced so that he begins to favor one particular variety at the cost of the others. None of these varieties, nevertheless, has an identifying or revealing function: none is his dialect, they all are registers. That the building-up of a varieties repertoire may be desirable is confirmed by the research on the EFL speakers in the San Francisco Bay Area (chapter 2.3). A (pedagogical) varieties grammar might be the instrument which might bring them to reach at least 'average communicative competence' (HYMES, 1968). The varieties to be included in a given speech repertoire can be classified taxonomically (as in Figure 4) as well as dynamically (as in Figure 5). In both cases the varieties are to be viewed as typolects, not idiolects. Knowledge of the pertinent variables and appropriate co-occurrence expectations, it is claimed, will make it possible to predict the use of a particular variety in a particular situation.

Part II: Introduction

Part II (Chapter 3) is basically an account, in terms of social dialectology, of the most prominent English language varieties currently in use in the San Francisco Bay Area. Its function within the overall plan of the study, however, is not so much to offer a synchronic description of the present-day varieties of English in the San Francisco Bay Area, as it is to provide the data of actual language varieties that might be found in the speech repertoire of real-world speakers and for which a varieties grammar might be written. Instead of sociolects, a bundle of different language varieties, e.g. text type varieties, might have been considered. However, it so happened that my research interests were drawn toward California social dialectology because in that area no previous research efforts are recorded. Whatever the kind of varieties selected, the purpose would have been the same: To establish, on the basis of primary observation of language in operation, what it takes to speak, understand or interpret language varieties; to establish also which levels of language organization are involved so as to determine how far the notion of 'grammar' in a varieties grammar has to be extended. The social-dialectological account of English language varieties in the San Francisco Bay Area is thus understood as a case illustrating the requirements of a varieties grammar.

Between the more speculative approaches of Parts I and III, Part II rightly occupies a central position. It is relatively easy to speculate about a varieties grammar in theoretical terms only, to review the relevant literature, and to suggest a new model. However, it is only first-hand experience in being exposed to diverse language varieties that will point out which parts of language should be included in a grammar for those varieties. My position, therefore, differs from that taken by many contemporary linguists. While CHOMSKY holds that only cognitivists are true linguists, whereas dialectologists and ethnographers are not (Immanuel Kant Lectures, Stanford, February 1979), I adopt the view that linguistics is a holistic discipline in which there is room for cognitivists *and* ethnographers, for psycholinguists *and* dialectologists, and in which the gathering of data in the field must precede theorizing, the «dirtying of our hands» (to make use of an expression from linguistic folklore) the speculative work at the desk. The account of English language varieties in the San Francisco Bay Area is meant to provide the real-world background against which the theoretical models for a varieties grammar presented in Part III can be checked.

CHAPTER 3

3 Varieties of English in the San Francisco Bay Area: An illustrative case

3.1 Towards a Social Dialectology of the San Francisco Bay Area

3.1.1 California Dialectology

For American dialectologists generally, the first motivation for investigative work was an antiquarian one. The goal of the first dialectologists – in 1889 – was to produce a dialect dictionary that would relate contemporary forms (sounds and words) back to their past forms in England. Their attempts reflect the search for linguistic roots by the descendants of the first Anglo settlers on the East Coast. Later, the newly established American Dialect Society decided to imitate the work of the European dialect geographers and produce a Linguistic Atlas of the United States and of Canada. Since the beginnings of this project – in 1929 – only the sections on New England (1933–43) and the Upper Midwest (1973–76) have been published. Five other sections are now in the process of being published (The Gulf States, 1972 –; The North Central States, 1976 –; The Middle and South Atlantic States, 1979 –) or at least in a state of 'progress' (Oklahoma; California-Nevada).[1]

The Atlas work is, no doubt, a superior scholarly achievement. Unfortunately, however, the practical value of the Atlas is somewhat doubtful, especially in the American West. As Raven I. McDavid, Jr., the leading American dialectologist says himself: «In linguistic geography it is necessary to choose informants from the longest settled and most stable elements of the population.» (1979b:3) While in Europe it was comparatively easy to locate

1 For information on the history of dialectology, especially dialect geography, in the United States I am indebted to various publications of Raven McDavid's, particularly McDavid, 1979.

such informants, in the extremely mobile society of California this proves more difficult. While in Europe dialect areas identified by means of isoglosses can frequently be interpreted as social dialect areas as well, such a coincidence appears to be near impossible in California. The data collected for the California Atlas 25 years ago by David REED and his crew (Berkeley) may reveal or at least corroborate some facts about the early settlement history of California, but with regard to the present-day spread and variety of the English language in California they are of little use.

A case in point is David DE CAMP's study of the English language in San Francisco (done under David REED at Berkeley, published 1958/59): Although DE CAMP was aware of the cultural diversity of San Francisco, he was not interested in the varieties of English created by the various social and ethnic groups, but in finding traces of East Coast dialects transplanted to the West Coast. He indeed succeeded in finding a Bostonese dialect in the area south of Market, and these findings have promtly made their way into accounts of California English although, twenty years later, there is hardly anything left of that East Coast dialect once spoken in San Francisco. In Carroll REED's updated edition of American Dialects (1977), we still read that «San Francisco maintains a class dialect to this day which is strongly reminiscent of Bostonese», a statement which is wrong from a present-day perspective even though REED tries to qualify it by adding that «the vast majority of the people there use a typical Northern Midland type of speech such as one might encounter in Illinois, Iowa, or Northern Colorado.» (1977:58)

This «Northern Midland type of speech» in turn has not received much attention by dialectologists. It was simply characterized as 'General American', 'Consensus English', 'Network English' or whatever label was found fitting for such an uninteresting variety. In the absence of more fascinating dialect forms – 13 years after DE CAMP, Elizabeth BRIGHT had to agree that many regional and local forms characteristic of the Atlantic seaboard had been lost in California – California English came to be characterized as lacking any special features, as being uniform and uninteresting. Characteristic is this quotation, again from MCDAVID (1975:114) speaking about Richard Nixon:

> When the White House was recently occupied by a native Californian, he and his fellow pranksters exposed the American public to the most aggravated kind of deregionalized faceless English.

This echoes a judgment made by Mario PEI eight years earlier (1967:192):

> If you want to hear the General American of the future, Hollywood and TV studio based, go to California and listen to the speech of the California-born younger generation. (. . .) Do you recall how in the presidential campaign of 1960 Kennedy's *ahsk* and *Africar* stood out like sore thumbs, while Nixon never drew a lifted eyebrow? Nixon spoke the general American of the future, an American shorn of all local peculiarities.

In 1980, TV commentators and journalists have made the same point all over again. Now it was Jimmy Carter's colorful southern accent that was compared to Ronald Reagan's bland, if correct, California English.

Dialectologists have repeatedly attributed the «deregionalized facelessness» of California English to the steady and substantial influx of immigrants from different parts of the United States and from various foreign countries. Because of the establishment of large urban centers and agricultural areas in this most rapidly growing state of the USA, dialect conditions have indeed been less tenuous than, say, in the Western mountain states. And Californians themselves have been found to exercise pressure towards the wiping out of dialect features in the speech of newcomers, especially New Yorkers, as the report about a speech therapist in Marin County quoted in chapter 2 documents. (p. 27)

In spite of such evidence for «blandness» (METCALF, 1977)[2], saying that California English is completely uniform and faceless is just as wrong as the attempt to explain present-day California English in terms of the Anglo settlement history. The «lively in-

2 In his 1977 account of Riverside English, METCALF notes a general blandness for California English, but moves away from Carroll REED's characterization of California (Anglo) English as a «typical Northern Midland type of speech» (1977:58) by showing a certain influence of Midlands and Southern pronunciations from the East.

termingling» of immigrant groups, of which Carroll REED is aware (1977:59), on the one hand has all but wiped out the remnants of East Coast dialects like Bostonese, and, on the other hand, has created new varieties of English for which there is no antecedent on the East Coast or in Britain. Today we have to note that there exists no adequate treatment of California English. The failure to deal with California English appropriately, as we see now, stems primarily from the narrow focus of traditional dialectological surveys of American English which restrict English to one ethnic variety only – Anglo English – and try to explain its varieties in terms of the original settlement history. Later population movements and other ethnic varieties are generally excluded.[3] Thus, accounts of California English do not speak about Chicano English, Black English, or Asian English, although ethnic varieties like these draw most attention upon themselves, not the hypothetical relics of East Coast dialects in Anglo English. What is appropriate to the language situation in California is an approach in terms of social dialectology rather than of dialect geography.

3.1.2 Demography of the San Francisco Bay Area

The claim that the newcomer to the San Francisco Bay Area (SFBA) is struck first of all by non-standard ethnic and other group varieties (cp. chapter 2) is substantiated by a closer look at the population of the area.

The SFBA is often understood to be identical with the San Francisco-Oakland Standard Metropolitan Statistical Area as identified by the US Bureau of the Census. As the map (next page) shows, it consists of Alameda, Contra Costa, Marin, San Francisco and San Mateo counties, covering 2.480 square miles boardering the San Francisco Bay. The larger Bay Area in addition includes

3 It has been calculated «that the typical informant for the Linguistic Atlas of the Pacific Coast would have been a Caucasian, a rural Californian, born in 1897 and educated through the eleventh or twelfth grade, a not-too-active member of a major Protestant denomination, and interviewed for the Linguistic Atlas in 1955.» (METCALF, 1977:23)

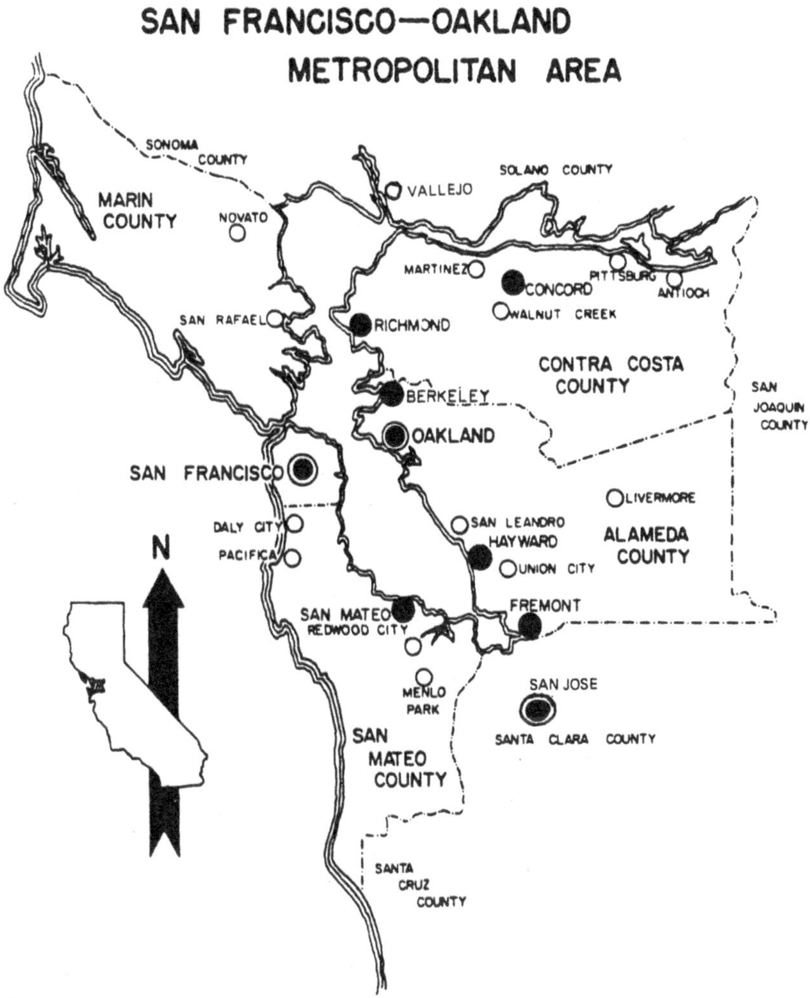

Sonoma, Napa and Solano counties to the north (boardering San Pablo Bay), and Santa Clara county to the south. San Francisco, San Jose (in Santa Clara) and Oakland are the largest cities of the area. Most of the population and industry is located in the flatlands around the bay and in the interior valleys of Contra Costa and Alameda counties. Least populated are the areas along the Pacific Ocean and in the coastal mountains of Marin and San Mateo.

In 1970, the population of the larger Bay Area was close to 4 000 000 (5 000 000 in 1978). The Report of the Bureau of the

Census, through the presentation of its data, acknowledges the large admixture of non-white ethnic groups. It not only has separate reports on Blacks (Negroes) and Chicanos (Spanish), but also separate entries for minority groups like American Indian, Japanese, Chinese, Filipinos. In 1970 the counties with the largest groups of non-whites were:[4]

San Francisco	28.6%
Alameda	20.2%
Solano	14.8%
Contra Costa	10.0%

The lowest percentages of non-white population were recorded in:

Napa	2.8%
Sonoma	3.4%
Marin	4.1%

Within the San Francisco-Oakland Standard Metropolitan Statistical Area the following cities had the largest ratio of non-white inhabitants:[5]

Oakland	40.9%
Richmond	40.1%
San Francisco	28.6%
Vallejo	21.8%

And these cities had the lowest percentage:

Sausalito	2.8%
Tiburon	2.3%

If one takes the population of the San Francisco-Oakland Standard Metropolitan Statistical Area projected for 1979, the following figures for different ethnic groups apply:

4 There are indications that the 1980 Report will show higher percentages for non-white population groups. (J. Fishman, personal communication)

5 Again, for 1980 the figures are expected to be considerably higher; additional cities will pass the 20% limit observed here.

White	2 486 410
Black	417 840
Chicano	387 980
Other	303 350

For the larger Bay Area only the 1970 figures are available.[6] These are presented here as rounded summations of the figures given for the San Francisco-Oakland, the San Jose, the Vallejo-Napa and the Santa Rosa statistical areas:

White	3 995 000
Black	370 000
Chicano	570 000
Chinese	100 000
Japanese	35 000
Filipino	54 000
Indian	18 000

3.1.3 Ethnic Language Varieties

From the viewpoint of demographic statistics there seems to be ample evidence suggesting a stratification of the English language in the San Francisco Bay Area according to social factors, especially ethnicity. According to the *International Encyclopedia of Social Sciences* (1968), an ethnic group is «a distinct category of the population in a larger society whose culture is usually different from its own. The members of such a group are, or feel themselves, or are thought to be, bound together by common ties of race, or nationality, or culture.» This definition is loose enough to accommodate not only such obviously ethnic varieties as Black English, Chicano English, Chinese English, or Japanese English, etc., but also Mellowspeak (see 3.2), the variety favored by many Whites, and even Gaytalk and Fraternity Talk (see 3.6; 3.7), although it may be safer to simply call these latter three 'social varieties' or 'group varieties'. Groups are separated by boundaries which help

6 No projections for the larger Bay Area have been made. First results of the 1980 Census may be available in late 1981. Final reports, however, are not expected before 1983.

to emphasize the cultures within these boundaries. In terms of language as an emblem of ethnicity, such boundaries clearly separate one language variety from another.[7] Within the larger social system of the SFBA, the English language is the vehicle of communication used by all the ethnic groups, both for intergroup and intragroup communication (cp. more generally FISHMAN, COOPER and CONRAD, 1977). Although in some cases, a group may have its own different language (e.g. Mexican Spanish, Cantonese, Tagalog), all the groups have created their own varieties of English. The point to be made with regard to this observation is that even without taking into account the original mother-tongue of, say, the Chinese, the Filipinos, or the Chicanos, ethnicity is mirrored in language, in the English language, i.e., which is the language shared by all the groups, though differentiated by each according to cultural heritage and folklore, according to favored topics and techniques of narration and conversation, according to the conceptualization of the world in vocabularies and semantic fields, and according to pronunciation habits often acquired through interference phenomena. Even if the grammar of English underlying the various varieties were identical for all those varieties – which it is only if a narrow definition of grammar is used and if a fairly rigorous TG view is adopted – the social meaning (the symbolic significance) of the alternate surface forms would still be different

7 This view is based on the sociolinguistic axiom that language is cultural behavior. Socio-cultural differences between population groups are not only manifested in non-linguistic behavior, but also in language; and language differences presume social-cultural differences. With WOLFRAM (1971a) I hold that language differences result from social-cultural differences among population groups. On the basis of this assumption, the research procedure in social dialectology is quite straightforward: (1) Isolate the population groups, (2) examine the kind of language used by them, (3) explain (2) in terms of (1). The description of linguistic differences is thus dependent – as HYMES (1969) says – upon an enthnographic description. Accordingly, it would be wrong to group speakers solely on the basis of linguistic differences – as done by DE CAMP (1968). WOLFRAM's 1969 approach seems to be more valid: He based the description of linguistic differences solely on the description of pre-determined groups. Although this second approach is to be favored over the first, the first should nevertheless be used in a second step in order to check the validity of the pre-determined socio-cultural group distinctions.

(GUMPERZ, 1977). In the study of ethnic language varieties, or more generally, in the study of group- or culture-specific language varieties, it is therefore just as important to look at the symbolic value of languages as it is to explain the formal characteristics of the language structure.

If the label 'ethnic' is restricted to population groups identified in demographic studies, a synchronic outline of the varieties of English in the SFAB ca. 1980 would cover:

Anglo English
Black English
Chicano English
Asian English

as the most prominent ethnic varieties. Asian English would be subgrouped into:

Chinese English
Japanese English
Filipino English
Korean English
Vietnamese English

Further, less conspicuous ethnic varieties might be added to the list:

Indian English
Italian English
Irish English

QUIRK et al. (1972), who recognize a separate Interference variety (see above, p. 52), would probably extend this list to include further groups like German, French, or Czech. However, while it is true that some characteristics of Chicano, Chinese, or Filipino English can also be explained in terms of interference phenomena, the case of the speakers of these varieties is clearly different from that of newcomers from, say, Germany or France. While the latter have arrived as individuals and quickly merged with the dominant (Anglo) Californian society, the former have arrived in extended family groups and generally not let themselves be fully assimilated into the dominant community, even as second or third generation

Americans. Although some of them, particularly from among the Irish, the Italians, the Japanese, and the Blacks have learned to speak General American in a way undistinguishable from the manner of Ronald Reagan, they have not simply adopted the patterns of white speech, but, instead, first created and then preserved their own variety of English. If they also speak the Standard Anglo variety, they can be observed to switch between what might be called their 'home variety' and what is their 'public or official variety'.[8]

In a geographical overlook of the SFBA it is not difficult to make out ethnically populated areas: The hills of the East Bay (white), the flatlands of the East Bay (black), the crammed sections of the South Bay (Chicano), Chinatown, Japantown, Boystown (where the Gay community lives) and Little Italy in San Francisco. It is in such areas that one would find the typical representatives of ethnic varieties. The city of San Francisco, which was populated earlier than the rest of the SFBA, reflects the situation in the Greater Bay Area on a smaller scale, as it were. When looking at San Francisco only, David DE CAMP (1958:388) gave the following description:

> San Francisco has always been quick to swallow but slow to digest its immigrants. This is particularly true of the foreign-born groups who have lived side by side in the city, generally, with little prejudice or intolerance but with little assimilation. Until World War II there was a distinct Chinatown, an Italian quarter, a Japanese section, a Negro district, etc. Each foreign and racial group tended to settle in its own district, not primarily because of such external pressures as zoning regulations and restrictive covenants, but because each wished to preserve its premigration culture. Consequently, San Francisco has never really been a 'melting-pot' like New York. The national and religious holidays of many countries are still observed in parts of the city. Foreign foods appear in its restaurants and grocery stores. Foreign languages are heard on its streets. Indeed, this cosmopolitan nature has always been the basis of the city's appeal to the tourist trade.

Twenty years later, DE CAMP's account is still valid basically. In the Greater Bay Area it is the Black, the Mexicans (Chicanos), the

8 An interesting example of such switching is discussed in GUMPERZ, 1979a.

Chinese, the Vietnamese and the Filipinos, and, to a somewhat lesser extent it appears, the Japanese, the Italians, and the Irish that have retained their cultural unity most intact. In addition, a sizeable portion of middle class Whites have recently created their own separate culture complete with their own language variety (Mellowspeak, 3.2). Recent immigration groups, like the Koreans, the Filipinos and the Vietnamese have again tended to move to the urban centers of the SFBA in extended family groups. Like the minority groups who came before them, they appear to settle close to each other and thus to form visible subgroupings of the population, with separate cultural organizations and developing language varieties of their own.

If a particular language variety is attributed to a particular ethnic group, this is not to say that the members of that group can express themselves in that variety of English only. After all, ethnic boundaries are permeable (BARTH, 1969). Depending on the networks of social interaction, members of an ethnic group can switch to another variety, as in these examples:

English Ethnic Variety	*Additional varieties*
Black English Vernacular	Network English, Standard Academic English, etc.
Chicano English	Network English, Chicano Spanish, etc.
Mellowspeak	Network English, Standard Academic English, Gaytalk, etc.

Ethnic language varieties, like other varieties, are thus seen as frequently making part of a speech repertoire comprising two or more separate language varieties. (Cp. chapter 2.5 and 4.4) As will be shown in the next section, ethnic and other group varieties are understood as typolects, i.e. language varieties typically associated with particular groups and having emblematic status for these groups within the scope of the English language in the SFBA.

3.1.4 *Linguistic Folklore and Typolects*

For the purpose of identifying typolects, especially ethnic and other group varieties, linguists and ethnographers profitably turn to folklore. Even a superficial inspection of the Berkeley Folklore Archives (Folklore Program, Department of Anthropology, University of California, Berkeley)[9] shows that there is ample evidence for ethnic varieties of English in the SFBA apart from that provided in demographic studies. In the SFBA, as much as elsewhere, the folk are aware of their own and especially of others' way of speaking. They are aware of some Whites talking in a particular, funny way (Mellowspeak, 3.2), of Black English (3.3) being different from Chicano English (3.4), of Asian English (3.5) being different again from Black English and Chicano English, of the Berkeley Fraternities and the San Francisco Gay communities employing vocabularies of their own, etc. Such a folk classification of English language varieties in terms of ethnic and social groups in general makes much more sense than a conservative dialectological classification of language varieties in regional terms. Although speakers of Mellowspeak predominate in Marin County (North West), and speakers of Chicano English in Santa Clara County (South), there is no point in distinguishing South Bay English from North Bay English or, for that matter, East Bay English from West Bay English. In most localities there are representatives of various social and ethnic groups and the speech repertoires of the communities are multivarietal. Instead of using a system of arbitrary regional classification, then, social dialectologists are better advised to follow the hints of folklore when attempting an identification and classification of the English language varieties in the San Francisco Bay Area.

Folklore materials may represent a group's image of itself as well as the representations of that image by members of other groups. Social and ethnic groups have traditional rivals and scapegoats for which the folklore acts as a unifying force by means of

9 Here is the place to express my gratitude to Alan DUNDES and his collaborators at the Berkeley Folklore Archives not only for having made the Archives accessible to me, but also for copiously and generously offered advice.

identifying the group and as a divisive force by means of molding or confirming a group's attitude toward another group. The genre of folklore most useful for this purpose is *blason populaire*, a genre comprising ethnic slurs, prejudiced attitudes and stereotype judgments (DUNDES, 1975). Examples of *blason populaire* can be used to illustrate the existence of boundaries between groups as well as to identify solidarity within groups. JANSEN (1965) distinguishes between the esoteric and the exoteric factor in folklore: 'esoteric' referring to what a group thinks of itself and what it imagines others to think of it; 'exoteric' referring to what a group thinks of another group and to what it imagines another group thinks it is saying about this other group. The stereotypes can be inwardly directed to establish strong in-group identification or they can be outwardly directed for the purpose of drawing attention to or depicting the characteristics of other groups. (1965:47)

When dealing with stereotypes of the kind represented by *blason populaire*, the question arises to what extent these can be taken to reveal something generally valuable. Since I claim that examples of *blason populaire* can be used to identify language varieties of social or ethnic groups, I obviously think that folklore stereotypes are of some validity. Looking back on the definitions of stereotypes in the United States, I find support for my view already in Walter LIPPMANN's classical account (1922). LIPPMANN characterized stereotypes as (1) means of organizing images, (2) fixed, simplex impressions, and (3) salient features chosen to stand for the whole. I am concerned mainly with the third point, the selection by the folk of a few salient features exhibited by another group, these features summing up in a short-hand way its characteristics in various areas, including language. (LIPPMANN also noted that such stereotypes are convenient, time-saving, and necessary; for without them man would have to interpret each situations as if he had never experienced any of the kind previously.)

A study more closely concerned with stereotypes and language is that by OGAWA (1969). OGAWA deals with the stereotypes in small-group communication. He shows how Caucasian UCLA students expect Japanese Americans to behave in discussions, and – this is the result I want to emphasize – that these stereotyped expectations are indeed represented in actual communicative behavior, i.e. the Japanese Americans indeed behaved as the stereotypes predicted they would. Equally, in my own research on examples of *blason populaire* and their relevance to social and ethnic varieties of English in the SFBA, I came to conclude that the materials stored in the Berkeley Folklore Archives do not only document the awareness of the folk that other social and ethnic groups are different from the one they themselves belong to and that the kind of English used by the members of these groups may differ from their own, but also that the points singled out by the folk turn up in linguistic accounts of the varieties in question as well.

In the accounts of English language varieties of the SFBA given in this chapter I will repeatedly quote examples of *blason populaire* in order to document from an ethnographic point of view the existence of such group varieties, at least as typolects. It is usually isolation due to different geographical and cultural origins, to differences in apparent behavior, countenance and customs, to differences in occupation, education, age, and social status, and, finally, to speaking the commonly shared language in a somewhat marked way that causes the creation of group stereotypes and of ethnic slurs. If language is addressed in *blason populaire* it is perceived not simply as any one of the cultural emblems marking off a group, but as the one emblem that can also include and express all the other emblems, like clothing, manners, diets, beliefs, myths, etc. *Blason populaire* can identify the cultural background and the characteristics of the kind of language typically used by the speakers in a certain group; it can point out the existence of what I call typolects. Folklore as a whole can establish the link between language and its function in different communities. «The ways in which language and folklore differ in function from one community to another are the most revealing,» is what HYMES (1972:44) says on the subject. Folklore, in general, may point to «the amount, frequency, and kinds of speech that are typical; the valuation of speech with respect to other modes of communication; and the valuation of different languages and ways of speaking.» (1972:44) *Blason populaire*, in particular, can reveal how ethnic and other social language varieties are valued and which of their features appear as the most salient ones. Since folklore is concerned above all with speech acts, genres, and phraseology, its comprehension of language is quite holistic. That is why I easily agree with HYMES on the point that folklore can «direct attention to essential features of language that are now neglected or misconceived in linguistic theory.» (1972:47) Indeed descriptions of language varieties like Black English, Chicano English or Fraternity Talk remain incomplete without proper considerations of those 'matters' that have so wrongly been termed 'extralinguistic'. Linguistic folklore appears to be particularly suited to reveal the cultural background relevant for a further characterization of the varieties in question. Where differences between language varieties are to be listed, it is insufficient to account only for what can be placed within the conventional narrow scope of linguistics: paricular of phonetics, of phonology, morphology, syntax, and certain aspects of semantics. A different notion of the scope of linguistics is required, one that can also accomodate variation in contextual and cultural frames.

3.1.5 Scope of survey

In the following survey of the English language in the SFBA I do not attempt a complete listing and description of all the varieties of English in use there. For one, completeness in this respect is unnecessary for the purpose of the larger study, and second, such a project would be a fragmentary one anyway: Nobody knows all the varieties of the English language; nor is the number of all the varieties of English occurring in the SFBA known. QUIRK et al.'s (1972:15) statement regarding the dialects of English is applicable here, too: «It is pointless to ask how many dialects of English there are.» Even for the most common varieties of American English, the data are still rudimentary. A source of reference like the *Linguistic Atlas of the United States and Canada* is of no help in identifying even the dominant varieties currently in use in the SFBA. The *Atlas* may contain information leading to the establishment of links between certain language items found in the SFBA and well-documented, but already historical dialects (cp. DE CAMP, 1958/59; BRIGHT, 1971). Since California English is still an elusive concept, there is no point in trying to consider

SFBA English as a whole and in establishing isoglosses separating it from other forms of California English. The traditional dialectological approach is therefore abandoned here in favor of a more strictly sociolinguistic one, which relates language varieties to social groups and speech communities. This more promising approach follows the impressions of the outsider (chapter 2) and considers the varieties of English in the SFBA not as regional, but ethnic-social and functional-situational.

The first variety to be described is 'Mellowspeak'. In many respects it combines characteristics of a group-specific variety like Gaytalk with those of a truly ethnic variety like Chicano English. 'Mellowspeak' is followed by a number of varieties that are much more easily correlated with ethnicity. Black English is dealt with in 3.3, Chicano English in 3.4, Asian English language varieties in 3.5. Varieties of English signalling group membership though not – at least not in conventional terms – ethnicity, are dealt with in 3.6 – (Fraternity Talk, Gaytalk and Juvenile Speech). In 3.8 the notion of Standard English is taken up; however, it is limited to Standard Academic English, a variety that is defined in functional-stylistic terms and can be correlated with contexts of application. In 3.9 some conclusions with regard to possible speech repertoires in the SFBA are drawn.

Research on the English language in the SFBA and in California in general is still in its beginning phase. (Cp. 3.1.1) Only in the case of Anglo English was it possible for me to check my material against that of other researchers. In the case of Black English, some comparison could be made to MITCHELL-KERNAN's (1971) Oakland-based work on Black language behavior. Chicano English is described in a somewhat impressionistic way, with comparison made to available accounts of Chicano English from Southern California and the Southwest. The section on Berkeley Fraternity Talk is based exclusively on material stored in the Berkeley Folklore Archives. The other varieties included are treated in a severely restricted way. Given this less than satisfactory research situation, the following survey of English language varieties in the SFBA should not be read as a definite account, but as a preliminary attempt to classify and describe in a synchronic way the varieties of English used in the SFBA ca. 1980. Within the scope of the whole study, these accounts are expected to establish the evidence that the English language in a region like the SFBA is indeed made up of several distinct varieties and that these varieties differ in more respects than a narrow grammatical approach would reveal.

3.2 Mellowspeak

Inhabitants of the SFBA themselves at times characterize California English as lacking special features (cp. 3.1.1). Talking like a native Californian is sounding as if you came from nowhere at all. This popular notion reflects what dialect geographers have found to be true about California English: It is said to be region-neutral and bland, close to, if not identical with the ideal of General American, Consensus English or Network English. In spite of this apparent facelessness, California as a whole (for additions to the vocabulary and praseology of American English from Mexican Spanish, cp. 3.4) and the SFBA in particular have shown linguistic inventiveness and productivity. Peter TAMONY, in a few colorful articles in *Western Folklore,* has demonstrated successfully that the SFBA has a tradition of producing its own special kind of English, especially in the realm of the lexicon, and then of exporting the innovations to the rest of the United States. In spite of the fact that Anglo English is said to sound so non-descript today, closer attention to it reveals that it can be quite different from the General American Standard. According to Tamony, the SFBA has always been good at coining new words and phrases. Indeed, a batch of Americanisms originated in or around San Francisco. To adduce a few:

shanghai, v.	'to kidnap sailors'
beatnik, n.	'member of the Beat generation'
sandlot, n.	'improvised or unofficial sportsfield'
malarkey, n.	'insincere, slightly pretentious talk'
hoodlum, n.	'urban ruffian, young rowdy'
Martini, n.	'a mixed drink'
Levi's, n.	'denim trousers'

All these vocabulary items are no longer restricted to the SFBA, but have spread throughout California and the United States.[10]

Given such evidence for linguistic inventiveness in the SFBA one should not be surprised to discover a new variety of Anglo English which is largely characterized by a phraseology of its own. Mellowspeak, as I call it following cartoonist Garry Trudeau, is different from General American or Network English in so far as it expresses through language the culture and lifestyle of a particular Anglo community, the center of which has been found in Marin County, just north of the Golden Gate. Marin County has a white population of 96%, in some of its cultural centers even of 98%. Marin is said to house a population dedicated to a life-style centering on self-awareness, on meditation, health food, and massage, on spiritual, social and physical communication (see documents inserted).

Mariners have been and still are the target of satire in California and the USA as a whole. Cyra McFADDEN's bestselling novel *The Serial* (1976) is just one, though maybe the most splendid example of such satiric treatment. McFADDEN reveals Marin culture through the speech patterns of those who participate in it. That is why the book has been exploited for linguistic analysis (LODGE, 1980; FALK and LAKOFF, in prep.). LODGE (1980) considers the novel «an invaluable guide to the dialect of the Bay Area, (. . .) a golden treasury of the slang that is spoken there by the educated middle classes.» (504) Basing himself on *The Serial* alone, LODGE has tried to comment on «the linguistic ingredients of this dialect», which he finds «varied and sometimes difficult to disseminate.» To him, the language of *The Serial* is an example of «psychobabble», a variety of the English language used to explore human relationships and states of mind; «it is essentially a language of psychological description and negotiation.» (504) LODGE then

10 This inventiveness contradicts David REED's rule of thumb for California vocabulary: the greater the use of a word throughout the East, the more likely it is to be the choice of Californians. (METCALF, 1977:12, based on REED, 1954:10–11) While this statement can be used to drive home the point of Californian linguistic blandness, it completely ignores the fact that there are highly popular words that have not originated on the East Coast at all, but were coined right there in California.

draws attention to the particular use of adverbs and prepositions in combination with verbs like *be, get, come;* he lists, among other expressions:

(1) to be into s'th.	as in	to be into Zen jogging
(2) to be at		this is where I'm at
(3) to be coming from		I know where you're coming from
(4) to be getting behind s'th.		People were getting behind marriages again
(5) to be coming down		What's coming down there?

LODGE notes that the language of *The Serial* is crowded with spatial-dynamic metaphors, most of which require translation into ordinary English. LODGE consequently translates

(1) as to be absorbed by Zen jogging
(2) This is the position I have reached in a particular process of change
(3) I understand what you mean
(4) People could accept and identify with marriage again
(5) What's happening?

He then proceeds, in his paper, to compile a tentative glossary of words and phrases that appear to require translation into ordinary English. He lists, among others,

To blow away	to surprise, astonish
to dump on	to inflict one's worries upon
to flash on	to notice, realize, think of
to run s'th. by	to show, explain
to swing with	to accept, tolerate
to munch out	to gorge oneself
to mellow out	to relax as a result of taking dopes
to wig out	to get very excited
to freak out	to go or cause to become very excited
to gross out	to disgust
to luck out	to find permanent good fortune
to hang	to act; behave, comport oneself
to lay	to inflict
heavy	serious, grave, important, powerful, oppressive
off the wall	spontaneously
far out	original, daring
upfront	honest, honestly
interface	relationship

trip	experience
to be into the pits	to have a depression

In his commentary LODGE points out that, generally, a special vocabulary «serves to define membership of a particular social or cultural sub-group, and to this end may be made deliberately mystifying to the uninitiated», but that «most slang, and certainly psychobabble is not deliberately exclusive in this way» (506). This is an observation I cannot back. The very fact that it is necessary to translate Mellowspeak into ordinary English shows that there is something «mystifying to the uninitiated». The foreign students subjected to examples of Mellowspeak (chapter 2.3) were unable to understand what was meant, although their fluency in Standard English was up to the TOEFL level. To the outsider, certainly, the variety illustrated in *The Serial* seems like the code used by the members of a culture to which he does not belong.

The language of *The Serial,* which LODGE calls «psychobabble», is labeled «Marin English» by LAKOFF (1979b) and FALK and LAKOFF (in prep.).[11] While «psychobabble» implies a negative attitude towards the variety,[12] «Marin English» implies a nar-

11 Robin LAKOFF presented her research on Marin English in a talk in a Charles FILLMORE seminar, Department of Linguistics, University of California, Berkeley, Winter Quarter 1979. Apparently I was collecting data concurrently with her and her collaborator Jane FALK. Since I began writing up my research only in August 1979, I could profit from LAKOFF's findings, check my material against hers and add additional points. Only later did I become aware of David LODGE's essay on the psychobabble of Cyra MCFADDEN's novel on Marin life *(The Serial).* Since LODGE's observations antedate both LAKOFF's and mine, he is to be credited with the original interpretation of Mellowspeak, even if LAKOFF and I might have arrived at the same or similar findings independently.

12 Satirist MCFADDEN is reported to call Mellowspeak «semantic spinach» and to accuse the variety of tyrannizing conversation, not only in California but increasingly throughout the country. Edwin NEWMAN, who, in *Strictly Speaking,* has profiled himself as a guardian of Standard English, is quoted as having made this statement on Mellowspeak: «It invents new phrases for old ideas, and sometimes new phrases for no ideas. (. . .) What worries me isn't so much the effect of Marin English on the language, but its larger effect on society. A society must be affected if a number of its members spend their time talking drivel.» (*Christian Science Monitor,* April 2, 1980, p. B16) Writer

row geographical definition. I therefore prefer the term «Mellowspeak». Both the lifestyle associated with Marin County and the language variety expressing it are no longer restricted to Marin County, but found all over the SFBA, and even beyond. A recent Doonesbury cartoon (Insert 1, p. 88) suggests that even New Yorkers are imitating the variety now. Once again, California and the SFBA appear to be trendsetters for the whole nation. In earlier cartoons (see Insert 2a, 2b, p. 89, 90), Garry TRUDEAU had made use of the Mellowspeak vocabulary with reference to Marin County and California only. The cartoonist's observation regarding the spread of Mellowspeak is confirmed by LODGE (1980:504), who, looking at Mellowspeak from Britain, finds that that particular variety of English is already «carried, by a kind of cultural gulfstream, to every part of the world where English is spoken», the reason being that «pop musicians, disc jockeys, top athletes and 'alternative' artists» tend to adopt and disseminate it around the world. Indeed, the diffusion of Mellowspeak beyond California throughout the USA and even abroad is also acknowledged by FALK and LAKOFF.[13]

Another reason for not giving Mellowspeak too narrowly geographical a label is that it appears to have its roots not only in Marin County, but in the whole SFBA. Mellowspeak seems to have developed out of the 1960's and reached its present-day form in the early 70's. One is tempted to trace it to locations throughout the SFBA: to San Francisco, the place of verbal inventiveness (cp.

Richard ROSEN is quoted as having said: «If psychobabble were a question of language alone, the worst one could say about it is that it is just another example of the corrosion of the English language. But the prevalence of psychobabble signifies more than a mere 'loss for words'. One never loses just words, of course, and so psychobabble represents a loss of understanding and the freedoms that accompany understanding as well.» (*Christian Science Monitor*, April 2, 1980, p. B17)

13 In a lecture entitled «Language in the Hot Tub: Talking Mellow», jointly delivered by FALK and LAKOFF in the heart of Marin County, the two linguists mentioned that «there are literal translations of 'Where your head is at' in Japanese and Hebrew». [Quoted in *Express* (Berkeley), May 2, 1980, p. 2]

Insert 1 G.B. TRUDEAU, Doonsbury, Cartoon. SF Chron., Oct. 14, 1979

Insert 2a G.B. TRUDEAU, Doonsbury, Cartoon. San Francisco Chronicle, January 14, 1979.

above),[14] of cosmopolitanism and multilingualism, the city that permits alternative lifestyles more than any other in the USA; to Haight Ashbury, where the hippies of the 60's established their

14 It was in San Francisco, at San Francisco State University, where she was a teacher, that Cyra McFADDEN was first exposed to examples of Mellow-speak. A student who had not read the assigned Ray BRADBURY short story, excused himself by saying: «I picked up the vibes and just couldn't get behind him.» When she threatened to flunk another student for not turning in any work, he responded: «I'm not into value judgments, so don't lay your power trips on me.» (Quoted from *The Christian Science Monitor*, April 2, 1980, p. B16)

counter-culture, where flower-children and beatniks found refuge in drugs and music; to Berkeley, where, again in the 60's, radical politics became manifest and the Free Speech Movement won a victory; to Mill Valley, finally, where membership in Human Potential Groups became a fashion and psychotherapy an addiction. However, I do not want to go too far in identifying Mellowspeak with particular places. Mellowspeak is not a local-regional dialect, but a social-cultural variety of English. It is more appropriate to say that it was created by and in the groups emerging from those places and the movements inspired or carried by them. Ultimately, it is never a place, but a group of speakers gathering in a certain location that create a new language variety.

Insert 2b G.B. TRUDEAU, Doonsbury. Cartoon. San Francisco Chronicle, May 18, 1979

LAKOFF (1979b) argued that the sources of Marin English (Mellowspeak) are mainly philosophical. This is surely correct if one thinks again of the Human Potential Groups, the groups of people leaning towards Eastern religions, the radical politics of the 60's and probably also the Drug Culture. However, the term 'philosophical' appears somewhat out of place if one would also include two of LODGE's «key sources»: Jazz and rock jargon, and sporting terminology. Yet, there is something loosely philosophical about those group activities I associate with the mellow lifestyle (Marin culture) and which are talked about in terms of Mellowspeak. It is helpful in this context to examine the SFBA monthly *Lifestyle*. All the 12 issues of 1979 checked by me have, with one or two exceptions, exactly the same entries. It is legitimate therefore to concentrate on one representative issue (November 1979). The monthly's table of contents list the following topics: Body Consciousness, Body and Mind, Bon Appetit, Health, Herbs, High Notes, Holistic Health, Meditation, Movies, Psychic, Religion, Rhythm, Singles, Spiritual Awareness, Theatre, Classified Ads, Lifestyle Events. Particularly interesting for a characterization of the mellow culture are the headings under 'Lifestyle Events': Alternatives, Awareness Training, Bioenergetics, Biofeedback, Body Consciousness, Business, Careers, Consciousness, Counselling, Couples, Education, Gestalt, Holistic Health, Hypnosis, Martial Arts, Massage, Men, Music, Nutrition, Performing Arts, Personal Growth, Primal Therapy, Psychodrama, Psychology, Singles, Weight Control, Women, Yoga. While many of these labels are themselves part of the Mellowspeak vocabulary, the texts announcing the particular events are even more revealing. Insert 3 (p. 92) contains some of these event announcements. The following verb phrases draw attention upon themselves:

have a flow of energy
open one's vision
affirm a commitment to human processes
emphasize flowing integration
relate beyond roles
become aware of deeper levels of meaning in life
reconstruct the inner movement of life
put oneself in touch with one's emotional, physical and spiritual body
share massage and enjoy good people
loosen up
ground
walk with one's feet firmly grounded
do centering exercises
do hot tubbing
give pleasure to one's partner and oneself
move through space
explore inner and outer relationships
align one's body
keep in balance
reestablish the bonds according to present needs and current life processes
change and transform
increase energy flow
stimulate one's senses
improve communication
celebrate being
have a good time

BIOENERGETICS
It is all right, gracefully, to walk with your feet firmly grounded to experience pleasure: Which is an appreciation of your body and all your vital functions, able to express a full range of emotion—to have a flow of energy, free of chronic tensions. A willingness to experiment, to open your vision, to recover your faith in your body, to affirm a commitment to your human processes. Gary Silverman, MA, MFCC (#12950), individuals, couples, groups. Grounded in Bioenergetics, emphasizing flowing integration between self and other. Sliding Scale. 334-4111

RELATING BEYOND ROLES
We often find ourselves relating to others from behind a role—male/female, expert/inept, aggressor/victim, happy/sad—which tends to keep us from a sense of genuine relating and sharing. It is possible to contact and project a more honest sense of who we are. Led by Steve Zolno, Self Center staff member, Director of Life Purpose Seminars, and creator of Effective Learning. Techniques for adults and children. At the Self Center, 555 2nd Ave., SF 8 pm. $4 includes wine party following.

INTENSIVE JOURNAL WORKSHOP
The Intensive Journal technique for self-realization, developed by Dr Ira Progoff, is structured in such a way that a person whatever his or her level of sophistication, can become aware of deeper levels of meaning in life. At your first workshop, the Life Context, you will receive a registered copy of the journal workbook, and you will be taken directly into experiences that will enable you to reconstruct the inner movement of your life. The sessions, led by John Leira of Dialogue House, will begin Friday evening at 7:30, continue through Saturday, and conclude early Sunday afternoon. Location is Russell College, 2300 Adeline Drive, Burlingame. Send $25 deposit to CRES, 25 W. 25th Avenue, San Mateo, CA 94403, or phone 341-1554.

INTEGRATED MASSAGE
Integrated Massage is designed to put you in touch with your emotional, physical & spiritual body to help you identify stress in these areas and release it through nurturing outlets such as: breath release, guided imagery, Gestalt, primal and meditation. Massage techniques such as Esalen, Shiatsu, polarity, Trager & reflexology are used to provide a complete approach to the whole body. A licensed graduate of the San Francisco School of Massage, Brian Silva has worked with the Buena Vista Doctors Clinic and has been teaching meditation & stress management and doing body work for the past three years in SF. For appointment call 641-0334.

DAY OF MASSAGE & HOT TUB FOR COUPLES & FRIENDS
Don and Catherine provide a warm safe environment in which to learn and share massage and enjoy good people. The day consists of introductions, loosening up, grounding and centering exercises, demonstrations, supervised practice sessions, hot tubbing and a pot luck lunch. The instruction focuses on basic and intermediate strokes of Esalen Massage with emphasis on giving pleasure to your partner and yourself. Don Spencer and Catherine Osterbye have been teaching together for over a year and Don has been leading massage workshops for over five years. Advance registration and deposit required. Phone: 658-4760 to register or to be on our mailing list

INTEGRAL COUNSELING CENTER
The Integral Counseling Center of the California Institute of Asian Studies offers crisis and growth counseling to individuals, couples and groups. Our services are available to anyone dissatisfied with his/her present way of life and wanting change and transformation. Our counselors have a wide variety of training in both Eastern and Western psychology—psychosynthesis, yoga meditation, Gestalt, Jungian dreamwork, humanistic, transpersonal and integral psychology. We have a sliding fee scale starting at $5, based on individual resources. All appointments can be made for days, evenings and weekends. Call 648-2644. 1780 Church St, SF 94114.

"EVERY BODY" WANTS TO MOVE
We will move through space exploring inner and outer spatial relationships between ourselves and others and focus on the breath, sound, and imagery in walking meditation. We will touch upon Oriental techniques in conjunction with movement for strengthening and aligning the body. Rachel Kraushar has taught movement, dance therapy and creative movement for 5 years & has taught Touch for Health for 2 years. At the Self Center, 555 2nd Ave., SF. 8 pm. 386-7027. $4 includes wine party following.

PRINCIPLES OF PERSONAL HEALTH TECHNIQUES
A very special evening with Jack Downing, who will lecture and demonstrate his own synthesis of numerous self-care techniques with emphasis on keeping in balance. By Jack Downing, Psychiatrist, Rolpher, Gestaltist, Arican and innovator. At the Self Center, 555 2nd Ave., SF. 8 pm. $4 includes wine party following.

RELATIONSHIP/COUNSELING
As healthy growing people we are constantly changing. Often this flux puts a great deal of stress on our relationships. Rather than leave or suffer along, forever wanting the relationship to be as joyous and exciting as it was when it was new, a better approach might be to re-establish the bonds according to present needs and current life processes. Gary Silverman, MA, MFCC (#12950), 334-4111.

A THANKS-GIVING
Join me in giving thanks for the body you are living in and the mind you have to balance. We will use techniques to increase energy flow, stimulate our senses, improve communication and have a good time, which is our purpose in life. Come and celebrate Being! No turkeys allowed. Led by Erna Ziegler who has practiced & taught Bio-Energetics, Gestalt & Movement for the past 12 years. Trained with Alexander Lowen at the Tulsa Psychiatric Center. At the Self Center, 555 2nd Ave, SF. 8 pm. $4 includes wine party following.

Insert 3 Lifestyle Events. From: Lifestyle. San Francisco, November 1979

It is with groups that engage in such and related activities that I associate Mellowspeak; i.e. with groups sharing interests in and concern for physical and psychic health and pleasure as well as with groups propagating alternative lifestyles (communal, gay, lesbian, feminist) and carrying political movements (environmentalists, conservationists, anti-nukes). Mellowspeak is spoken, I would suggest, by people who participate in activities of the kind advertised in the 'Lifestyle Events' announcements.

Without answering the question, LAKOFF (1979b) wondered whether 'Marin English' (Mellowspeak) can be considered a dialect. If HALLIDAY's definition is applied (1978:185) – a dialect being «who you are», indicating «your place of origin and/or adoption» – Mellowspeak could indeed be called a dialect of English. In the classification of language varieties proposed in chapter two, however, the term 'dialect' was restricted to the denotation of regional varieties. Since the use of Mellowspeak is not limited to Marin County but extends throughout the SFBA and even beyond, it makes more sense to treat it as a code selected by people who share the same culture. In this respect, Mellowspeak could be considered something like an ethnic variety, comparable to Black and Chicano English, especially since it is used by middle and upper class whites mainly (an observation also made by LODGE 1980). As in the case of the other ethnic varieties occurring in the SFBA, there are examples of *blason populaire,* jokes and satiric comments by means of which outsiders to the lifestyle expressed in Mellowspeak pass stereotypical judgments on the speakers of this variety. In SFBA folklore, the following joke is well-known:

> How many Mariners does it take to replace a bulb? – One to actually do the replacing, two to consider the implications, and three to share the experience.

Apart from Cyra MCFADDEN's *The Serial,* itself a satirical comment on Mellowspeak and the culture expressed through it, there are cartoonists and newspaper columnists who play on Mellowspeak in a way which, though much more sophisticated, is nevertheless reminiscent of linguistic *blason populaire.* The *Christian Science Monitor* cartoon (Insert 4, p. 94) contains six illustrations of the spatial metaphors characteristic of Mellowspeak:

> I'm not into value judgments.
> I'm getting into like a new reality.
> I said – Don't lay your power trips on me.
> I'm getting clear on where I'm coming from.
> I'm getting behind being an exercise freak.
> I picked up the vibes and just couldn't get behind him.

How to babblespeak in the hot tub

Insert 4 Christian Science Monitor, April 2, 1980, p. B16

The Doonesbury cartoons (Inserts 1, 2a, b) define the culture in which such language is used as mellow ('Mellow's own Dr. Dan Asher') and the language as 'Mellow-Speak'. Items often elaborate on the central concept of space: We learn that for speakers of Mellowspeak it is important to create and have a space, that «space is where your head is at», and that «space creates a context for im-

ART HOPPE

Small Was Beautiful

"MISSION CONTROL? Mission Control? This is Jerry Brown. Do you know where my head is at?"

"By our calculations, Governor, you should be touching down on Mars in five minutes, eight seconds."

"Wow! What a far out trip. And they laughed back in 1978 when I included $6.3 million in the State budget for our very own space program."

"Congratulations, Governor. You've won the space race by beating the Russians to Mars."

"And the Americans, too, Mission Control. Let's be upfront about this. It's one small step for mankind and one giant step for Californiakind. Can you relate to that, Mission Control?"

* * *

"WE CERTAINLY CAN, Governor. And how are your two fellow Californianauts doing?"

"Frankly, Mission Control, there's been a few bad vibes since Ralph came out of the closet three weeks after blast-off. I told Ralph, 'Wow, that's beautiful! I really know where you're coming from.' But George was very uptight about it. I told George that he and I didn't have to share Ralph's trip because we weren't into gayness, but we should be proud to be sharing space with Ralph because he was now such a beautiful person."

"Well put, Governor."

"Go with the flow, George, I said. But he said he couldn't groove on sharing such a damn small space for two months with, as he put it, 'a lousy faggot.'"

"We checked on him, Governor, and you were right. He recently immigrated to California from Cedar Rapids."

"I flashed on that right away. For when I told him that while small was beautiful, the possibilities were limitless, he called me some kind of nut. No true Californian would say that. He would say, 'Your head's really in a funny place, you know.'"

"Good thinking, Governor. Where's George now?"

"In a focal position in the observation bay. Definitely a defensive posture. Ralph and I have been working on getting him clear by taking turns reading him *The Complete Works of Khalil Gibran*, which we brought along for spiritual emergencies. But he won't come out."

"Good heavens, Governor, you'll need his help for the landing."

"Don't worry, Mission Control. Ralph and I are really laid back about this landing business. I'm going to plant the State flag and make a long forty-second speech pointing out that the whole purpose of our space program is to prove the California lifestyle is way out and that I, as its leading representative, should therefore be elected President."

* * *

"THAT'S WONDERFUL, Governor. But our computer data shows that you must fire your retro-rockets in exactly 6.2 seconds."

"Don't lay your authority trip on me, Mission Control."

"But you must fire your retrorockets to slow your descent or . . . "

"Now you're intellectualizing, Mission Control, and, worse yet, making value judgments. As a true Californian, I know how to mellow out and go where the psychic energies are in a crisis."

"But, Governor, your velocity is 18,500 miles per hour. What are you going to do?"

"Ommmmmmmmmmmmmmmm . . ."

"Governor, fire the rockets! Governor, fire . . . Governor . . . Governor?"

Insert 5 Art Hoppe. «Small Was Beautiful», *San Francisco Chronicle*, June 15, 1978

pacting your environment.» And again there are examples of spatial metaphors. The piece by columnist Art HOPPE finally (Insert 5) makes California governor Jerry BROWN himself a mellow speaker. Surely, the variety of English used by BROWN in this fictitious interview is not General American, but a variety of its own. If an uninitiated reader were to go through the text, most of it would require translation.

So far, all the textual evidence – with the one exception of the advertisements for lifestyle events quoted in Insert 3 – might suggest that Mellowspeak is a fictional language variety only. Indeed, there are vexed Californians who claim that 'Marin English' as defined by LAKOFF does not exist (response to LAKOFF, 1979b). To them it is always others, especially New Yorkers, who talk in a «funny» way (cp. above p. 27). Yet, the outside observer again and again notes that people are heard and reported to use Mellowspeak. From time to time a quotation in one of the local mass media will be in Mellowspeak. Witness the extract from an ordinary journalistic report on the death of the Peoples Temple aid Michael Prokes quoted in Insert 6. What this text adds to the list of variety

By Michael Taylor
Chronicle Correspondent

Modesto

The grieving family of Michael Prokes, stunned by the suicide of the top Peoples Temple aide, secluded themselves at home yesterday while federal agents swooped down on this town in reaction to the loss of a key figure in their investigation of the cult.

At the Prokes house on Concord avenue, members of the family cracked the front door a few inches for visitors. One member, his eyes red from weeping, said softly, "We're going through an intense grieving process and we're unable to give a clear statement."

Insert 6 San Francisco Chronicle, March 15, 1979. Extract from cover story.

specific phraseology is something sounding even more gross than what the satirists could think of. The fact that somebody was able to say «We're going through an intense grieving process» when others would say nothing at all or, maybe, «We are in mourning», proves that people actually do use Mellowspeak, not only in the relaxed setting of the hot tub, but also when under stress. The examples of personal advertisements listed in Insert 7 in addition

MELLOW male wants to meet mellow woman. Share camping, hiking, jogging, swimming, companionship, affection, friendship and feelings. Write to GG, PO Box 163, Milpitas, CA 95035.

SERIOUS. attractive, caucasian male, 33, 5'6," 130, brown hair, deep blue eyes, mellow & laid back. Enjoy movies, quiet dinners, hot tubs, etc. Lady, 20 to 35, share my apt, life & love. Serious, open and aware are qualities I like. David: (415)843-2985.

ATTRACTIVE, slender man looking for a woman to share and feel with. To communicate with life's rhythm and contribute a note of our own. I'm 35 years old with a capacity to add knowledge and dimension to that figure. I'm in quest of an inner knowledge for an outer reality. What better way to consummate this desire than in the form of a lady that in her own emotional sphere is sensitive and communicative. Write Ad No: A1116

SHY but gregarious young woman, 24, wishing for loving husband and children. I am a teacher, model and gourmet vegetarian cook, 5'7," 118 lbs, chestnut hair, blue eyes. Solar Moonchild, lunar Sagittarian, Virgo rising. I love the ocean, wilderness and San Francisco too. Religious background. Christian Science, Krishnamurti, Advaita Siddhanta. I would love to meet you if you have similar and complementary programing and if you are honestly willing and able to support a family. Please be older, at least 6', nonsmoker/ drinker/ doper, and have a positive, humorous and serious outlook on life. Write Ad No: 9C132

I'M a positive, alive, W/M, 35, 6', 140 lbs. with good job. I am also starting my own publishing business. Well educated. Religious leanings: Buddhism/TM. Non smoker/drinker/doper. I'm looking for a very attractive, intelligent, creative woman 21-31 with similar interests for lasting relationship. Photo appreciated. Write Ad No: B0193

BLUE-EYED, brown-bearded, Berkeley businessman, 32, 140 lbs, 5'6." Excellent sense of humor, trained architect and photographer. I enjoy films, cooking, motorcycling, wine tasting, and moderate jogging. I appreciate trim, full-figured women who are independent-minded and unhung-up in conventional ideals of success, morality, and "Prince Charming relationships." Write Ad No: B0207

EAST BAY W/M, 30, Taurus, vegetarian, single, 5'10½", 150 lbs., honest, sincere, warm, open-minded, altruistic, into humanity, growth-oriented lifestyle, outdoors, consciousness raising, seeks open-minded woman. Write Ad No: B0197

MALE, W, 31, 6'2," 178, warm, mellow, hip, hot, seeks woman; age, looks not foremost. Music, dining, quiet evenings. John: (415)347-4387.

HANDSOME Jewish man, 33, 6'2", 190, financially secure and living in Sausalito. Enjoys tennis, jogging, biking, quiet beaches, midnight cruises on the Bay, movies, concerts and new experiences. Would like to meet attractive and mellow lady, 25-35, for an intimate sharing relationship. Write Ad No: B2202

Insert 7 Classified Ads: Personals. From: Lifestyle. San Francisco, November, 1979.

show that people in the SFBA make use of Mellowspeak when wishing to establish contacts with other people sharing the same cultural background and participating in the same lifestyle. In these announcements Mellowspeak is clearly used as a code to reveal and recognize who belongs and who doesn't.

The list of adjectives used in these advertisements

mellow	sincere
laid back	warm
open	open-minded
aware	altruistic
sensitive	into humanity
communicative	growth oriented
positive	outdoors
alive	blue-eyed
creative	trim
independent-minded	consciousness raising
unhung-up	hip
honest	hot

indicates the qualities treasured in people (oneself and others); that of nouns lists the goals to achieve in life:

companionship	affection
friendship	feeling
knowledge	dimension
emotional sphere	

and that of verb phrases points to the activities considered important:

programming	jogging
share (with)	feel (with)
communicate with	contribute a note of
life's rhythm	one's own
be in quest of an inner knowledge for an outer reality	

Obviously, Mellowspeak is not simply fictitious; it actually exists as a separate variety of English in the SFBA. A comparison of the non-fictitious examples with the fictitious ones shows that the satirists did not have to exaggerate much. The characteristics of «psychobabble» worked out by LODGE apply not only to *The Serial*, but to non-fictional Mellowspeak as well.

Evaluating the material presented – evidence had to be adduced and discussed because, apart from LODGE 1980, no account of Mellowspeak has been published yet – the following remarks can be made:

Mellowspeak differs from Standard English and other varieties of English not only with regard to the culture from which it stems, but also with regard to its realization in areas of linguistic organization. (1) Phonology: Whereas in Standard English careful pronunciation is a goal to achieve, Mellowspeak does not mind slurred and careless speech. The tempo of delivery is generally slow, pauses and features of hesitation are not infrequent. A certain degree of inarticulateness seems to be as much a virtue as in the kind of English spoken by the British aristocracy. In terms of GUMPERZ' conversational analysis[15] mellow speech also has a function in pragmatics, signalling e.g. the unimportance of speaker status, the importance of «camaraderie» (LAKOFF, 1979a), the tentativeness of statements, the transitoriness of everything within vague spaces.

(2) Morphology and Syntax: Mellowspeak follows the rules of Standard English grammar, but extends these to also accomodate features shared by vernaculars in general. Thus, the passive is virtually absent; double negatives may occur; complex sentences are rare. This seems to be in keeping with the anti-rationalist basis of Mellowspeak, and also extending into pragmatics.

(3) Lexicon: Most obviously, the mellow culture is expressed in the vocabulary of Mellowspeak. A speaker of Mellowspeak has to know a lot of terms and the values attached to them. Sometimes these terms (words and phrases) illustrate the creativeness in word-formation typical of the SFBA (cp. above); but more often, they are not new to the lexical inventory of the language as such, but have been re-interpreted to suit new communicative functions. (Similar processes have been noted for Black English and lingos

15 GUMPERZ' work has been pioneering in detecting social and pragmatic meaning in conversation, mainly through close analysis of prosody, intonation, and paralinguistic cues. (GUMPERZ, 1978)

like Fraternity Talk and Juvenile Speech (see below)). If one runs through the examples adduced, it becomes clear that *mellow* is the key word of Mellowspeak. It is an adjective expressing positive value, referring to the principle of mellow culture that a relaxed attitude toward life and speech is of central importance. A speaker of Mellowspeak should thus be *mellow* or *laid-back* (synonym) rather than *uptight* or *hung-up* (antonyms). Further social meaning is expressed in verbs like *be beautiful, be open, relate, reach out, share,* which refer to non-verbal activities performed in groups. The heavy use made of spatial-directional metaphors (like *be into, come from, get behind*) indicates that nothing is expected to be static, but everything in process, while at the same time attempting to set abstract notions into concrete images. Thus, people are said to be *together* (positive), *fragmented, unglued* or *pushed out of shape* (all negative). FALK and LAKOFF (in prep.) also note that Mellowspeak has its own set of linguistic backchannel signals. They mention *wow, heavy, I hear you,* and *far out* as items replacing comparable Standard English items like 'yes', 'I see', 'I understand you', all expressing not intellectual, but emotional interpersonal accord.

Most of these examples document that Mellowspeak is very much concerned with turning emotions into processes, so that these can be talked about in more concrete terms. Thus, instead of saying 'I feel bad' or 'The family is mourning', the member of the Prokes family in Modesto (inserted example 6) could say *We are going through an intense grieving process.* In Mellowspeak fixed expressions are developed for feelings people usually do not talk about. Hence the many words describing abstract thought and human relationship. «Marin English aims for emotion, not ideation; for spontaneity, not articulateness; mandala, not line; intuition, not ratiocination; concrete, not abstract; camaraderie, not distance.» (LAKOFF, 1979b, quoted from notes taken)

In a grammar that would truly reflect the linguistic and communicative knowledge of a fluent speaker of Mellowspeak the rules commonly indicated for Standard Modern American would have to be modified, not so much in the area of syntax, but in the areas of prosody and suprasegmental phonology, in semantics and pragmatics. A comprehensive dictionary of words and phrases could not simply be attached to that grammar, but would have to become integral part of it. For descriptive purposes, the cultural roots of Mellowspeak would have to be indicated and the grammar to be squarely set within and related to the particular social-cultural frame of Mellowspeak. (For a general discussion of these aspects, see chapter 4.)

3.3 Black English

The settlement of California and the SFBA by Blacks goes back to the middle of the 19th century. Like other immigration groups, Blacks were first attracted by the economic advantages promised by California in the Gold Rush days. Later it was work in agriculture and the possibility of new and numerous jobs in manufacturing and service industries that brought Black laborers and their families to the West. Most of them settled in the rapidly growing urban centers where they found work first as longshoremen, construction workers and railroad workers, later and up till today as employees of the increasing number of large factories. Although the western migration of Blacks was outnumbered by the large parallel migration to Harlem, Chicago and Detroit, many Californian cities experienced sharp increases in their Black population as early as 1930 (TAYLOR, 1977). Fifty years later, California has the fourth largest statewide Black population. The metropolitan Bay Area houses about half a million, most of them in Oakland, San Francisco, Richmond, and Berkeley. As almost anywhere in the United States of today, interaction with Black speakers of English is an everyday experience for members of the non-Black population; Black English is a living reality. In the SFBA, Black English received special promotion during the 1960's. The Black Panther movement originated in Oakland, and its leaders, Eldridge Cleaver, Huey Newton, and Bobby Seale, first addressed Bay Area residents, and then the whole nation. There is no doubt that the rhetorics of the Black Panthers helped to establish Black English as an important variety of English not only in Black-dominated Oakland, but also in the neighboring campus city of Berkeley and in San Francisco, as well as in the whole SFBA.

The rich materials stored in the Berkeley Folklore Archives point out the awareness of the folk of Black English being a separate variety of English in the SFBA. Examples both of esoteric and exoteric kinds of *blason populaire* as well as of other genres of folklore help to outline the demarcation line between the Black ethnic group and other ethnic groups. It would be wrong to assume that boundaries exist only between the white (Anglo) and the Black communities; esoteric examples of folklore illustrate that Black groups capitalize on their being ethnically different from all the other ethnic groups, whether Anglos, Chicanos, Chinese, or whatever. Equally, it is not only the Anglo community, but also the Chicanos, the Chinese, the Japanese, etc. that use ethnic slurs directed against the Blacks. The stereotypes, however, are the same in the *blason populaire* of all the non-Black groups.

Anti-Black *blason populaire* deals with skin color (blackness being associated with ugliness, dirt, baseness, evil, sin, hell), body size, sexual licentiousness; with animal-like behavior, lack of civilization and education; poverty, crime and political agitation. Where so many points of culture and social behavior are singled out for *blason populaire,* it is not surprising that language, too, is included in the catalog. Witness this joke (recorded in Oakland):

> Rastas and Mandy had been married for a little while, and one day they were just sitt'n out on the porch talk'n, and Mandy says, «Rastas, when we all goin to Florida?» Rastas looks at her funny and replies, «Goin to Florida? Who says we goin to Florida?» Mandy says, «Why, you did, honey. You said when we got married, you was gonna take me to Florida.» Rastas shakin his head says, «No, Mandy, I never said notin like dat. I say dat after wes get married. I was gonna tampa wi' you.»

This is an example of exoteric *blason populaire.* The non-Black folk usually tell the joke with what they think is a typically Black accent. Thus, and by also observing other linguistic characteristics of Black English, they can prepare their audience for the linguistic pun on *Tampa/tamper.* The text points out these features of Black English:

> Absence of postvocalic [r]
> Replacement of dental fricatives by stops
> Complete dropping of final consonants
> Denasalization of[ŋ]> [n] in word-end position

gonna
was conditional
Contamination of *we* with *us*
Unmarked past tense with *say*
Get-passive
Copula deletion
Double negation
Question without inverted word order

As a comparison of this list with the more exhaustive one given below indicates, the use of folklore materials may indeed lead a (socio)linguist to features typical of a language variety, while at the same time also providing him with information about the cultural background of that variety against which the linguistic data must be read.

Black English is viewed here as being on a continuum with other varieties of English. Although, apparently, it cannot be denied that, from a historical point of view, Black English derives in part from a non-English system,[16] the process of assimilation has made Black English, now from a present-day synchronic point of view, a variety of English whose rules could be treated as derivable from the rules of English in general. This is also the view adopted by many American linguists, notably William LABOV, while a few others, like STEWART (1969) and DILLARD (1972), insist on the separateness of Black English.

As a variety of English, Black English is more homogenous than, say, British English or American English. Black English is part of American English; and, although it is spoken all over the United States, it is not usually divided into several regional dialects. First of all, Black English is an ethnic variety in use wherever Blacks gather. Being younger in history and having developed out of ghetto-like conditions, it has been less exposed to disruptive forces than Anglo English. If it shows internal differences today, as between North-Eastern Urban Black English (New York) and Southern Rural Black English (Memphis, Tennessee), these differences are due less to geographic provenience than to local social

16 «The evidence (. . .) suggests Black English originated in creole and ultimately pidgin lects.» (TRAUGOTT, 1976:58)

and economic factors. There are, indeed, no fundamental differences between the Urban Black English of Harlem and the Urban Black English of Oakland or Richmond. When Claudia MITCHELL-KERNAN (1971) was studying the language behavior in West Oakland, she found that the speech of her informants exhibited «a great deal of similarity to the speech of Blacks as reported by researchers in a number of geographical areas.» (15) In particular, she found that the phonological and grammatical patterns closely paralleled those emerging from LABOV's New York study. There seem to be good reasons, then, to claim, as LEGUM et al. (1971) do, that there is a «national dialect» of Black English.

The kind of Black English I want to isolate as a distinct variety of English in the SFBA is Vernacular Black English. The vernacular is used orally and informally, at home and in the street (MITCHELL-KERNAN, 1971); it is the typical form of English used by Black speakers of English in everyday interaction among themselves.[17] Differences between Black English and other varieties of English were first assumed on the levels of phonology and lexicon only – as in the traditional assumptions about the relationship between dialects (SAPORTA, 1965) –, more recently also on the levels of morphology and syntax (LOFLIN, 1969). Today it is fairly easy to find descriptions of the linguistic characteristics of Black English. They would usually include the features presented below. The following list is my own compilation, checked against FASOLD and WOLFRAM, 1970; TRAUGOTT, 1976:81–93; MOULTON, 1976: 149–170; and LURIE, 1978:78–93. I was also able to check this list against the notes on California Black English taken by METCALF (1977:34–35) and the list set up by MITCHELL-KERNAN based on her West Oakland data (1971:19–29), as well as against the rich collection of documents of Bay Area Black English stored in the library of the Department of Rhetoric and the Language Behavior Research Laboratory, University of California at Berkeley.

17 Like white speakers, speakers of Black English may switch from the informal vernacular to the more formal, mainly academic and written variety of Standard English. Equally, Vernacular Black English should not be mistaken for the jargon employed by juvenile Black street gangs exclusively.

Characteristics of Black English

Phonology	Forwarding of non-initial stress Absence of word final consonant clusters Absence of postvocalic [r], [l] Avoidance of [ð] [θ]; systematic use of [d] or [v], and [t] or [f] instead Devoicing of syllable-final [d] Raising of [ε] > [I] before nasals Loss of glides [I], [U] Denasalization of [ŋ] > [n] in word-end position Lowering of [I] and [U]
Grammar	Predominance of active voice *Get*-passive Frequent iteration of subject Occasional {Ø} marker for plural nouns, yet, on the whole, generalization of {s} Signalling of possessive by means of {s} optional Frequent use of objective personal pronouns in subject position Copula deletion or contraction Frequent lack of number agreement between subject and verb Present tense unmarked through whole verb paradigm Past tense unmarked in common verbs like *say, come*, and also if phonological constraints work against the formation of clusters Aspect marking by means of *done* for completion; by means of *been* for remote past; by means of invariable *be* for the distribution of events over time; by means of {Ø} for permanent identification Absence of auxiliary (mainly *do*) in content questions; general simplification of word order in questions Multiple negation, negative concord, *ain't* Expletive or presentative *it* Extended use of contact clauses Greater insistence on personal nominal reference through extended use of possessive

Considered together, the examples of speeches (taped) delivered by Black Panther leaders and of conversations (both taped and transcribed) of Black highschoolers are probably more representative of the speech patterns of the whole Black community than the speech patterns of teenage gang members studied by LABOV, COHEN, ROBBINS and LEWIS in 1968 or the mother-child interactions analyzed by ENGLEMANN in 1970. The fact, actually, that the checking of New York and Chicago derived rules of Black English against SFBA Black English as used both by political leaders in public oratory and adolescents in informal conversation does not yield any significant deviations, increases the overall validity of group-specific studies of Black English carried out so far.

Yet, two qualifying remarks are necessary. First, while the phonological characteristics conventionally indicated do appear with high frequency in the SFBA data, the grammatical features do so less consistently. This may be due to the fact that the speeches collected in the Department of Rhetoric at the University of California, Berkeley, illustrate stylistic levels – an observation also made by Susan ERVIN-TRIPP, personal communication –, each not only pragmatically different, but also showing slightly modified grammatical structures.[18] One should therefore caution against relying too heavily on the rules of Black English grammar listed so often now without indicating possibilities for modification. Although there is little reason to assume diatopic variation in Black English, there appears to be variation in both the diastratic and, especially, the diatypic dimensions of language.[19]

Second: What appears to be highly important, too, in an account of Black speech are informations about intonation and suprasegmentals in general, about vocabulary and phraseology, and about discourse conventions and speech genres. A description of Black English is far from complete if these aspects are neglected.[20] Unfortunately, only very few and quite limited studies have been carried out in these less accessible areas so far. TARONE (1973) comments: «While the semantic, syntactic, and segmental phonemic structures of black English have all been described in some detail, its suprasegmental characteristics – stress, rhythm, and inton-

18 The collection of speeches in the Department of Rhetoric, University of California, Berkeley, provide ample material for research on style in Black English – so far unused.

19 Without using the label, GUMPERZ (1979a) has amply documented the existence of diatypic varieties in Oakland-based Black English.

20 Black English capitalizes on social meanings frequently expressed only through means of prosody, intonation, and speech genres. Cp. GUMPERZ (1979a), FOLB (1980).

ation – have been largely overlooked in most studies. At the same time, investigators have consistently recorded the impression that these suprasegmental features are probably just as distinctive in black English as the other, more carefully described, features of syntax and segmental phonology.» (29) In an investigation undertaken in Seattle, Washington, in 1972, TARONE compared the intonation patterns of speakers of Vernacular Black English with the intonation patterns used by speakers of Vernacular White English and speakers of Formal Black English. She found that Vernacular Black English was characterized by:

> 1. A wider pitch range, extending into higher pitch levels than in white English or formal black English and often shifting into a falsetto register.
> 2. More level and rising pitch contours on all sentence types in an informal situation.
> 3. Apparent greater use of falling final pitch contours with *yes/no* questions in formal, threatening situations, but level and rising final contours in informal, familiar situations.
> 4. The use of nonfinal intonation contours, without the use of the lexical item *if*, to mark the dependent clause of some conditional sentences. (1973:35)

TARONE concludes that intonation is certainly «one of the most important features for the communication of attitude in all social situations. (. . .) Thus, when the characteristic intonation patterns of black English differ from those of white speech, we may expect some fairly serious miscommunication of attitude between black and whites.» (1973:29)

More information than about the suprasegmental part of Black phonology is available about the lexicon of Black English. Yet, according to students of Black culture (TAYLOR, 1976), neither the *Dictionary of American Slang* (WENTWORTH and FLEXNER, 1960) nor *An American Dictionary of Slang* (WEINGARTEN, 1954), nor the *Dictionary of Afro-American Slang* (MAJOR, 1970) are exhaustive in their treatment of the Black English vocabulary. In parts, this lack of documentation is due to the speedy change to which the Black English vernacular is subjected. Especially in urban areas (like those of the American North-East or the SFBA) vocabular items and idiomatic phrases are quickly outdated. A law which applies to Juvenile Speech (see below) also applies to Black English: No sooner is a term borrowed into Anglo speech than it becomes *passé* in Black speech. As TAYLOR reports, it is very difficult for non-Black lexicographers to penetrate deep enough into Black culture to produce an accurate dictionary of Black English. Yet, updating existing wordlists seems to be even more difficult a task. It has also been observed that often, if there is overlap in lexicon between Black and White vernacular, the meaning of a given word or phrase would be different in the two varieties. With regard to word selection, Geneva SMITHERMAN (1980:164) attributes the failure of Black English dictionaries to represent the lexicon of the variety accurately to the fact that lexicographers have not been able (yet) to deal with one important question: «what are the psycho-cultural processes that guide our selection of certain words out of the thousands of possible words in the Anglo-Saxon vocabulary?» The consequences of insufficient information about the vocabulary of Black English again is that «a Standard English speaker or a person that is not familiar with Black English (. . .) might misinterpret a speaker of Black English.» (TAYLOR, 1976:224)

In order to understand Black English, knowledge of phonological and grammatical rules (of the kind illustrated in the list above) is clearly not sufficient. Some knowledge about Black culture appears to be equally necessary. KOCHMANN (1969) has pointed out a central aspect of Black culture which, as it seems to me, also fashions the discourse conventions of Black English. He noticed the existence of a linguistic tradition which centers on oral-aural skills rather than on reading and writing. Similarly, TAYLOR (1976) claims that the differences between Standard English and Black English are «differences between a literate culture and an oral culture.» (212). She explains: «Communication – its meaning and the forms in which it takes place – is different in the two cultures. (. . .) without a medium, such as the written word, the act of communication becomes more intense, emotional, and expressive.» (212) For oral speakers, rhythm, body language, and imaginative allusions are mandatory. Intellectual detachment is not expected; important are improvisation and spontaneity; if you are witty and a fast talker, you are a winner. Folklorists and sociolinguists have identified several narrative forms which exploit these qualities: tales, proverbs, jokes, rhymes, toasts, signifying.[21] Understanding the discourse conventions of Black English also means being aware of the narrative possibilities of such speech genres and approaching them not from a literary but an oral point of view.

If misunderstandings and gaps in communication are to be avoided, Black English cannot be explained simply in terms of phonological and grammatical characteristics. A grammar of English that would also include Black English would have to extend its scope considerably. It would have to include speech genres like those now documented for California Black English in FOLB (1980) and for SFBA Black English in MITCHELL-KERNAN (1971). It would have to relate its rules to up-to-date dictionaries catching the idiomaticity of Black English (a first attempt is made in FOLB's glossary, 1980:227–260). And it would have to contain information about prosody and intonation of the kind now worked out by GUMPERZ (1979a). Ultimately, it is only some knowledge about Black culture that makes the understanding of Black English possible. Thus, what is essential about Black English, are not only the features linguists have concentrated on so far, but something deeper, culture-specific. Indeed, speakers of Black English in the SFBA mention that a summary of the characteristics of Black English like the one presented above, while not wrong, does not capture what is central to that variety of English. They see the essence of Black English in the worldview and the lifestyle projected through it. In this respect, Black English is on a par with Mellowspeak.[22]

21 Cp. ABRAHAMS (1962 and 1964) for the pioneering studies from a folklorist point of view; MITCHELL-KERNAN (1971) for a sociolinguistic account of signifying in Oakland; REYNOLDS (1974) for an ethnographic account of toasts in Los Angeles, and FOLB (1980) for a wide-scope presentation of speech genres current in Watts.

22 WILLIAMS (1976) lists some of the cultural elements mirrored in Black English: «The critical criteria for Blackness include intimate knowledge of greens, chittlins, corn bread, and sweet potato pie. The profanity of the streets has to punctuate phrases appropriately, and other words have to be manipulated to achieve the proper effect. Positive virtues are found in the high style of dress that distinguishes the lower classes.» (12) In Oakland, MITCHELL-KERNAN (1971:12) found «obvious examples» of an ethnic cultural heritage in preferences in diet, dress and entertainment, in religious practices, the socialization of children, and family organization.

3.4 Chicano English

Chicano English[23] is a variety of English which should be explained and analyzed slightly differently from Mellowspeak or Black English. METCALF, one of the few experts on Chicano English, defines it as «a variety of English that is obviously influenced by Spanish and that has low prestige in most circles, but that is nevertheless independent of Spanish and is the first and often only language of many hundred of thousands of residents in California.» (1974:53) It is this contact with another language that establishes the difference to both Mellowspeak and Black English. The characteristics of Chicano English can be grasped better if its origin in bilingualism is understood. It has been noted (e.g. by MA and HERASIMCHUCK, 1968; GUMPERZ, 1966; WOLFRAM, 1974) that coherent linguistic systems can develop in bilingual communities. Chicano English is such a system. Historically, its evolution can be explained by reference to the substratal theory, in whose terms linguistic change is explained by the retention of features of a language spoken at an earlier stage, before language shift has occurred (cp. LEHMANN, 1972:174; BLOOMFIELD, 1933:470). According to the substratal theory, three stages must be distinguished: At stage 1, a certain population speaks language A; at stage 2, this population also takes up language B; it becomes bilingual; at stage 3, the population gives up language A and becomes monolingual in language B. Yet, and this is crucial for our discussion of Chicano English, the variety of language B spoken by the population formerly using language A is different from the standard form of language B or other varieties of B.

Chicano English, for which language A is Mexican Spanish, will therefore show differences from other varieties of English that can be classified as retentions or adaptations from Spanish. In studies devoted to the English of originally Spanish speaking populations in the USA (Latinos, Hispanics), it has been stressed repeatedly that the varieties under discussion are varieties of English, not varieties of Spanish or of any compromise language. In his report on

23 «Chicano» is a term used for self-identification by Mexican-Americans and their descendents, now in general use to refer to the Hispanics in California.

the speech of working-class Puerto Rican adolescents in New York City, WOLFRAM (1974) was definite about the rule of pleonastic tense marking being an English dialect rule which can be described without reference to Spanish at all. Similarly, EDWARDS and DOVIAK (1975) treated Z-devoicing in the speech of Mexican-American fourth-graders in New Mexico as a rule of a variety of English. For me too there is no doubt that Chicano English is a variety of English. I do not claim, however, that the speakers of Chicano English in the SFBA do not use Spanish. Actually, it would be difficult to find a second generation speaker who is not bilingual. Since the influx of Mexicans into California continues at a steady pace, stage 3, the second monolingual one, has not been reached yet generally. Even among third generation speakers a certain degree of bilingualism is still normal.[24] Nor do I want to claim that English speaking Chicanos do not make use of Mexican-Spanish vocabulary items in everyday communication. However, this is also true of most Anglo speakers. After all, California was under Spanish and Mexican rule for quite some time. Both the Spanish mission and the Mexican occupation have left their traces on the land, linguistically above all in California place names. How far-ranging this list is is well documented in GUDDE's (1969) work on California toponymy.[25] The day-to-day impact of Spanish upon the speech habits of the English speaking population is documented as early as the mid 19th century. HUSTVEDT (1948) lists words of Spanish (Mexican) origin appearing in an otherwise English context without explanation or gloss in the Los Angeles *Star*. Obviously, the editor of the paper could assume his English speaking readers to understand the Spanish items without difficulty. The way in which items of Spanish find their way into Chicano English and other varieties of English is paralleled by the way in which English items creep into Chicano Spanish. REYES (1973) mentions many nouns: *el clutch, el income-tax; la welfare, la application.* He shows the occurrence of English adjectives, adverbs,

24 Benji WALD (1976) notes that contact between children and grandparents is usually in Spanish.

25 Word lists of similar value are *Cowboy Lingo* (ADAMS, 1936) and *Western Words* (ADAMS, 1944).

verbs, prepositional phrases and conjunctions within Spanish syntactical frames: *que dirty!, especially ora que estoy malo; nomas vino a find out; por two hundred dollars; quero ir, but, no puede,* etc. Chicano bilinguals (stage 2) may use words and phrases which are phonologically and semantically part of the English language in a variety of Spanish syntactic environments. English items are especially frequent when their Spanish counterparts are not of common everyday usage in California. It is such switching among bilingual speakers of Spanish which is sometimes mistaken for Chicano English, although it belongs with the study of Chicano Spanish.

So far, research interest has centered more on Chicano Spanish (cp. HERNANDEZ et al., 1975) than on Chicano English. The descriptive material on Chicano English (formerly also called Mexican-American English) is therefore very limited and scanty. The neglect of Chicano English like that of other ethnic varieties in the West goes back to the 1950's when David REED and his crew conducted their language survey for the *Linguistic Atlas of the Pacific Coast.* Chicano English was deliberately excluded and does not figure in the only important account of California English attempted so far (cp. 3.1.1). At the time it was assumed and even voiced that Chicanos do not speak any language at all (METCALF, 1972:14), neither English, nor Spanish, but a mixture of the two. More recently, however, close analysis of recorded conversations (as in the pioneering study by GUMPERZ and HERNANDEZ, 1971) has revealed beyond doubt what was hinted above: What might have been heard as «language mixture» is in fact the natural code-switching of bilinguals. Today, at last, Chicano English is being accepted as a variety of English in its own right.

When speaking of the Chicano English of the SFBA, I have in mind the language used by the members of the Mexican-American population at the substratal stages 2 and (mainly) 3. I do not consider the English speech of recent immigrants for whom English is still a foreign language; I only consider the speech of the mass of Chicanos who are second or third generation Mexican-Americans. Their variety of English is stabilized and has «as much claim to be a legitimate dialect of English as that spoken by Blacks, Anglo Riversiders, Bostonians, or college teachers» (METCALF,

1972:15). This dialect is «the fluent English spoken as a native language by many of the Mexican-American community, (. . .) not just English with a Spanish accent. It is a fully developed variety of English, and serves as the only means of communication in the many Mexican-American communities where Spanish is no longer spoken.» (METCALF, 1972:15)

In 1970 Chicanos constituted the largest minority group in the SFBA (close to 600 000; estimation for 1980: at least 800 000 in the San Francisco-Oakland Metropolitan Statistical Area alone). Statewide their population numbers 3.3 million (1976), not counting undocumented illegals estimated at ca. 1 million. By 1990, the Chicanos are expected to constitute a majority in California. In the SFBA most Chicanos live in urban communities, predominantly in the South Bay and Peninsula counties. Given their large number and strong ethnic identity as a minority group, it is not surprising that the Chicanos (or Mexican-Americans, or Hispanics) are singled out for *blason populaire* as much as the Black inhabitants of the SFBA. The rich folklore material stored in the Berkeley Folklore Archives has both esoteric and exoteric examples of *blason populaire,* which leaves no doubt that the Chicanos, like the Blacks and the Asians, recognize themselves and are recognized by others as a separate ethnic group. The following terms are used by non-Chicanos to refer to Mexican-Americans: *pepperbelly, beaner, taco, tortilla; greaser; wetback; Manuel Labor.* Reference here is made to Mexican food, greasy hair, and employment. *Wetback* is understood both as referring to the frequent sweating of Chicanos due to work and to their having reached the USA illegally by swimming through the Rio Grande. All the terms, including the punning *Manuel Labor,* view the Chicanos as bums and hoodlums.[26]

26 These are some typical jokes bringing out further characteristics of the Chicanos in the form of stereotypical judgements:
(1) Why do Chicanos have a cake at a wedding?
To keep the flies off the bride. (Berkeley)
(2) How do you change the color of the water in the swimming-pool?
Throw in a Mexican! (San Jose)
(3) What's the difference between a hypodermic needle and a Chicano?
Nothing, they are both a pain in the ass. (Berkeley)

In spite of all these – and many more, and worse – ethnic slurs, Chicano English itself is rarely singled out for *blason populaire.* There are stories like this one:

> Riding on the trail with sidekick Pancho, Billy could smell this terrible odor. «Hey, Pancho, did you poo in your pants?»
> «No,» said Pancho, «I no poo in my panz.»
> They rode on a little further and Billy could still smell this shit. «Hey, Pancho, are you sure you no doo doo in your pants? I smell something awful.»
> «No, Billy, I no poo in my panz.»
> Well, Billy really got perturbed. «Come on, Pancho, are you really sure you no poo in your pants?»
> «No, Billy, I no poo in my panz.»
> Well, Billy told Pancho to get off his horse and pull down his pants. Of course, these two turds fell out of his pants.
> «Pancho, I thought you said you no doo in your pants!»
> «O, Billy, I think you mean today!» (Berkeley)

The language used by Chicanos is represented as primitive. In the text, *doo doo* and *poo* emphasize the infantile ring of the passage. Pancho, the Chicano, leaves out the verb in his sentences *(I no poo in my panz),* a feature which is echoed, for purposes of further ridicule, by his companion, Bill. The only feature that can be considered relevant with regard to a description of Chicano English is the absence of tense marking *(I think you mean today),* while the simplification and voicing of [ts] > [z] appears to be typical of any English vernacular. The example illustrates, however, that it is

(4) How many Chicanos does it take to rob a bank?
One to hold the gun and four to write the note. (Oakland)
(5) Do you know why Christ wasn't born in Mexico?
Because they couldn't find three wise men and a virgin. (Fresno)
Although examples of *blason populaire* like the ones quoted are frequently heard in the SFBA, their points of reference (or attack) are not identical with those most often used to demonstrate Chicano ethnicity. It appears that low-riding (the ritual street cruising in intentionally lowered cars by adolescents and young adults), Machismo (the projection of Latin virility), catholicism (religious profession with unifying ethnic force) and the politically oriented Chicano Power movement become increasingly more important as features denoting Chicano ethnicity. It can be assumed that Chicano English will acquire additional symbolic significance as it serves to express these movements and values.

pronunciation which is most reliably noticed by the folk. Witness also this riddle-joke:

> What is a pee-cup?
> It is what a Chicano drives to work every day. (San Francisco)

In this item of *blason populaire* the tensing of /I/ in closed syllables characteristic of Chicano English makes for a new reading of *pick-up*. The fact that the folk rarely include other linguistic points in their catalog of observations about Chicano English does not contradict my claim that folklore materials point out what is typical about language varieties. According to METCALF (1972, 1974) it is precisely in the areas of phonology that the characteristics of Chicano English appear most distinctively. Nevertheless, it is true that the folk characterization of Chicano English is less precise than that of Black English. Judging from documented folklore materials alone, it appears that the folk are better informed about the peculiarities of Black English than about those of Chicano English. It is possible for non-Blacks to list linguistic items of Black speech to a degree not reached when non-Chicanos imitate Chicano English. The same point must be made about the scholarly assessment of Chicano English: While linguists have little difficulty to list the rules of Black English, their accounts of Chicano English look haphazard and impressionistic.

While there are many studies on Black English, Chicano English is still «Virgin Territory» (ORNSTEIN and DUBOIS, 1977). There are only a few tentative attempts to list the features of Chicano English, many of which are not reliable in a more general context. DUBOIS and HOFFER (1975), e.g., present a list of mistakes frequently made in essays written by Spanish-dominant college bilinguals. Such mistakes which are due to interference phenomena or imperfect fluency in English should not be identified as characteristics of Chicano English. More general in its validity and therefore also more reliable is ORNSTEIN and PENFIELD (1980). The authors list 27 variant features, but are careful enough to attribute dialectal status to only 14 of these. 4 others are explained as idiosyncratic occurrences, while the final classification of 8 further features is left open («interference or dialect?»). If one also includes the research reported in METCALF (1979) and in ORNSTEIN and DUBOIS (1977) the following list of Chicano English deviant features can be suggested:

Characteristics of Chicano English

Phonology, Segmental	Tensing of /I/ Lowering of [æ] to [ɑ]. Homophony for *tab:tub* Merger of /č/ and /š/ Devoicing of final stops and fricatives [b] > [p], [d] > [t], [g] > [k]; [v] > [f]; [z] > [s] (limited) Dentalized realization of alveolar stops Bilabial instead of labiodental fricative: [oƀər]
Phonology, Suprasegmental	Compounds stressed on second element, or equally on both elements At the end of declarative sentences pitch and loudness do not fall off rapidly (pitch 2) Yes-No questions end on level pitches, rather than on raising glides Emphasis placed by means of raising glides
Grammar	To some degree: lack of verbal inflection to mark tense or third person singular To some degree: lack of nominal inflection marking plurality or possessive Frequently: deletion of dummy pronominal subjects

Many of the reports on Chicano bilinguals would add a number of entries under the heading of 'grammar'; yet, these are either attributable to lacking competence in English or typical of vernacular English in general. I agree with METCALF (1979:16) who concludes: «When the Spanish influence extends to vocabulary, idiom, or syntax to any notable degree, the speaker is likely to have English as a second language only.» However, «when the Spanish influence is confined to the intonation pattern and the pronunciation of consonants and vowels, but does not result in un-English word choice or syntax, the student is more likely to be a native speaker of English.» If comparison is made not simply to Standard Textbook English, but to other English vernacular dialects, the grammar (syntax and morphology) of SFBA Chicano English certainly does not differ much from that of other varieties of English.

Nor is the difference established in the lexicon (although there may be group-specific semantic shifts in certain words and phrases). As has been hinted, California Chicano English does apparently not have more Spanish vocabulary items than the white varieties; indeed, even the many Spanish place-names are often pronounced in an angliziced way. While METCALF noticed that speakers of Chicano English in Riverside tend to use rather old-fashioned, book-learned expressions of English and seem to be cut off from the language trend of the day (1972:15), I did not receive the same impression. If one accepts that Mellowspeak is the special variety spoken by a group ethnically closed off against Blacks and Chicanos (though open towards Jews and Muslims), it is not surprising that the vocabulary of Mellowspeak is largely absent from Chicano speech. Trendy terms that have permeated all-American English, however, Anglo as well as Black, are also found in Chicano English.

As the list of Chicano English characteristics illustrates, the main differences between Chicano English and other varieties of English are not found in grammar and lexicon, but in segmental and suprasegmental phonology. While the points of segmental phonology are relatively easy to describe (cp. METCALF, 1972:17ff.), those of suprasegmental phonology are somewhat more difficult to grasp.[27] METCALF (1974:55) comments: «I am now more convinced than ever that the most distinctive, persistent, and important characteristic of Chicano English is its intonation. To speakers of other English dialects, the Chicano English speaker often sounds uncertain, wishy-washy, and a little crazy – because of intonation patterns that make it seem as if he is asking a question where he should be making a statement, expressing doubt when he should be certain and putting stress on the strangest words for no apparent reason.» Better than any other linguist so far, METCALF (cp. also 1972:18) has described some of the reasons that may create misunderstandings between Chicanos and non-

27 In a paper presented to the American Dialect Society meeting, 16–17 July 1980 (University of New Mexico), Joyce Penfield showed that it is possible to work out the particulars of stress and intonation in Chicano English quite accurately. (PENFIELD, 1980)

Chicanos and favor the rise of anti-Chicano ethnic slurs (as reflected in *blason populaire*). METCALF has also commented on more general speech habits of Chicano speakers of English: «There are some indications that the range of styles of a speaker of California Mexican-American English is different from that for the local Anglo English speakers, with the Mexican-American norms always somewhat less formal than the Anglo norms for the same situation. Thus to the Anglo speaker, the Mexican-American speaker may sound too casual, and to the speaker of Mexican-American English the Anglo speaker may seem overly formal or haughty.» (1972:19) I am not aware of any investigative work on Chicano English speech genres and discourse conventions. Listening to Chicano students on the San Jose campus (California State University) as well as to various other speakers of Chicano English on Bay Area television, however, has convinced me that there may be more to Chicano English stylistics than degrees of laxness and looseness.

In conclusion we may say that descriptions of Chicano English should not look for points at which Chicano English syntax and morphology deviate from Standard English, but emphasize those areas in which Chicano English clearly differs from other colloquial and non-standard varieties of English. These areas would include segmental and suprasegmental phonology (the «Chicano accent»)[28] as well as discourse conventions and speech genres (stylistics). A full understanding of all these areas, however, is possible only if the description also covers some cultural and folkloristic background. As has been observed by JORDAN DE CARO (1972), this background creates a set of linguistic reference not shared by speakers of other English dialects. Once again, then, learning a particular variety of English would mean not simply internalizing rules of 'linguistics proper', but familiarizing with a lot of 'extra-linguistic matter'.

28 In another paper presented at the same 1980 ADS meeting Manuel GODINEZ and Mona LINDAU found that Chicano bilinguals systematically differentiate between English and Spanish phonology. They consequently suggest (as I do) that rather than being determined synchronically by interference from Spanish, Chicano English represents an autonomous social dialect with distinct characteristics (GODINEZ and LINDAU, 1980)

3.5 Asian English

I do not intend to deal with Asian English at any length here. However, it ought to be pointed out that the varieties of English created by Asian immigrants – Chinese, Japanese, Vietnamese, Korean, Filipino – are important additions to the repertoire of English language varieties current in the SFBA and in California. I would also like to show that *blason populaire*, including linguistic *blason populaire*, exists about these groups as well, not only about the Blacks and the Chicanos. And I would like to hint at those areas of linguistics that most need commenting in a manual on these varieties of English. The research situation for Asian English is worse still than that for Chicano English. Not even about the Chinese-American community of San Francisco (which is the best-known of all of them) is there any reliable information available today. The social dialectologist must again be grateful for the material he finds in the Folklore Archives. As restricted in applicability as they are, they at least point out the directions to be explored in future research.

3.5.1 Chinese English

It is still unclear when the first Chinese settled in the USA. Chinese sailors probably visited colonial ports in the 18th century. It is certain, however, that Chinese servants were living in Philadelphia by 1796 and in San Francisco by 1840. The immigration records that claim that only 43 Chinese entered the USA before 1849 are hardly accurate since they do not include the more considerable influx on the Pacific Coast, which was under Spanish and Mexican rule until 1846. The large wave of Chinese immigration into the USA, however, did not start before the California Gold Rush necessitated a great number of cheap laborers. Chinese settlements in the USA originally took one of three forms: Chinese camps, Chinatowns, or Chinese centers. Chinese camps, once common in frontier America, began to fade as Chinese railroad workers, miners, fishermen, farm laborers, laundrymen and shopkeepers were driven out of many rural communities by racial violence during the last three decades of the 19th century. Many refugees sought shelter in large cities like San Francisco, where traditional institutions had provided for their security and employment. Social enclaves – Chinatowns – emerged to serve the everyday needs of displaced and oppressed newcomers. The Chinese were confined within Chinatown by local laws and customs and by their own communal needs. Those Chinese who wished to venture beyond the obligations and restrictions of the San Francisco Chinatown headed for the East Bay cities of Oakland and Berkeley, where loosely knit community centers could grow to meet the periodic needs of a dispersed Chinese population. Such community centers, although much less colorful than the Chinese camps of the Old West and the Chinatown of San Francisco, were the most pervasive form of Chinese settlement along the Pacific Coast. Today the population of Chinese descent in the SFBA numbers ca. 100 000 (1970), about three quarters of which live in San Francisco, two other strong groups in the East Bay cities of Oakland and Berkeley.

Although the Chinese population no longer lives in ghetto-like conditions and may be well integrated into American society, the Chinese have not lost their ethnic identity. Like the Black and the Chicanos they promote their interests in politics and business and are conscious of their cultural heritage.[29] Ethnic slurs directed at

29 A recent documentary on National Public Radio entitled «Chinese Americans: An Emerging Political Power» examined the growing political clout of San Francisco's Chinese American population and analyzed how this development will affect the city and the political future of other minority groups. Chinese-American political history was traced back to the days of open racist discrimination in the city when politicians built political power with phrases like «The Yellow Peril» and «The Chinks Must Go». It has taken generations to overcome that attitude. Ten years ago, e.g., there was not one Chinese-American holding elected office in San Francisco. Today there are five. The documentary pointed to several factors which help to explain this change: the emergence of an educated, professional middle-class willing and able to bear the sacrifices that political leadership demands; an increase in political awareness and activism among young Chinese-Americans; the integration of Chinese into all of San Francisco's neighborhoods; and an increase in population number. While listening to the speakers of the Chinese-American community it also became obvious that language no longer functions as a barrier between the Chinese and the non-Chinese. Chinese English was fully understandable as English.

the Chinese are frequent. Even today a Chinese-American may still be called a *fob* (acronym for «fresh off the boat»), especially if something exotic can still be traced in his behavior. More derogatory names as in *There once were two Chinese men, Go Taka Shiti and Hoo Flung Dung* are less often heard.[30] School-children know rhymes like

Chinky Chinky Chinaman
Sitting on a fence
Trying to make a dollar
Out of fifteen cents. (San Francisco)

Ching Chong Chinaman
Sitting on a rail
Along came a white man
Cutting of his tail. (Palo Alto)

These are traditional rhymes that go back to the 19th century. They are still current in present-day folklore although the Chinese in the SFBA are no longer so poor and although one rarely sees a Chinese-American with a long thin beard. What makes these two examples of *blason populaire* interesting for our purposes is their reference to and use of Chinese names. Indeed, it is often the strange sounds of Chinese names that is exploited in folk jokes.

Why don't the Chinese use telephone books?
There's too many Wing Wongs and they might wing the wong number.
(Inglewood)

How do the Chinese name their babies?
They throw a bunch of silverware in the air and the noise it makes as it hits the floor are the the names for their babies.
(Berkeley/Los Angeles)

How Long is a Chinese!? (Berkeley)

30 Reaction among the Chinese-Americans against ethnic slurs is still strong, however. A recent Hollywood movie project featuring Charlie Chan, a fictitious San Francisco sleuth, caused violent protest throughout the SFBA. A spokesman for the Chinese for Affirmative Action called the Chan character a racist depiction of Chinese, citing Chan's «chop suey pidgin English, fortune cookie proverbs and bowing». (San Francisco Sunday Examiner and Chronicle, May 11, 1980, A-11)

This last example can be used to illustrate the fact that speakers of Chinese (Cantonese) English experience difficulties in grasping the particulars of English intonation patterns such as used in question. The sentence *How Long is a Chinese* is disambiguated only if accompanied by the correct intonation pattern. Since Chinese is a tone language, speakers of Chinese English find it hard to attend to the patterns of sentence intonation characteristic of English. While TUCKER (1978) also mentions deviating intonation patterns as characterizing the Chinese English of San Francisco, I cannot fully back his other observations. Neither phonology nor syntax are noticeably deviating from the Anglo norm in the speech of Chinese-Americans of my acquaintance. Consonant clusters may be simplified and verb forms may occasionally lack inflectional marking, but these are features also found in other varieties of English. According to my observations, significant differences might be located in the number and kinds of speech genres and conversational routines employed by speakers of Chinese-American – a point also suggested by John J. GUMPERZ (personal communication).

3.5.2 Japanese English

The first main influx of Japanese into California was between 1850 and 1866, when Japan made it illegal for her citizens to leave the country. By 1880 there were only 86 Japanese in all of California. After the lifting of the Japanese emigration restrictions in 1891, however, the Japanese began to arrive in large numbers. Even before Pearl Harbor (1941) there was a good deal of dislike for the Japanese all through California. The War events saw all the Japanese, including the Nissei (American-born US citizens of Japanese origin) in concentration camps. Although today the Japanese are well integrated into American society, racial difference and past history have given them a clear-cut ethnic identity. Like the Chinese the Japanese in San Francisco have their own cultural and business center. Within esoteric forms of *blason populaire* a Japanese who emulates white American values is known as a *banana:* yellow outside, but white inside. Exoteric forms of *blason populaire* include *Jap-flap, Jap-in-the-Box, Buddha-head* and *Joj* (acronym for «Just off the jet»). Jokes like the following play on the imperfect phonological realization of English in the speech of Japanese-Americans:

> A jovial Japanese man was standing on a corner in San Francisco on a particularly chilly day. An elderly, though staunch appearing caucasian lady approached him and they stood together at the corner waiting for the light to change. The Japanese man, wishing to be friendly, made a cheerful comment on the weather: «Bely, bely cold today, yes?» The woman replied indignantly, «Well, your belly wouldn't be so cold if you'd tuck your shirt in!» (Berkeley)

> What goes crick-crick?
> A Japanese camera! (Berkeley)

Folklore does not note much else beside the mixing up of [r] and [l] or [v] and [b]. Lurie and Conklin (1978) also draw attention to possible mergers, especially [r] and [l] [s] and [š], [z] and [ž], [t] and [č]. They also point out that due to the fact that Japanese has a five-vowel system only, speakers of Japanese English may fail to realize all the eleven vowels of American English perfectly, that they may insert extra vowels to break up English consonant clusters (extreme case: /bosotany/ for *Boston,* 1978:56), and that stress may not be used to differentiate between word classes. However, all these points appear to be characteristic again of the Japanese-American who is not a native speaker of English. The fluent speaker of Japanese English will show only minimal deviations from the Anglo norm, noticeable only in fairly level intonation patterns and even stressing and in the pragmatic area of linguistic behavior showing politeness, deference and the like.[31]

3.5.3 Filipino, Korean, and Vietnamese English

While the Chinese-Americans and the Japanese-Americans are in general best known to non-Asians as representatives of Asian Eng-

31 This is the unmistakeable outcome of an informal study of a Japanese-American student, living in our Berkeley home during the academic year 1978/1979.

lish, in recent years immigrants from the Philippines, from Korea, from Vietnam and other countries have greatly added to the number of Asian-Americans both in California and in the SFBA. Of these, the Filipino community is currently the fastest growing ethnic group in California. Already in the 1970 census they were given separate treatment. In the Larger Bay Area they numbered more already than the Japanese (54 000 compared to 35 000). While the Koreans have arrived in steady numbers since the 50's, the influx of Vietnamese has been formidable since the end of the Vietnam War. A substantial group has now settled in the South Bay area.

What happened to the Chinese and Japanese before them is now happening to the Filipinos, the Vietnamese and the Koreans. Racial differences, past experiences, cultural heritage and settlement history establish them as ethnically distinct groups. They are developing a language situation characterized by switching from their mother-tongues to English. While many of them are still at bilingual stage 1 or 2, for future generations their own varieties of English – Korean English, Vietnamese English, Filipino English – will gradually assume the functions and symbolic meanings now still carried by their native tongues. Neither of these dialects will be considered interference varieties any longer, but separate social varieties of English, fully understandable in the light of the cultural load carried by them.

3.6 Fraternity Talk

A variety of English much more restricted in scope than any of those discussed before is the slang used by the members of fraternities and sororities (hereafter fraternity also implies sorority) on the campus of the University of California at Berkeley. Fraternities have existed on the Berkeley campus since 1870. They are chartered with permission of the university and together form what is known as «the Greek system». This label was originally meant to reflect the dedication of the fraternities to the ideas of democracy first voiced in ancient Athens. During most of their 110 years in Berkeley the fraternities were fairly popular among the Cal students. But during the 1960's Berkeley political activism brought them to a steady decline. While in 1960 still 23% of all the undergraduates were members of fraternities and sororities on the Berkeley campus, affiliation decreased during the 60's down to 8%. The trend of the 70's, however, was again upward. While the number of fraternity and sorority houses in 1971 was 43 (down from 70 in 1961), their number was again up to 51 in 1979. Today the Greek system is again a part of the Berkeley campus which cannot be overlooked. It is no longer a shame to be a Greek. Students no longer feel that they have to hide their pins. Some new pledges do not even seem to be aware that belonging to a fraternity house was once considered a social liability.

The fraternity section of Berkeley is a hodge-podge of impressive older mansions and recently constructed apartment buildings. Some of the more beautiful houses are on Piedmont Avenue or «frat row». On warm days – of which there are many in Berkeley – some kind of partying is sure to be going on outside those houses. There is a wide median of grass in the middle of the street where a fraternity boy can be seen throwing a football or a frisbee any time any day. Although the Interfraternity Council claims that academic goals are just as important to them as social events, non-members nevertheless view the Greek system as mainly dedicated to partying and strange, outlandish customs. The houses are seen as a kind of fantasyland untouched by problems of the real world. Their inhabitants are ridiculed in terms of *blason populaire:* Fraternity boys are called *freddies,* which implies their being conceited, rich, boisterous, fad-addicted and often drunk; sorority girls are called *sallies,* which implies their being snobbish, rich, fashion-conscious, proper and prim.

Within the loose definition of ethnicity given in 3.1.3 fraternities can be considered ethnic groups. They are social units closely bound together. They have their own culture, their own traditions, their own folklore. They have their own emblems of ethnicity in customs and dress, as well as in speech. All this is confirmed by the existence of *blason populaire* about them.

It can be assumed that much of what seems so particular about Berkeley Fraternity Talk is also shared by fraternities elsewhere in the USA, since most houses on the Berkeley campus are chapters of national organizations. Nevertheless, it is possible that Berkeley

Fraternity Talk has a flavor of its own; not in the terms borrowed from Greek, which help to establish the fraternities as something different from the ordinary, not in the traditional expressions used to refer to rites and ceremonies, but in periphrastic phrases used instead of conventional terms, in vocabulary and phraseology developed for less formal activities. I would submit then that there is a kind of national core to the lexicon of Fraternity Talk with a number of fringe vocabularies added at and characteristic of the various campuses in the USA. However, I cannot test this hypothesis because I am not aware of any published material on Fraternity Talk from any campus. The data I have collected about Berkeley Fraternity Talk are all culled from the Berkeley Folklore Archives. Some background information I could gather from fraternity materials stored in the archives of the Bancroft Library, University of California at Berkeley. The fraternities, more than most other groups, try to keep their lives, their rituals and ceremonies, their various social activities, their folklore and their language secret. That is why it is so difficult to get at Fraternity Talk and why no accounts of Fraternity Talk have been given yet.

Like Gay English, Juvenile Speech, and, to some extent, Mellowspeak, Fraternity Talk is adopted language. It is a conscious acquisition on the part of a brother. A student can only become a member of a fraternity if, apart from other initiation processes, he also learns the new language variety. Fraternity Talk acts as a signal of membership and as a symbol of ethnicity. A newcomer to a fraternity will have to know more than the Greek letter names of the various houses: *Alpha Chi Omega, Alpha Delta Pi, Alpha Gamma Delta* (which are three of the 14 sorority houses); *Sigma Alpha Epsilon, Sigma Chi, Sigma Nu* (three out of the 37 fraternity houses); he will have to learn the nicknames of members present and past. In many cases this includes knowledge of the story about the origin of the nickname in question. In each fraternity there are lots of stories which are part of daily reference. Communicative competence is achieved only if these areas of reference are known to the newcomer. In Chi Psi, e.g., he reportedly has to learn about a fictitious *Count* and his role during initiation. In Kappa Delta Rho he has to know who the imaginary *Roscoe* is so as to understand what is meant when a brother says *Oh, shit, my girl-*

friend is out with Roscoe (solution: she has let him down). Pledges have to learn the frozen formulas used in ceremonies, as in this example from an opening ceremony (anonymous fraternity):

> Omega: Brother Warden, what is the hour?
> Alpha: Most excellent Omega, it is midnight among the profane, but the sun is at its meridian height in this place.
> Delta: Most excellent Omega, it is the ... hour of the ... day.

Whereas ceremonial discourse like this is written down in a secret book, most other formulas are not codified in written form. Drinking songs, e.g., are orally handed down from one generation of brothers to the next. Equally, proverbial sayings are part of the fraternity tradition. A few examples:

> The whole world is a picnic if you can stand the ants.
> A beautiful woman is like a fine horse: useless unless you can ride her.
> There is nothing so over-rated as a bad lay, and nothing so under-rated as a good shit.

There are other fixed expressions a new member has to learn. In some cases there is also a particular intonation pattern to be mastered, as in the formulaic expression of surprise *I'm not q u i t e believing that,* or in the expression of pleasure *I'm – liking – it – a lot,* which is marked by pauses between its constituent items.

My efforts at coming to grips with Berkeley Fraternity Talk have concentrated on producing a first, obviously still tentative glossary of words and phrases. It is based on the archive materials mentioned, and also includes the terms published by the Interfraternity Council and the Panhellenic Council in the annual fraternity and sorority rush guides. To the extent possible (given the secret nature of Fraternity Talk) the data were checked against occurrences of Fraternity Talk in the *Daily Californian* (student-run campus paper) and fragments of speech overheard on the Berkeley campus in 1979. It is assumed that the following glossary includes expressions used by brothers and sisters among themselves. Not surprisingly, many entries circle around such activities as partying, womanizing and beering, activities also captured in parodying house names coined by non-members: *Grabba Thigh, Wanna Mastur Beta, Ata Bita Pie,* and *Un Kappa Keg.*

Obviously, a good deal of Berkeley Fraternity Talk can also be found in other varieties of SFBA English, particularly in juvenile slang. Yet the blend of a terminology inspired by classical antiquity and initiation rituals with that of juvenile street-lingo is unique to Fraternity Talk. Any language variety is bound to have areas of overlap with other varieties. Nevertheless, it is usually possible to get a fairly clear idea about its shape. Fraternity Talk can be identified by studying the language used by brothers in the fraternity setting. Outside that setting, if not again in the company of another brother, fraternity members will switch to other varieties of English. Such possibilities have been mentioned before and will be discussed again in 3.9.

By describing Fraternity Talk mainly through a glossary I acknowledge the fact that this particular variety of English needs translation, as much at least as Mellowspeak. As in Mellowspeak and Black English, the terms listed in the glossary also give access to the culture and lifestyle expressed in the language variety. It is only such ethnographic knowledge which will produce full communicative competence in Fraternity Talk. While the semantics of words, phrases and whole speech routines are important to Fraternity Talk, the areas conventionally covered by grammar (morphology and syntax) do not need explanation. Fraternity Talk makes use of structures used both in informal (vernacular) and formal English. One would have to detail, however, which speech events require the one, and which the other. Unfortunately, limitations beyond my powers have not allowed me to proceed that far. I have also indicated that deviating patterns of prosody and intonation may again signal special meaning. Even if the glossary given here were complete (which it isn't), the description of Fraternity Talk would still be incomplete. The following glossary is meant, therefore, only as a one-sided introduction to Fraternity Talk. At the same time it should make the point that certain varieties of English cannot be described without extensive reference to the lexicon.

A glossary of Berkeley Fraternity Talk

active, n.	member of a fraternity who has successfully undergone the initiation process. As a full member he is subject to the dues of the National Fraternity Association, but excluded from housework chores and not subject to study rules.
alumnus, alumna, n.	Member (m., f.,) of a fraternity or sorority who has graduated from college.
ash, n.	a Black prostitute
to get one's ashes hauled	pay an ash for her services
ass, n.	girl with certain masculine features (women libber) and not impressed with her potential of attractiveness. Ranks 6th among the 10 girl-types identified.
ass bandit, n.	boy who sleeps around with any girl
badge, n.	token given to a brother after initiation
to be on the ball	be alert, knowing, quick to grasp new matter
to be beaked *to have a huge beak*	be in a mood, sulk, be angry
beat, v.	bother
beer run, n.	an active's getting drinks for the whole house
to turn belly-up	quit, give in, give up
bid, n.	invitation to join a fraternity, addressed to a rushee
to bird *to shoot bird* *bird*, n.	vomit vomit vomit
to bleed one's lizard	urinate
bogie, n.	someone who takes more than his share; selfish, greedy person; person who keeps smoking his joint without passing it along
bong, n. *to bong*	guy or girl who hasn't made it into a fraternity/sorority; unattractive, unappealing person refuse a rushee
boogie, n.	girl with a small weight problem; ranks 5th among the ten girl-types

to book it	study
to have big books	have a lot of reading to do
bro, n.	fraternity brother
bro-jug, n.	beer drinking of two or more bros
buddy-fucking, adj., n., v.	getting better results than the average of the fraternity
brownie, n.	excrement
to hide the brownie	play a dirty trick on someone
to receive a brown helmet	be refused a date by a girl
to have a buzz on	be slightly drunk
to buzz	annoy and wake up other people when walking home from a drinking spree
cat's ass, adj.	good, very good
to catch a bucket	to be turned down by a girl when asking for a date
to catch a heater	get mildly drunk
chapter, n.	local group representing a larger national fraternity organization
closet case, n.	bro whom the fraternity does not want to show; unattractive or uninteresting person
to crash and burn	fail in one's studies; give up the books for booze or balls
cunt, n.	girl who is unattractive, aggressive, artificially made-up, fairly responsive to sexual proposals. Ranks 7th on a scale of ten.
dog, n.	ugly girl
doggy decorations, n.	dog shit
doink, n.	physically attractive (athletic) male who does not demonstrate macho lifestyle, though.
to go down the tube	get bad grades in class
to dump on someone	refuse a date; turn someone down; terminate a relationship
dump job, n.	date refusal; termination of relationship
elephant, n.	girl, both ugly and fat
face man, n. *face woman,* n.	boy/girl accepted into a fraternity/sorority only for their looks; they can be shown off; contrast *closet case*

fanny, n.	vaguely promiscuous sorority girl
fanny fanny chi, n.	sorority with reputation of promiscuity
to flag	fail an exam; receive an F grade
to flick it in	1. to give up; quit 2. fuck
to fold	yield, give in to suggestions made
fox, n.	desirable girl; girl a bro would like to catch
freddy, n.	fraternity man seen from the viewpoint of non-members; implies being conceited, drunk, boisterous, fad-addicted, rich. (Exoteric form of *blason populaire*)
fuck flick, n.	pornographic movie
function, n.	activity involving the whole fraternity
class function	party put on by an ex-pledge class
drink function	event or activity involving heavy drinking
exchange function	parties organized alternatively at two different houses
fountain function	throwing somebody into the fountain on Kroeber Plaza
Fenton's function	having ice-cream at Fenton's
horny function	watching fuck flicks
kegger function	beer party at a (sorority) house
little sister function	party with affiliated sorority girls
munchies' function	getting and sharing after-study food late at night
pinning function	engagement party run for a bro
pledge function	entertainment put on by pledges
rasty function	group drinking avoiding excesses
rush function	fraternity entertaining prospective members
shitty function	getting drunk together, singing songs, telling dirty jokes
tube function	watching television
funky, n.	girl-type number one; girl who is perfect in terms of sex-appeal, looks, intelligence, natural beauty
good woman, n.	casual, informal, easy-going girl
greek, n.	member of a fraternity/sorority
gross, adj.	too much of something; horrible; ugly; outrageous; extreme
to grovel	act in a disorderly way; behave as if drunk

gypo, n.	member of the street culture; gypsy, beatnik, hippie; Telegraph Avenue creature
to hang in there	not give up; keep up doing whatever one is doing; go on pursuing a girl; keep sexual drive going
hasher, n.	boy/girl employed in sorority/fraternity house for kitchen work and serving dinner
to hash	prepare food, wash dishes
heat, n.	alcoholic intoxication
to have a good heat on	be in a condition of drunkenness
hell week, n.	period of pledge initiation at the end of which pledges might either be bonged or accepted as actives.
honkey, n.	outgoing, often boisterous girl; ex high-school cheerleader type; ranking fourth among the ten girl-types
hole, n.	extremely undesirable girl. Type number 10.
to hook a few b's	go and have a couple of beers at the local beer joint
housed, adj.	sick due to drunkenness
shit-housed, adj.	very sick
hurt me!	I like that girl over there; I feel the sting of love
I.F.C., n.	Interfraternity Council. The representing governing body of all the fraternities
initiation, n.	the solem ceremony through which the pledges become actives
induction, n.	the ceremony in which a prospective pledge is formally pledged
independent, n.	person who is not a member of a fraternity/sorority
jungle juice, n.	punch made of a quart of rum, a gallon of orange-pineapple juice and some grenadine
a keg of the bull	a can of Schlitz beer
kip, n.	establishment frequented by fraternity/sorority members
lambda sigma delta	L.S.D. (lysergic acid diethylamide)
line, n.	group of girls who pledge at the same time

legacy, n.	rushee who is the son or brother of a (former) member
mama, n.	attractive, sexually appealing girl; ranks 3rd among the ten girl-types
hot-chocolate mama, n.	bro who prefers studying to partying and drinking
mark book, n.	book in which rule violations of bros are recorded
mick, mickey, n., adj.	easy; easy work; easy course
moon-eyes, n., adj.	someone drunk; drunk
more than a handful is waste	My girl's breasts are large enough
nato, n.	no action – talk only: a virgin girl
nugget, n.	boy/man courted or shown off by fraternity members
O.T.L., n.	out to lunch: someone who does not pay attention, who does a bad job, is absent-minded
O.T., excl.	out!, get out!
panhellenic council, n.	coordinating and controlling body for all the member sororities
pin, n.	sign of fraternity membership
pig, n.	low-ranking girl-type (number 9 on the scale of 10); obese, ugly, shy girl
pig-run, n.	sorority rush
pimp job, n.	doing something mean to a bro for no apparent reason
pledge, n.	uninitiated member; is to be subservient to the actives; has to do housework chores and is subject to study rules
pledge class, n.	group of pledges who have joined the fraternity at the same time
pledgeship, n.	period during which one is a pledge
pop, n.	drink
presents, n.	the event of introducing new pledges to the campus community
pyramid, n.	girl who has been formally pledged but not yet initiated
pyramid club, n.	group (line) of girls who have pledged to join a sorority

puke, n.	someone who makes you vomit; a pledge
puss, n.	boy with some characteristics of a girl: orderly, obeying; a boy who is dominated by a girl
pussey-whipped, adj., n.	dominated by a girl
rack, n.	bed
to be racking it	sleep
to be racking it with one's baby	having sexual intercourse with one's girl-friend
rasty, n.	boy who has drunk but still feels good
rat, n.	establishment where fraternity and sorority members meet
rat, n.	pledge
rat-fuck, n.	sophisticated trick played on pledges during initiation
raving, adj.	being in a state of extreme emotional involvement: happiness, madness, frustration
red death, n.	ravioli with red (spicy) sauce: a punch made of Champagne, white wine, red wine, vodka, grenadine, Hawaiian Punch and Maraschino cherries
rookie, n.	pledge
rush, n.	the activity by which a fraternity seeks new members
rushee, n.	student interested in becoming a member
sally, n.	sorority girl seen from the viewpoint of non-members; implies being snobbish, proper and prim.
to screech	sing when drunk; fraternity boys singing dirty songs
to screw up a wet dream	be incompetent, not able to live up to expectations
secret sauce, n.	punch made of champagne, vodka and Bali-Hi wine
to shake hands with the wife's best friend	urinate
shitty, n.	boy who has been drinking and is beginning to reel
shit-faced, adj.	heavily drunk, just before passing out
dont shit the shitter!	watch out! be careful!

to siphon the python	urinate
smelly, adj.	due to luck alone
sneak, n.	phase during the initiation period
snow job, n.	making a good show, impressing someone
sookie, n.	highly attractive, naturally good-looking, but not necessarily intelligent girl; ranking 2nd.
S.O.S., n.	Shit on a shingle: leftover food mixture on toast
to get on the stick	start working; get going; do something
to streak	run down the street naked
I think we're there!	I agree to your proposal of going there; I will join you.
turkey, n.	fool; looser
twat, n.	bad-looking girl responsive to sexual proposals. Ranks 8th on a scale of ten girl-types.
upper class, n.	former pledge class now handling the initiation process of pledges
what are the odds of . . . ?	What about . . . ?
what is the story?	please clarify! Can I have the details?
wimp, n.	boy/man who is not attractive physically
Z-baggers, adj.	boring

3.7 Gaytalk and Juvenile Speech

Group varieties of the kind exemplified by Fraternity Talk exist in greater number than one commonly assumes. Here two more are briefly mentioned, two that belong to the speech repertoire of many inhabitants of the SFBA.

3.7.1 Gay English

San Francisco is known to house and attract more homosexuals than any other city in the USA. Indeed, there is a large gay community living in and around an area that is now popularly known as «Boystown», the center of which is Castro Street. Like other minority groups, homosexuals are politically active, they defend their rights and fight for power on various levels. Today they have their representatives in the administration of the city and the county. As a group they have also developed their own kind of speech.

Julia STANLEY (1970) has conducted research on homosexual slang all through the USA, including San Francisco. She considers it possible to speak of homosexual slang in terms of a homogenous speech community. Indeed, the homosexual group in San Francisco is certainly a subculture community possessing a language variety capable of linguistic description. Research into San Francisco Gay English was also made by RODGERS (1979), whose *dictionary of gaytalk* confirms and details the findings of STANLEY concerning the characteristics of Gaytalk. Gay English is largely identifiable as a specialized vocabulary developed by the members of the community for purposes of self-identification and communication within the subculture. Gaytalk, like Fraternity Talk, is a conscious acquisition on the part of the speakers; «it acts as a signal of membership within the group and as a method of unifying the members» (STANLEY, 1970:55). STANLEY also examined the question whether there is a vocabulary common to the homosexual subculture and attempted to determine its boundaries on the basis of usage. She found that there is «a core vocabulary that consists of terms borrowed from the theatre and from the slang of prostitutes and the criminal underworld, as well as several stock phrases common to the slang of adolescents and homosexuals.» (1970:55) Gay English has a fondness for compound formations, including rhyming compounds, for exclamations, puns, blends and truncations. (STANLEY, 1970:53–55) It also has a number of speech genres and conversational routines comparable to those of Black English. The main routines and the items of the core vocabulary are known by homosexuals in different geographical areas. In addition, there is a fringe vocabulary, which is «undoubtedly more colorful and creative than the core, but it is not known at all levels of the homosexual community» (STANLEY, 1970:55). The Gaytalk of San Francisco can thus be viewed as consisting of the national core and its specific fringe part. It is this mixture which is detailed in RODGERS (1979). Linguistically, Gaytalk seems to be characterized mainly by semantics and pragmatics deviating from the Anglo norm (Standard English would have to be characterized as straight, I guess), learnable through lists of words, phrases, and routines relating to the gay lifestyle.

3.7.2 Juvenile Speech

Every person who has to do with adolescents knows that the informal language used by the young may differ from that used by adults. Peer group pressure forces adolescents to acquire rapid competence in the lingo of their streets and schoolyards. Reaction to school doctrine helps to establish Juvenile Speech as an alternative to Academic Standard English, the language of the schoolbooks. EFL students abroad are eager to pick up what comes to them as the latest juvenile slang through the channels of rock and pop music, of songs, books, cartoons, and films. That American English has its own youth lingo is not a point to be made; nobody will deny it. However, what is true about Fraternity Talk and Gaytalk is probably also true about Juvenile Speech: In addition to a national core, there are certainly also fringe parts characteristic of various places, maybe even individual school-yards. A few examples of juvenile slang currently in use in the SFBA will show that youth lingo should also have its place in an account of the varieties of English spoken in the SFBA. The following three examples were recorded by LUDLOW (1979):

> We booked on past the Impala, and it was a total face. (Mill Valley)
>
> You may think you can hang with me in math, my man, but you're late. (San Francisco)
>
> You chargin' me? (Berkeley)

The point about this kind of slang is that the words do not look or sound unfamiliar; indeed, *book*, *face*, *hang*, and *charge* have entries in standard dictionaries. Nevertheless, the meanings of the three examples are not clear without further comment. Obviously, the dictionary meanings do not fit the slang use of the words. In SFBA Juvenile Speech, *book* is a verb meaning «to drive one's wheels (automobile) with effectiveness»; *face* means «success»; *hang with,* a term also recorded in Mellowspeak, though with a slightly different meaning, translates as «copy from»; *late* as «mistaken», and *charge* as «address». Current adjectives are: *keggage, totally fine, bad, wicked* (all denoting fun, pleasure, enjoyment), *dyno, primo, bad, the ultimate* (all referring to something wonderful and great), *grungy* and *grubby* (meaning «shabby»), etc. (cp. LUDLOW, 1979). There is, then, clearly an in-group vocabulary, probably also whole speech routines, by means of which membership is defined. Like Fraternity Talk and Gaytalk, Juvenile Speech is not correlated with racially defined ethnicity. Whereas Black English is obviously Black, and Chinese English Chinese, the youth lingo of the SFBA is spoken by adolescents of all colors. It is just one language variety in the speech repertoire of high-schoolers who also have competence in Standard Academic English and the variety of the ethnic-social group their families belong to. If compared to Standard Academic English, differences show up not only in word semantics (cp. BRENNEIS, 1977), but also in syntax and discourse conventions (cp. LABOV, 1972e). Suprasegmentals and segmental phonology, however, are bound to be impressed by the home variety of the individual youth.

3.8 Standard Academic English

Kurt VONNEGUT is credited with having defined Standard English as «that kind of the language (the folk) do not speak» *(Breakfast of Champions).* This may be true in so far as the standard language is understood as an ideal norm against which the performances of individual speakers are checked. I do not intend to include this notion of Standard English here, since it allows for variation itself. The standard language has functional and stylistic offshoots, both written and spoken forms. Often, it is identified with 'national language' and serves purposes of interdialectal communication.

When Standard English is understood as the norm of English used by educated people, it can be defined descriptively with reference to social and stylistic parameters. Mostly it is written; if spoken it is used in highly formal situations. It is always the kind of English presented in textbooks of English as a first or second or foreign language. It is in this respect that the more general notion of Standard English is frequently confused with what should be more narrowly labeled Academic Standard English or Textbook English. English language programs geared towards college entrance exams (see chapter 2.2) naturally stress this one aspect of Standard English without taking due notice of the wider range of the notion 'standard language'.

If Textbook English is something fictitious for most native speakers of English, it is surely a reality for all speakers of English as a second or foreign language. But Academic Standard English becomes important, too, for native speakers of English, because mastery of it is required before admittance to colleges and universities is granted. For the many students enrolled or about to be enrolled in the many educational/academic institutions of the SFBA[32] Standard English is much more real than VONNEGUT thinks. As Academic Standard English it is an everyday experience. As such it is defined as the variety of English suiting educational and academic purposes, as the medium of book learning and extreme formality. Standard Academic English is the variety of English used by students and scholars in their academic writings and, occasionally, in the form of a lecture. As LABOV (1972d) has reminded us, it is quite different from Vernacular English of whatever ethnic coloring. Although the teaching of Academic Standard English may give students «Precision in spelling, practice in handling abstract symbols, the ability to state explicitly the meaning of words, and a richer knowledge of the Latinate vocabulary», LABOV questions how much of it is really useful. «In high school and college middle-class children spontaneously complicate their syntax to the point that instructors despair of getting them to make

32 The number of colleges and universities in the SFBA is staggering. The most important are: University of California at Berkeley, University of California at San Francisco, Stanford University, University of San Francisco, San Francisco State University, San Jose State University, Hayward State University, Golden Gate University, University of Santa Clara, Notre Dame University, Mills College, Merritt College, College of Marin, etc.

their language simpler and clearer. In every learned journal one can find examples of jargon and empty elaboration – and complaints about it.» (1970:11f.) Thus, Academic Standard English (cp. BERNSTEIN's original definition of «elaborated code») may be «flexible, detailed, and subtle» (JENSEN, 1968:119) on the one hand, and «turgid, redundant, and empty» (LABOV, 1970:12) on the other.

There is no need here to launch into a description of Academic Standard English. Of all the varieties of English, this is certainly the best known. Grammars and dictionaries of English detail its rule apparatus and its lexicon; handbooks of stylistics demonstrate how it is effectfully organized into texts. Every (advanced) textbook of English is devoted to describing the features of Academic Standard English. In the SFBA it is the same as elsewhere in the USA.

3.9 After-Babel-Babble in Bagdadh-by-the-Bay

Like few other cities in the world, San Francisco has attracted people from many nations, speakers of many different languages, representatives of diverse cultures. In Bagdadh-by-the-Bay, as the folk call San Francisco when they want to refer to its exotic charm, the curse of Babel would certainly have had drastic effects upon communication if the many immigration groups had not all accepted English as *lingua franca.* There are still many members of ethnic groups – especially among the Chinese and the Mexicans – who stick to their original mother-tongue. Other speakers have had less reservations about taking up English as their second language and handing it on to their children as their first language. But even where the original mother-tongues have lost ground, the cosmopolitan character of Bagdadh-by-the-Bay is still noticeable linguistically: in the various varieties of English that have emerged in the SFBA.[33]

33 Inhabitants and visitors of San Francisco know that there are two further important population groups in that city: the Irish and the Italians. Both groups, however, are no longer given separate treatment by the US Census.

Since English is the language used by all the groups, and since a particular variety of English is taught at school to the members of all those groups, communication between population groups in the SFBA is not impossible. Nevertheless, some differences between the various group-specific varieties persist. These differences can be traced on the various levels of language: suprasegmental and segmental phonology, morphology and syntax, text structures and discourse conventions, lexicon and speech genres, semantics and pragmatics. On the surface, the points of difference may seem insignificant at times; in their totality, however, they are bound to be of some consequence. Recent work by John GUMPERZ (1978, 1979b) has shown that miscommunication between speakers of English from different cultural or ethnic origins are very frequent. In England, e.g., speakers of English English and speakers of Indian English were found to lack understanding for each other's way of using English. Both groups needed help in the form of hints as to how to decode each other's speech. It could be demonstrated that many prejudiced judgments made by members of different ethnic groups about each other had their roots in lacking knowledge of each other's way of speaking English. (GUMPERZ et al., 1979) The fact that there are so many examples of *blason populaire* in the folklore of the SFBA suggests that misunderstandings of the kind reported by GUMPERZ are probably quite common in California, too.

A knowledge of the various varieties of English in use in the SFBA can certainly help to relieve such misunderstandings and some of the resulting tensions. Where people from different cultural, ethnic, social or educational backgrounds have to interact, they are in need of information about the factors that might cause breakdowns in communication. The factors that produce communication difficulties cannot be attributed only to problems of ac-

Linguistically, Irish English can no longer be identified in San Francisco, while Italo-American English can still be heard. Italo-American English might have been included among the varieties of English in use in the SFBA; Irish English not. Linguistic *blason populaire* exists only about the Italians using English, not about the Irish. Some research on Italo-American English is reported in Correa-Zoli 1970 and Simonici 1959.

cent, lack of adequate knowledge of vocabulary or the structure of English. They also stem from different conventions in the use of English, conventions that – as much as accent or syntax – are variety-specific. Accent, vocabulary, and syntax are three levels of language where varieties may differ; but they do not comprise the source of all the differences. Equally important are the cultural conventions associated with particular varieties. It is not only when a phoneme is mistaken for another, when the meaning of a word or phrase is interpreted wrongly, when grammatical categories are realized differently, but also when attitude and meaning are conveyed through one set of conventions and interpreted through another that breakdowns in communication may occur. Any successful interaction between members of different groups depends on each party interpreting correctly what the other has tried to convey. These interpretations, GUMPERZ holds, are what judgments about the speaker's ability and intention are based on. If the speakers in the interaction are using different strategies and signals from each other to convey attitude and meaning, wrong inferences are likely to be drawn. Over a period of time, these tend to build up into stereotyped attitudes and produce the folklore of *blason populaire*.

Because the varieties described in the preceding sections were presented as group varieties, it was possible to approach them in terms of *blason populaire*, giving folklore an ancillary function within sociolinguistics. This also reflects the fact that in the SFBA ethnic and other social varieties are most distinct, not local-regional ones. All these varieties are varieties of English, i.e. clearly related to and part of a whole represented by the English language (American English), each of them overlapping in certain areas with other varieties, but still having its own distinct identity. Given a network of interactive ties an individual speaker of English in the SFBA is placed somewhere among a number of these varieties, with one functioning as his home variety. We could thus imagine, e.g., a Black student, having as his home variety Black Vernacular English; as a student he would also have command of Academic Standard English; as a member of a fraternity he would also be able to use Fraternity Talk when appropriate; and, depending on our imagination, we could easily associate him with further varieties of English, including some not listed in the survey given. The speech repertoire of a white lawyer, to launch into another imaginary example, might include Mellowspeak as his home variety, Standard Academic English and American Legal Jargon as his professional varieties, and Gaytalk as the variety used by him after work when visiting certain San Francisco bars. Since some of his clients might be Black, Chicano or Chinese, he would at least have to have a passive knowledge of these varieties, too.

Individuals like these two fictitious characters will have acquired full or partial competence in varieties of English other than their home variety by long exposure to and regular interaction with speakers of these other varieties. Yet, as the research of GUMPERZ has mede clear, even native speakers of English are in need of further elucidation about varieties of English encountered by them in daily interaction. A guide to various varieties of English is required not only for the benefit of the outsider, the nonnative speaker of English, but also the insider. Only if such a guide is made available will the disruptive effects of the curse of Babel be removed, removed, too, from the cosmopolitan center represented by Bagdadh-by-the-Bay.

Part III: Introduction

In the description of the varieties of English of the San Francisco Bay Area given in Part II, it was repeatedly pointed out that knowledge of grammar in the conventional narrow sense of the term is not enough to overcome the linguistic barriers existing between the various groups speaking those varieties of English. Great importance was attributed to suprasegmental phonology, especially to intonation patterns, to the semantics of variety-specific lexicons, and to pragmatics. While differences between varieties can also be observed on the levels of syntax and morphology, it has become obvious that syntax cannot obtain a central position in a varieties grammar as it would in a CHOMSKY model. Like segmental phonology, and the areas already mentioned, syntax is just one part of that grammar. To say, on a general level, that one area of language is more important than another seems to be problematic. With regard to specific varieties, however, it would be possible to say, e.g., that for A lexicon is dominant, for B suprasegmental phonology, etc. In both cases, such dominance could be explained by pointing out the impression of cultural phenomena, in the case of A mainly on the lexicon, in the case of B mainly on intonation. Indeed, in the account of the language varieties given, cultural factors were often mentioned explicitly. Lifestyle was seen as a key factor shaping not only Fraternity Talk and Gaytalk, but also Mellowspeak and, at least to some extent, Black English and Chicano English. Certainly, the lifestyle of a community is also expressed in the language variety employed by that community. Varieties, as GUMPERZ has repeatedly reminded us (e.g. GUMPERZ and HERASIMCHUCK, 1972), thus come to be expressive of social and cultural meanings. Since these meanings seem to be the crucial ones in intergroup communication (cp. 3.9), it is inconceivable for a varieties grammar to exclude them from its scope. That is to say, a varieties grammar will also have to include those areas of linguistics on which social and cultural meanings operate most clearly: lexicon, suprasegmentals, and pragmatics.

Part III, therefore, is written to argue for the necessary holistic nature of a varieties grammar, based on the evidence of variety descriptions given in Part II. It is also meant to discuss the usefulness of a number of approaches and models recently suggested in American sociolinguistics, given the holistic frame of a varieties grammar. It is also expected to point to a way out of an apparently unsolvable situation. Accepting the proposals suggested at the end of the study – eclectic procedure and *ad hoc* varieties grammars –, however, requires an openness of mind not usually found in linguistics today.

CHAPTER 4

4 Language Varieties and Notions of Grammar

4.1 Some Basic Notions

4.1.1 Holism

> Suppose we assume that some minor god wishes to cross the line, wishes to pass as a member of the human community. It has the Standard Divine Sensorium by which it is able to perceive in an instant all of space and time, it is able to assume any form or to occupy and control any existing creature, but it needs to be told how to talk and what constraints it needs to impose on its unlimited potential in order not to give away its divine origin. It will need to acquire the local grammar, or maybe more than one local grammar, and a large portion of the lexicon of that language or those languages. It will need to identify itself as a member of the community with respect to age, sex, family position, social status, educational background, occupation, geographical origin, etc., and it will need to equip itself with a fairly coherent set of opinions about the world and a set of affective preferences, together with a strategy for changing these, though this last is not necessary for an adult. It will need to perceive among its interlocutors whether they are people it is supposed to know, how its biography is shared with theirs, if and how they are related to it, and so on. It will need to notice what sorts of social occasions it finds itself in or what sorts of social settings its own actions has put it in. It will need to know what linguistic conventions and routines govern conversations on these occasions, what it and its interlocutors are expected to accomplish with each contribution to the conversation, when it can appropriately talk at all and when it should remain silent. And it will apparently need to know how to vary its speech from time to time and how past decisions to vary its speech in some respect might require it to vary its speech in some other respect more often or less often so that certain proportions come out right.
>
> (FILLMORE, 1972:284–285)

In his address to the 1972 Georgetown University Round Table on sociolinguistics, Charles FILLMORE recalled the richness of language and pointed to the difficulties and limitations encountered by a grammarian attempting to go beyond the definition of conventional grammar. He expressed some doubt as to whether conventional grammar might ever succeed in grasping language as a whole. Yet, he still thought of «the grammarian's job as that of discovering and describing the elements, the structures, the processes and the constraints which are somehow made available to the language user as instruments for communicating.» (1972:282) He found himself, however, «more and more tending toward the study of how and for what purposes and in what settings people 'use' their grammars.» (1972:282) FILLMORE here accepted a distinction between 'grammar' on the one hand, and 'use' on the other. In a varieties grammar, however, as will be seen, these two realms are not easily separated. A varieties grammar is also a grammar of use, a grammar with a functional dimension. FILLMORE's «proposal for determining the boundary between linguistics and other disciplines connected with a speaker's control of language use» is to start «a project for writing an instruction manual for an Immigrant» like the minor god wishing to cross the line and wishing to pass as a member of the human community. (1972:285) Something similar to this «Instruction Manual» is what I expect a varieties grammar to be.

Above, in chapter two, I have pleaded the case of the usefulness of such a manual for the EFL speaker, an outsider to English language varieties almost like FILLMORE's minor god. I have made the point that from the outside point of view and in the more generally valid process of variety selection language varieties are equalled with registers which are selected by speakers according to certain criteria. The varieties are described in terms of the region they are typical of, the social group (ethnic, economic, occupational, age, sex, etc.) they represent, the topic they are used for, as well as other less dominant variables. There is no use, it seems to me, giving a grammatical description of any variety without clarifying – in further descriptive statements – its particular diatopic, diastratic, or diatypic labels. Linguistic analysis (in the narrow sense) can only be done profitably after the variety in question has been firmly embedded culturally, so that the linguistic facts can be understood as on a continuum with cultural factors. We thus have to envisage a varieties grammar as holistic in nature.

When speaking of a varieties grammar as a holistic grammar, I want to go beyond a definition of grammar in Chomskyan terms. Linguists who have broken off from the orthodox generativist position have begun to see the limitations they have themselves been accepting. FILLMORE may be quoted as one of these; George LAKOFF as another.[1] More conventional definitions of grammar would suggest an approach towards a varieties grammar dealing mainly, if not exclusively, with syntax and phonology, and some semantics. It has become obvious, however, that the information needed by a user of a varieties grammar as a source of reference for appropriate linguistic behavior cannot be limited to the conventional narrow scope of grammar in linguistic theory. In order to understand language varieties and in order to achieve active competence himself, a speaker of English – whether native or foreign-born – is dependent on information about language in a broader sense. 'Grammar' in the label 'A Varieties Grammar of English' obviously means something else than the abstract formalism creating all and only English sentences (as in generative grammar). It, too, reflects the knowledge of the speaker-hearer; but it reflects the full knowledge a *fluent* speaker-hearer has of his language *and its uses.* As such it is a collection of statements to which a speaker or writer can turn for information about the appropriate way of encoding language in a variety-specific way, and a hearer or reader can refer to when decoding discourse or text in a given variety of English. These statements would go beyond rules of phonology and sentence formation into the fields of discourse structure, lexicalization, and cultural impact on language generally. This, at least, is suggested by the insights gained about language varieties in chapter three. There the characteristic features of language varieties of English were found not simply in different

1 Recently FILLMORE has taken up the notion of fluency in a way that approaches my understanding of holistic competence (1979b). In (1979a) he exposed the innocence assumption inherent in much of contemporary semantics and showed that speaker-hearers have not only be idealized once, but twice; for they are so innocent as not to know idioms, fixed expressions, metaphors and the like. George LAKOFF has moved away from generative semantics into pragmatics and is now trying out a new approach to language through metaphors and image schemas. (1979, 1980)

patterns of phonological and syntactical structure, but, to a large extent, in different selections from the stock of lexical items and varying attribution of meaning to such items; they were also found to reside in so-called extralinguistic matters of which phonology, syntax, and vocabulary are not always separate, but may, indeed, be expressive. Frequently it may even be the case that conventional areas for grammatical investigation do not indicate marked differences between varieties although such differences are strongly felt to be present. In these cases, the differences seem to appear more significantly in the areas of suprasegmentals, discourse conventions, and speech genres, if not in the cultural load generally expressed through the variety in question. Given this assessment, a varieties grammar should not only fulfil the expectation of bringing together all the language varieties in a unifying apparatus, but also of accounting for all the distinctive features of the individual varieties, including 'extralinguistic' ones.

Linguists know – or should know – that grammatical regularities are only one aspect of linguistic behavior. As such they cannot be considered in isolation. From an empirical point of view, it is not possible to separate the grammarian's grammar (morphological and syntactical regularities of a natural language; formalism defining a language) from other parts of linguistics. If such a separation is made nevertheless, it has to rely on a theoretical construct. Linguists have been faced with the dilemma of either doing justice to language as a whole and doing without an adequate theory or presenting a formalism and neglecting certain aspects of language. The kinds of grammatical analysis linguists are familiar with presupposes a rather narrow hypothesis about the nature of language as a discourse system, one, actually, that leads to limitations unacceptable within the framework of a varieties grammar. As SILVERSTEIN has put it, «the explicit principles of grammar construction and grammatical theory in the Western tradition are all variants of the assumption that speech instantiates a grammatical system, or *langue,* whose elements contribute to speech events of pure reference or denotation.» (1978:140) SILVERSTEIN turns himself against the notion «that grammatical analysis and description can be carried out independently of the sociocultural organization of speech, i.e. of the fact that speech is a culturally constituted form of social action.» (1978:139) One of SILVERSTEIN's cases is the incorporation of a specification of the personal pronouns into a grammatical description. He shows that this leads the grammarian into the realms of social anthropology because the referential value of the pronoun *I*, e.g., presupposes the constitution of a social role in an instantiation of a certain recognized social action. (1978:142) Basing himself also on a discussion of performative utterances, SILVERSTEIN concludes that «the kind of context-independent referential potential that is the prerequisite to grammatical analysis under the assumptions of traditional theories is thus a very small part of the analysis of a grammatical system.» «There seems to be no way to do grammatical analysis, let alone to justify it, without making its cultural prerequisites explicit.» (1978:145; 151)

The reason why the «narrow-scope approaches» are unsatisfactory lies with the fact that they do not do justice to language as a whole. Research done on varieties of English such as Black English has only very recently begun to concentrate on areas other than the structure of the language although – as Geneva SMITHERMAN has repeatedly reminded linguists (1977, 1979, 1980) – what is needed is research on «the characteristics of black speech relative to the use and function of language (i.e. language in social context)» (1979:204). SMITHERMAN is quite specific with regard to the kind of research now called for: «In describing the actual speaking behavior of blacks, we must be concerned not simply with theoretical concepts having to do with structural variables. Rather we need to broaden our conceptualization of language so that our theories will speak to variations in language functions, to interactional norms and rules governing language use, and to developmental patterns in the acquisition of communicative competence.» (1979:204) What she advocates is a synthesis of theoretical and socio-ethnographic linguistics. It is exactly such a synthesis of approaches which I call holistic. A holistic grammar would not abandon the listing of rules about the structure of a language, but would also include rules detailing communicative competence. As said before, there is more to linguistic competence than just knowledge of syntactic patterns and «correct» pronunciation. Language is a complex game. Its many-natured rules are only now being discovered by linguists working in various research areas, although most people who participate in the language game seem to know them anyway. It is when they move out of familiar territory that they are at a loss; it is as outsiders, like FILLMORE's minor god, that they are in need of a guiding manual explaining to them the language game and its rules. A varieties grammar of English would attempt to become such a manual, by at least stating rules for constructing utterances which native speakers of particular varieties would judge appropriate. Since appropriateness is a value attached not only to the structure of sentences, but also to choice of lexical items and speech genres, to pronunciation including suprasegmental phonology, and observations of discourse conventions, the grammar should include information on all those parts of language as well. This requirement of a holistic varieties grammar, however, is at odds with the narrow definition of grammar, its being «independent of meaning» (CHOMSKY, 1957:17).

That there are links between language and culture, however, is not seriously disputed any longer today. Yet, how language and culture can be connected is subject to debate. HYMES (1964) has pointed out two kinds of links: One is associated with the work of MALINOWSKI and emphasizes the interdependence of culture and language as aspects of the same event. The other, associated with LEVI-STRAUSS, emphasizes the congruence of language and culture as parallel systems. The case of parallelism is also argued by GUMPERZ and HERASIMCHUCK: «Just as grammatical knowledge enables the speaker to distinguish potentially meaningful sentences from non-sentences, knowledge of the social values associated with the activities, social categories and social relationships implied in the message is necessary in order to understand the situated meaning of a message, i.e. its interpretation in a particular context.» (1972:99) The account of English language varieties in the San Francisco Bay Area (in chapter three) reveals that cultural information is crucial to an understanding of language varieties. The cultural context in which these varieties operate cannot be separated from the meaning expressed in their linguistic structures; analysis of «sound patterns» and «phrase structures», «componential analysis» of phoneme-, morpheme-, or phrase-related units of meaning is not enough. Linguistic structures must also be examined as to social or cultural meaning. (BLOM and GUMPERZ, 1972; GUMPERZ and HERASIMCHUCK, 1972) It appears, then, that «the structure of language and the structure of the context of language (the rest of human culture) are coded along the same lines, derive from the same source and, consequently, are subject to similar types of analysis» (DURBIN, 1972:52). 'Extralinguistic' matters are thus put on one and the same level with grammar. It is only small step from here to suggest that language be seen on a continuum with culture. For years now, HALLIDAY has indeed argued for abandoning the strict separation of grammar and cultural units. Particularly he has argued that social structure and grammar offer the speaker a set of options and that therefore utterances are the result of a selective process in which speakers choose among a network of social, semantic, syntactic, and phonological alternatives to express their intent. (HALLIDAY et al., 1964; HALLIDAY, 1978)

A holistic perspective is adopted explicitly by Charles FERGUSON. As a linguist he is no longer satisfied with viewing linguistics as a branch of psychology mainly. He prefers considering linguistics a branch of anthropology. By means of the term 'holistic', FERGUSON refers to the study of language in terms of a whole culture or society. It means that «linguists turn their attention to the social contexts in which language behavior occurs, to whole acts of expression and communication in which language typically has a central role, and to the whole community or society in which the norms and expectations of language use are shared.» (1977:3) It would be wrong to think that holism is a new idea. It had only gone out of fashion. Up to the first part of our century, a holistic approach to language studies could be taken for granted. A unified perspective on linguistics, anthropology and folklore was present in HERDER's work and – in the USA – still in that of SAPIR. It was only after the split of linguistics and anthropology that linguists seemed less and less interested in the sociocultural roots of language. The «assertion and pursuit of disciplinary autonomy on the part of linguistics» (BAUMAN, 1977:15) contributed to the undoing of the integrated approach in modern times. In linguistics, as BAUMAN says (who himself is committed to a unified vision of language, culture, and verbal art), «the focus of interest and analysis was (. . .) on the patterning of linguistic features in texts», giving «primacy either tacitly or explicitly, to the referential function of language, the propositional content of utterances.» (1977:16,17) Work in anthropological linguistics, sociolinguistics and linguistic pragmatics, as well as continuing work in stylistics and text linguistics, has prepared the way, once again, towards a holistic view of language. Today, as HYMES says, «some linguists are beginning to attend to a conception of linguistic structure as interdependent with social circumstances.» «Much of philosophy and some of linguistics seem to have found their way back to an open-ended conception of the modes of meaning in language.» (HYMES, 1973:59, 72)

I have argued the case of holism at some length because a varieties grammar of English can be approached only in holistic terms if it has to have any success at all. Of course, a holistic approach towards a varieties grammar cannot be but eclectic. It most probably will have to do without the beauty of a single abstract model. It would have the ragged looks of a tool geared towards practical use. As SMITHERMAN has put it with regard to the educational implications of the holistic approach, teaching and learning about a language must come from an «interdisciplinary, synthesized theoretical-socio-ethno-linguistic perspective». (1979:207)

What linguists need, then, is a higher-order concept from which a holistic grammar can be derived. For sure, some such higher status has been claimed for various concepts, and I will discuss some of them with regard to their relevance to the notion of a varieties grammar in the following sections. Some sociolinguists have staked their hopes on generative dialectology, others on variable rules and other methods ultimately derived from a Chomskyan notion of grammar. It will be shown that all of these models yield useful results indeed, if the traditional definition of grammar is kept, they lead to results that are at least formally satisfactory and can be used to explain differences between varieties in relation to each other and to a higher order unit. Yet, if truly contextual questions are asked, these models cannot fulfil the needs of a varieties grammar. A satisfactory model for a varieties grammar is found only if the narrow definition of grammar is abandoned for a wider, holistic one; if the varieties in the grammar are related to HYMES' notion of 'ways of speaking' (see 4.3.3.3).

Instead of attempting to redefine 'grammar', one might, of course, give up the term itself. As DI PIETRO (1976b) has pointed out, linguists in the past twenty years have been living in the age of grammar. Grammar indeed seemed to dominate linguistics. The importance still attributed to the notion of grammar is probably also the reason why I stick to the term 'varieties grammar', although doing so may mean to extend the definition of grammar considerably or occasionally substituting alternative terms like 'guide', 'instruction manual' or 'storehouse of information'.

4.1.2 Typolects

4.1.2.1 Homogeneity within Heterogeneity

Like the work of the variationists discussed in 4.2, the present approach towards a varieties grammar of English goes back to a feeling of uneasiness about the static nature of the synchronic model in general use until quite recently. The variationists were reacting against the 'freezing' of language at a given point in time and against the idealization of the speaker-hearer; against what was called 'artificial homogeneity'. As a result of this attitude, variationist studies were and still are concerned with heterogeneity in language, with finding dynamic, instead of static, models for language description, and with integrating the rules of the various 'lects' (i.e. idiolects or dialects) of a language into a unified description of that language. Variationists tried to develop a metatheory capable of incorporating variation at the center of language study (especially: LABOV, 1969; DE CAMP, 1971a; BICKERTON, 1971; BAILEY, 1973; CEDERGREN and SANKOFF, 1974). As much as I agree with them about the need for the study of variation in language, I cannot follow them into condemning the static model completely. It is true that traditional synchronic linguistics has largely excluded types of variation from the purview of the discipline; and some of the most interesting aspects of linguistics, like language learning and language change, can be studied most insightfully only if the homogeneity hypothesis is abandoned. For the purpose of a varieties grammar, however, a certain degree of language freezing, of homogeneity within heterogeneity is still necessary.

I base my approach to a varieties grammar not only on the notion of holism, i.e. on doing justice to the whole of language, including the cultural background of speakers expressed in it, but also on that of the variety as a typolect. This means that I am concerned with variation in language not on the level of the individual and idiolectal, but on the level of the supra-individual, the typical; with language that is group-specific, indicative of recurrent situations or classes of genres.

Where typolects represent the speech behavior of social groups, it might be helpful to clarify their relation to language in a 'community grammar'. A varieties grammar is conceived as a community grammar in more than one sense. Conventionally, grammars written by linguists are supposed to be grammars not simply of individuals, but of speech communities. In this tradition, language structure is assumed to be homogenous and invariant so that any speaker-hearer in the community would have the grammar internalized, thus making it possible for a linguist to pull the community grammar out of any speaker-hearer, as it were. If this speaker-hearer is replaced by a statistically idealized one – as in variationist theory – then the emerging community grammar is equalled with that of a typolect in a varieties grammar; i.e. it is assumed that a number of constraints are shared by all the speakers of the typolect. There is, however, a second interpretation to 'community grammar'. It may be assumed that within any real community of speakers there is more than one variety of a language (or of more than one language). In a varieties grammar, the typolects occurring in any community can be related to each other; the varieties that make up the speech repertoire(s) of the members of a given community can be represented within a unifying theory. Community grammar (sense 2) is thus defined as a polylectal grammar, each part of which also has supra-individual validity as a typolectal community grammar (sense 1).

4.1.2.2 Typolects in popular interpretation

Something like the notion of typolect I have in mind is represented in what one might call a popularized and applied varieties grammar of English: *The People's English* by James Hamilton (1975).

HAMILTON's book purports to be «a guide to the six great social classes in the United States – and more particularly, to their speech and writing standards.» (1975:i) It is written as a course-book for the student of English (as a native speaker), introducing language at the lower-class level and then progressingly adding more elements of grammar and vocabulary for the middle and upper-class levels. It does not give a complete description of either of these varieties of English, but selects from them those items that should be part of the linguistic repertoire of Americans who want to upgrade themselves socially. As will be seen below, a course-book built up like *The People's English* can be used to illustrate the working of implicational scales, since it presents social varieties as on a continuum, the end point of which implies all the earlier points. As they move from low-level English to upper-class Standard English, students are expected to enlarge their apparatus of grammar. (HAMILTON does not discuss any theoretical questions.)

Although I do not share a view of English as consisting of inferior and superior varieties, I do believe that social classes in both the USA and in Great Britain speak different varieties of English. As is well known, the strongest claim for the existence of socially differentiated varieties of English was made by Basil BERNSTEIN. In his work (e.g. 1971) he compared the speech behavior of secondary school boys from working class backgrounds and from middle class backgrounds. BERNSTEIN concluded that the language of these two groups of boys exemplified two different codes: One, the 'restricted code' of the working class boys can be described as limited in scope and predictable in its lexicon, and as being marked by the absence of syntactical complexity. The second, the 'elaborated code' of the middle class boys, can be described as having wider scope and lesser lexical predictability, as being marked by greater syntactical complexity, lengthier utterances and by subordination patterns. For the USA, similar claims were made by BEREITER and ENGLEMANN (1966). They noticed that ghetto children lag behind their more advantaged middle class peers in exactly the same respects as the British working-class school-boys investigated by BERNSTEIN: limited size of vocabulary, short sentences, simple grammar. Both BERNSTEIN and BEREITER/ENGLE-

MANN, and, in the field of application, HAMILTON, argued that lower-class children must be given better education. They also claim that the language variety used by the lower-class children must be classified hierarchically below that of the middle-class speakers; they qualified it as 'deficient' (BEREITER and ENGLEMANN) or 'restricted' (BERNSTEIN). While I do not adopt their viewpoint, I still make the assumption that varieties of the kind discussed by BERNSTEIN and BEREITER/ENGLEMANN do exist and are widely, even popularly, understood to be expressive of social class (in this instance), or ethnic groups, occupational fields, particular situations, etc. (in other cases), and that they can be isolated as homogenous units within the larger heterogenous complex of English.

4.1.2.3 Varieties as Typolects

When speaking about a varieties grammar of English I have in mind a kind of grammar than can accomodate various types of English language varieties; i.e. a grammar that allows for language differentiation according to the units of subclassification suggested in chapter two: diachronically, diatopically, diastratically, and diatypically.

Figure 1 Language varieties of English

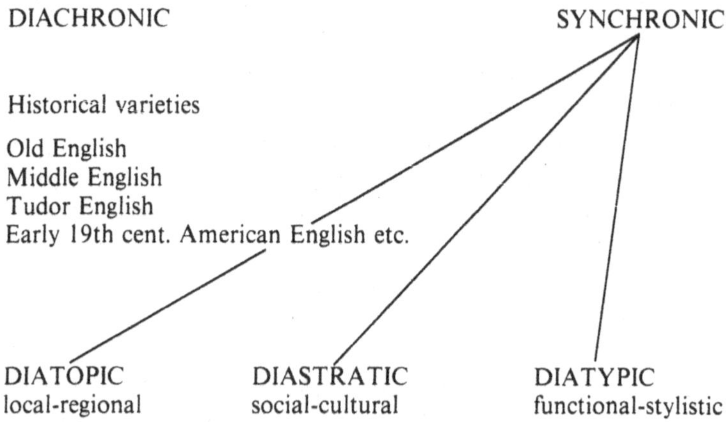

This chart would allow for diachronic and synchronic comparison of varieties. Accordingly, if a varieties grammar were written, it could be used to show the differences between the Academic Written English of ca. 1100, 1500 and 1900; it could be used to relate the characteristics of the speech of Sam Weller (in *The Pickwick Papers*) to a certain sociolect, or those of the rhetorics of Hrothgar (in *Beowulf*) to a certain genre. In these cases as well in those depicted in the account of present-day San Francisco Bay Area varieties, the salient features of the varieties in question would be indicated. Obviously, the notion of a varieties grammar with such a vast span cannot be developed within the synchronic-static model. Yet, in spite of the apparent need for a heterogenous model, the homogeneity hypothesis is not abandoned completely. It is simply relegated from the level of the language to that of the variety. The individual varieties come to be considered typolects. Terminologically, 'typolect' expresses that a variety is not simply the language of a certain individual, but that typical of a group, a situation, a place at a given point of time, etc. A Black inhabitant of the San Francisco Bay Area, e.g., does not represent Black English by himself; however, he most probably participates in the variety called Black English. Black English, like other typolectal varieties he may have command of, exists through the use several speakers make of it as a group. For sure, there are individual features that make it possible to distinguish the speech habits of speaker A from the speech habits of speaker B, even when both use the same variety. There is still considerable variation left between speaker-hearers in the way their individuality shapes their speech habits and in the way they organize their speech repertoires. Such differences, of course, are also examples of variation in language – actually, they have been studied foremost by variationists – but they belong to a level below that of the typolect; they are idiolectal in nature and thus not part of the central concerns of a varieties grammar working with typolects.

Typolects characterize a variety through what, by common agreement, is viewed as typical; by features and rules that are characteristically observed by the average speaker. It is by sticking to single language varieties at a time, by comparing how these are made use of by various speakers or in various texts, and by relying on statistical methods of discovering what is the average with regard to inventories and usage, that one may succeed in describing a variety as a typolect. What a varieties grammar relies on are the regular areas of social and cultural agreement where individuals extend their roles in predictable ways, not individual behavior. Or to say it in Saussurean terms: A varieties grammar is based on *langue* rather than on *parole*. SAUSSURE, by the way, was one of the great linguists violently attacked by variationists for having forced the homogeneity hypothesis upon linguistics (cp. BAILEY, 1973). It is interesting to note, however, that even variationists have to confirm the existence of typolects, and thus of areas of homogeneity in language. Without being able to account for the phenomenon, LABOV, e.g., has noticed that individuals are fairly consistent in their use of linguistic variables. He noticed that their patterns of frequencies are quite stable. Individual informants do not vary significantly from the speech patterns characteristic of the whole group. And when, in any of the many corpuses of sociolinguistics data available now, these data are scanned by looking at individual scores, the broad patterns for grouping become very distinct.

The relation between English, the whole language, its varieties (typolects) and individual language (idiolects) can be represented like this:

Figure 2 Typolects in relation to idiolects and total language

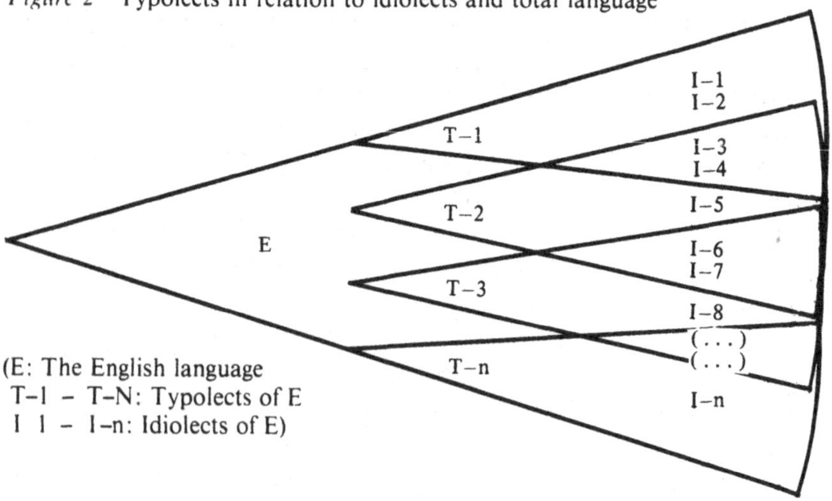

English (the English language) as a whole is viewed here as consisting of all the varieties in the language. A variety, on the other hand, is not defined as consisting of all the idiolects in the language. The range of the idiolectal language repertoire of a speaker may let him participate in one, two, three or even further varieties; but no one would have a speech repertoire that includes all the varieties of English. Varieties are therefore defined as consisting of the idiolects of a number of people that are linked through shared cultural background or networks of interests and/or activities. Communication within such groups regulates the use of language. The selection of linguistic items from the whole of English is approximately the same for all the speakers participating in a typolect. Individuals are seen to fit into the regular patterns of typolects; there, possible idiolectal variation is eliminated through statistical idealization.

4.1.3 *Family of Varieties*

4.1.3.1 Common Core and Potential

The relationships among the varieties of a language can be likened to that of members in a family. This notion is at least as old as SCHLEICHER's *Stammbaumtheorie* (1861) and has been repeatedly exploited by linguists. It has been pointed out (by WUNDERLICH, 1974) that there are two reasonable ways of picturing how the total language can be understood to comprise its individual varieties, both in terms of set theory:

(1) English is defined as the set-theoretical intersection of all the varieties of English;[2]
(2) English is defined as the set-theoretical union of all the varieties of English.

2 Application of this model to English was made by SVEJCER (1978). He considers the English language a complex system consisting of overlapping subsystems.

If, for purposes of illustration, we limit the number of English language varieties to, say, six, the relationship of varieties and total language can be represented like this:

Figure 3 Intersection and union of varieties

(1) Intersection of varieties (2) Union of varieties

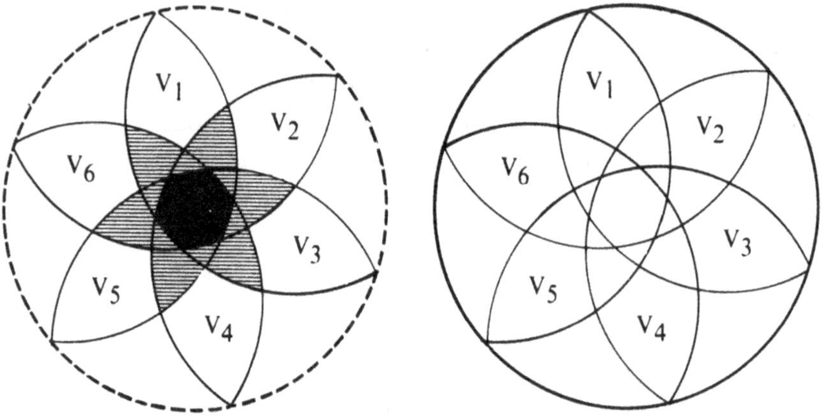

Kanngiesser (1972) has used the terms 'standard' to refer to (1) and 'potential' in reference to (2). 'Standard' appears to be an unfortunate term because what it designates is not the standard language. More helpful here is Hockett's (1958) term 'common core', if it is understood to be that part of the language which is shared by all of its varieties. Although Quirk et al. (1972) do not distinguish between (1) and (2) and do not always use the term 'common core' consistently, their initial definition of the term comes close to what is meant here: «however esoteric or remote a variety may be, it has running through it a set of grammatical and other characteristics that are present in all others.» (1972:14)[3]

3 Cp. Svejcer's interpretation of 'Common Core' as «the aggregate of identical elements of two microsystems» (1978:19). I extend this interpretation to a reading of «the aggregate of identical elements of two *or more* micro-systems.»

It is important to note that the intersection of all the varieties does not constitute a variety by itself, but, as a kind of 'common core', the set of language items shared by all the varieties can be useful as a point of reference. If its contents are known, individual varieties can be described by listing the features particular to them, but not found in the 'common core' and thus not shared by all the other varieties. As an instrument measuring the degree of commonness among varieties, the 'common core' might indeed be called the 'standard' of the language.

'Potential', the term KANNGIESSER applies to (2), is less ambiguous than 'standard'. Again, the summation or union of all the varieties does not constitute a variety by itself. Viewed synchronically only, it is theoretically possible to imagine a speaker who, at a given time, has a repertoire of all the varieties of a language. However, if we take English as the language in question, it seems utterly improbable that any human being could ever have such a vast repertoire. And since nobody knows how many and which varieties there are in English, even a computer could not realize the whole potential. Yet, as a theoretical construct, the 'potential', like the 'common core' can be of considerable use as a source of reference.[4] The 'potential' contains the total set of rules that could potentially be selected in individual varieties. It gives a maximal definition of the language because it contains every possible variety. It can function as a supergrammar (see 4.2.5). If the varieties of English are viewed as members of a family, it will be possible to characterize them not only in their own terms (e.g. Chicano English, Standard Academic English, Courtly Ricardian English) or in relation to the standard language – as is mostly the case when varieties of English are described – but also in relation to the 'common core' or to the 'potential' and thus also to each other. Two or more varieties can be described by referring them back (1) to the

4 It seems appropriate at this point to recall that in general, universalist, and comparatist linguistics, too, it has been found useful to presuppose that each language selects from the universal stock of semantic features in its own ways and that the particular selection of features in each language depends to a large extent on how speakers interpret their environments and on how they structure the communities in which they live. An analogous presupposition is made here with regard to the varieties of one language.

'common core' or (2) to the 'potential' and then listing the differences that define them as what they are, as (1) additions to the 'common core', or (2) particular selections from the 'potential'. (Cf. Figure 4)

Figure 4 Representation of variety by reference to common core (1) or potential (2)

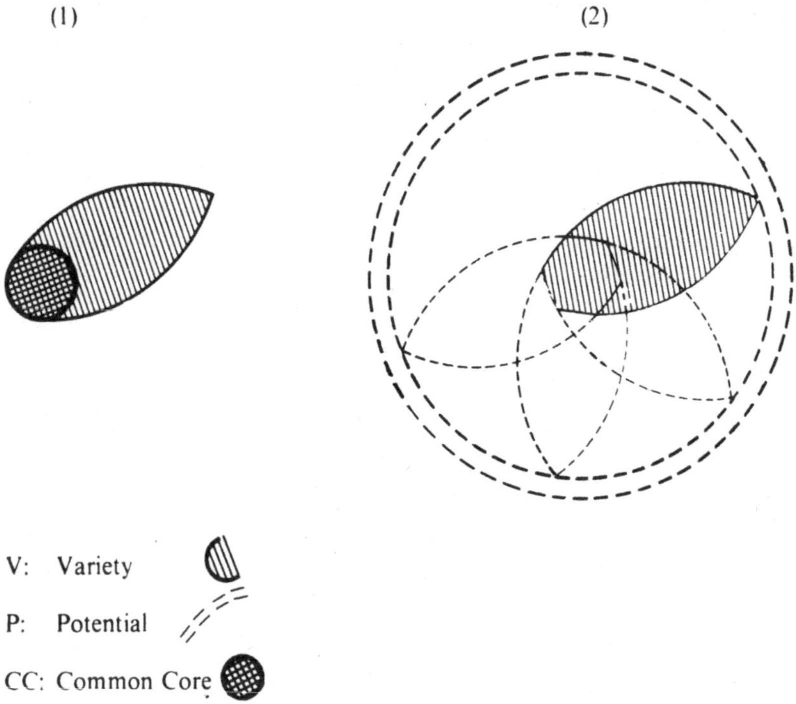

4.1.3.2 Grammar Family

Within linguistic theory, KANNGIESSER seems to have made most explicit use of the family assumption. (1972; cp. also 1971) Like LABOV, KANNGIESSER starts out by stating the need for modification within the original conception of language description held in generative grammar. CHOMSKY's «speaker-listener in a completely homogenous speech community» (1965:3) is considered too much of an idealization. The assumption of language homogeneity is removed in so far as the whole language community is seen as consisting of individual groups of speaker-hearers, each having its own grammar, shared by members with identical competence. KANNGIESSER argues that a large speech community cannot be homogenous and stable for social, geographical, psychological and generational reasons. Yet, although he fights the homogeneity hypothesis on the level of the whole language, he still works within it on the lower level of the language variety. He appears to accept what I have called the principle of 'homogeneity within heterogeneity'.

He argues that the theory of any language must be built not on one grammar only, but on a system of related and coexistent grammars. KANNGIESSER thus replaces the one grammar derived of the one idealized and innocent speaker-listener by a system of distinct parallel grammars, each reflecting the competence of distinct groups. Such a system of grammars is called a 'family of grammars'. Since the varieties are related through this grammar family, they together create a language with a 'standard' ('common core') and a 'potential' for common reference. In these terms, the English language, e.g., can be viewed as an agglomeration of related language varieties (family), each having a grammar co-existent with the grammars of the other varieties, and each grammar reflecting the competence of one group of speaker-listeners. The rules of any of these variety grammars are a selection from the total set of rules contained in a supergrammar ('potential') valid for the whole language family. There are features that are common to the grammars of all the varieties. These features indicate the existence of areas of contacts between the individual grammars as between members of a family. Extensional rules applied to one variety (in terms of application or non-application) make it possible to equate this one variety with another variety in the same family. The listing of such extensional rules can also show the differences existing between varieties before their equation.

KANNGIESSER's theoretical proposal, as will be seen, is also voiced by other variationists. None of them, however, has made it as explicit as KANNGIESSER. His concept is certainly highly attractive. If it is applied to a language like English, it allows us to preserve the notion that English, after all, is still one language. Particular varieties, like those pointed out in chapter three, can be viewed as members of one family. The rules of their grammars are part of a large set of rules which makes up the whole apparatus of English. Each variety is characterized by its own set of rules, only part of which is shared by other varieties. Unfortunately, KANNGIESSER does not take the step into the field of application. The only examples he adduces are simplified rules taken from canonical generative texts.[5] For further elaboration and application of KANNGIESSER's theory, we will have to look elsewhere, notably in the work of KLEIN (1974) and of the American variationists.

4.2 Variationist Approaches

4.2.1 Introductory

Although in recent years linguists have increasingly come to work on variation in language, the notion of a varieties grammar is still quite unfamiliar. To my knowledge, there has only been one attempt at setting up a varieties grammar for some specific language: It is the grammar developed by Wolfgang KLEIN (1974). KLEIN proposed to represent the gradual acquisition of German by foreign migrant workers in the German Federal Republic in what he called a *Varietätengrammatik.* Within the work of variationists who often appear to be concerned with details of individual speech to the extent of losing sight of what is more generally significant in a speech community, KLEIN's model can be considered a step ahead. KLEIN paved the way for a kind of varieties grammar that can concentrate on the typical, instead of on the individual, a grammar that is concerned with showing the differences between typolects more than with the working of variation on particular features of speech. The many studies that have emerged in the wake of the variable rule and scalogram analysis models have been directed at very small points of difference between the speech be-

5 The lack of application is a failure even in KANNGIESSER's own terms: «Das letztlich entscheidende Kriterium einer jeden Sprachtheorie ist das Kriterium ihrer Anwendbarkeit; jede Theorie muss sich an der Erfahrung bewähren können, wenn sie als Entwurf überhaupt akzeptierbar sein soll.» (1972:177)

havior of individuals and have almost exclusively looked at phonological data only, although the models might be powerful enough to indicate variation of a typical kind and on all the levels of language organization. It seems to me that it is time now to evaluate their possibilities with regard to a large-scale and holistic varieties grammar.

The models discussed in the following sections are examined with regard to the three notions introduced in 4.1: grammar family, varieties as typolects, and holistic description. In a varieties grammar of English, as I envisage it, the various language varieties are to be related to each other as belonging to one and the same family. The individual varieties are to be described with regard to what is typical and superindividual about them, and the scope of that description has to go beyond the traditional definition of grammar.

4.2.2 Parallel Grammars: Generative Dialectology

There are two assumptions in KANNGIESSER's model (see 4.1.3) that deserve further consideration:

(1) the view that the grammars of the varieties of a language are co-existent or parallel with each other,

and

(2) the view that all these grammars select their rules from a kind of supergrammar (the 'potential') and therefore also have a certain amount of rules in common (as reflected in the 'standard' or 'common core').

The idea of language varieties having a common deep structure forwarded in generative dialectology is nearer to the notion of 'common core' than to that of 'supergrammar'. While the common core can be understood as being represented by a set of underlying propositions common to all the varieties of L, of being, so to say, a kind of kernel or deep grammar of L, the supergrammar could only be thought of as being represented by a combination of all the surface grammars of the individual varieties, as being, thus, a total surface grammar of L. (see Figure 5)

Figure 5 Co-existent grammars in generative dialectology

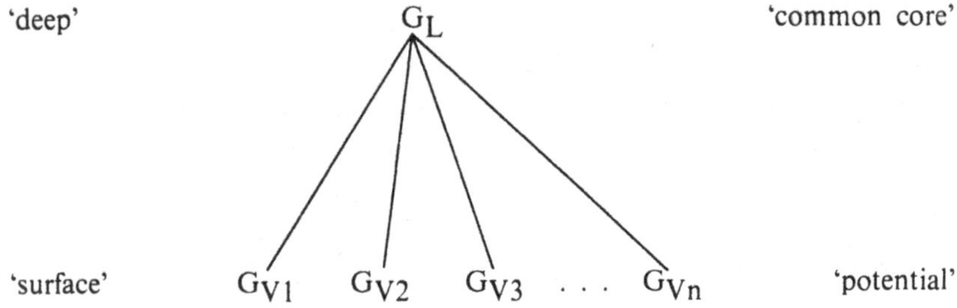

G_L: The grammar of a language, deep structure form, comparable to 'common core'

G_V: The grammar of a variety of that language (V1 to Vn), surface structure form, the total of all the G_Vs comparable to the 'potential' or 'supergrammar'

The parallel grammar model is assumed in most of the more recent work on the relationships of diatopic and diastratic language varieties. LOFLIN (1970) puts the model of co-existent grammars squarely within the framework of generative-transformational grammar: «Two or more language varieties V1, V2, V3, . . . , Vn are *dialects* of the set L1 if (. . .) the categorical subcomponents of the bases of the grammars postulated for V1, V2, V3, . . . , Vn are identical. Identity of categorical subcomponents is necessary to define the membership of language varieties, V1, V2, V3, . . . , Vn in the set L1; language varieties which have identical categorical subcomponents also, of necessity, have identical deep structures.» (1970:27) CARDEN (1973) establishes the link to contrastive analysis: «Given a set of informant response patterns defining a dialect system, you assume that the dialects have grammars that are identical except at points relevant to the articulate response patterns that you are trying to analyze. At these points the analysis explicitly displays the ways in which the dialects are similar and different, so that the stated differences in the grammars generate the observed differences in the response patterns. (...) This method of parallel grammars is successful in the same sense that it has been used to give insightful descriptions of similarities and differences within system of social, geographical, and randomly distributed dialects.» (1973:8f.) CARDEN here refers to approaches developed in generative dialectology. Evaluating the studies in question (KAYSER, 1963; KLIMA, 1964; LOFLIN, 1969; LABOV, 1969) from our perspective, we can say that generative-transformational grammar, although criticized by some for not accounting for language variation, has nevertheless stimulated research on the interrelationship of language varieties. It appears that generative theory might indeed have developed a descriptive framework within which the varieties of a language can be placed. It certainly offers a convenient apparatus for the comparison of the rule inventories of varieties, especially encouraging to contrastive analysis. So far, however, work in the generative tradition has excluded many levels of language, centering above all on phonology. Since HALLE's article (1962) several studies have appeared which seemed to show that a generative approach to dialectology can reveal relationships between genetically related dialects not so easily represented in structuralist approaches. In some cases, individual grammars for every dialect were constructed and then compared; in other cases a common set of underlying propositions was set up, which was then connected with different sets of rules to the respective surface forms of the dialects in question. It is this second approach which seems to have most in common with the notion of a language as a family consisting of members with co-existent grammars related through a common deep structure, a special kind of 'common core'. One of the more recent iterations of the position is NEWTON's (1972): «Because dialects arise from an originally more or less uniform language, it is possible to show that they can for the most part be described in terms of a common set of underlying forms.» (1972:5) This is surely a very attractive hypothesis. If it were true, it would allow linguists to write the grammar of language varieties as a succession of rules (from shared deep structure to varying surface structures) given in different order and different degree of applicability for each variety. One fundamental question is, however, whether the grammarian can know for sure what the underlying form common to all the varieties is. HAUSMANN (1975) has argued convincingly that even within phonology, where matters appear to be simplest, this is not possible. According to him, the Identity Hypothesis (i.e. the postulation of underlying identical representations) is too strong. In other areas of language organization, especially semantics and pragmatics, lexicon and speech genres, where the cultural load of individual varieties appears most forcefully, the Identity Hypothesis is certainly doomed to collapse as well. Another drawback of studies in generative dialectology (published so far) is that they do not make any attempt to relate the differences observed on the surface of individual varieties to what their authors would call 'extralinguistic matters'. Holism is still foreign to generative dialectology.

4.2.3 Variable Rules

4.2.3.1 Categorical, optional and variable rules

Today, the model of variable rules developed by LABOV and elaborated upon by CEDERGREN and SANKOFF (1974) and SANKOFF (1975) is probably the most popular means for accounting for variability in language. It has been shown in a great number of investigations that variable rules can describe variability in language both synchronically and diachronically; and that variable rules seem to work not only for phonological data – although disproportionately much work has been done in phonology – but also for syntax and certain aspects of semantics. (G. SANKOFF, 1974; D. SANKOFF et al., 1978).

LABOV and his followers understand variable rules as belonging within the framework of generative-transformational grammar. It is important, however, to distinguish variable rules both from optional rules (considered to be in free variation) and from obligatory rules (considered to apply categorically). The occurrence of variable rules, on the other hand, is neither random nor unpredictable (like optional rules), nor absolute (like obligatory rules). Although LABOV has distinguished variable rules both from optional and obligatory rules (LABOV et al., 1968, I:88–90), it is helpful to preserve the notion of optional rules when approaching the notion of variable rules. For, to some extent, variable rules can be considered a special kind of optional rules governing variation.[6]

As introduced by LABOV, variable rules are affixed with indices indicating the probability of their application in a certain context. The attachment of probability statements makes these rules something else than merely optional (BERDAN, 1973). Vagueness of application is replaced by exactly indicated variability of application. In order to know whether such a rule operates or not, and if yes, to what degree, its probability of application must be known. The probability of application itself depends on intra- and extralinguistic factors. In this way, LABOV succeeds in developing a method to systematize the optionality of non-obligatory rules. In generative-transformational grammar, categorical rules (obligatory rules) are those rules which are always obeyed by speakers; not following them creates ungrammatical utterances. In TG analyses, however, it had been largely ignored that the existence of various and differing language varieties might affect the judgment of certain rules as either categorical or optional; or the occurrence of certain utterances as either grammatical or ungrammatical. Based on such observations, the notion of variable rules was developed. Rules are no longer simply categorical or optional; whether they operate, depends on contextual factors, among others, factors like those that constitute language varieties. LABOV showed that the application or non-application of optional rules is not a matter of chance, but is, indeed, predictable. (LABOV et al., 1968)

If the concept of variable rules is taken over into the framework of a varieties grammar consisting of a super or reference grammar and a number of individual variety grammars, it becomes clear that there are certain aspects that seem to fit quite well. Given the stock of rules contained in the supergrammar ('potential'), it is possible to select some of these rules for variety 1, some for variety 2, and so on. It would be wrong to say that the application of a rule out of the overall inventory of rules is either categorical or option-

6 In TG terms, different ways of saying the same thing are explained in terms of rules that either do or do not operate: these are the optional rules. But transformational grammar does not go beyond this explanation, particularly it does not account for optionality being a function of context – whether extra- or intralinguistic.

al; but it would be correct to say that the rules are variable, their application being dependent on certain conditions. These conditions are linked to the characteristics exhibited by the varieties in question. In a varieties grammar, instead of speaking of a large set of optional rules which might or might not operate, it is more desirable to have a mechanism which indicates which of all the rules of the supergrammar are selected as making up the grammar of any particular variety.

4.2.3.2 Probabilities of rule application

In order to know whether a variable rule operates or not, one has to know its probability of application. This can be calculated according to one of four models proposed so far: (1) additive, (2) multiplicative application, (3) multiplicative non-application, and (4) logistic.[7] KAY (1978:78) gives the respective defining equations:

$$(1) \quad p = p_o + \cdots + p_n$$

$$(2) \quad p = p_o \times p_a \times \cdots \times p_n$$

$$(3) \quad p = 1 - (1 - p_o) \times (1 - p_a) \times \cdots \times (1 - p_n)$$

$$(4) \quad p = \frac{p_o \times \cdots \times p_n}{[p_o \times \cdots \times p_n] + [(1 - p_o) \times \cdots \times (1 - p_n)]}$$

(where *p* is said to designate the probability of application, *po* the input probability, *pa* the constraint selected from the first linguistic constraint family, . . ., and *pn* the constraint selected from the *n*th linguistic constraint family.)

7 Of the various models quoted, it is (2) and (3), the multiplicative ones, and (4), the logistic one, that have real probabilistic foundation. Keeping to the multiplicative model (the standard one, today), the assignment of probability numbers to variable constraints can be illustrated with the example of the well-known rule for the deletion of word-final alveolar stops in English. Since it is known to be sensitive to the nature of the initial segment of the following word, in that rule a probability value is assigned to the presence of a following consonant. «This value,» as FASOLD (1978:86) explains, «taken together with the values for the other constraints on the rule in a given environment, can be used to compute the probability that an alveolar stop will be deleted in that particular environment.»

The formulations of variable rules look rather complicated because they include many aspects of the linguistic environment *(pa* to *pn)* apart from the 'extralinguistic' input probability *(po)*. The application of a rule is affected by constraints appearing, e.g., in the preceding or following phonological segment, the grammatical status of the morphological unit containing the element in question, its position relative to word boundaries, etc. Although, ultimately, such intralinguistic constraints may be considered as being caused by the extralinguistic environment making up the input probability, variable rule formulations consider them separately, the apparatus thus becoming highly refined. The mathematical assumptions inherent in variable rule analysis propose that intralinguistic and extralinguistic constraints operate independently, that is, as KAY and MCDANIEL emphasize, «that there is no interaction between linguistic and social constraints» (1979:175). This assumption, however, is certainly wrong. KAY and MCDANIEL agree: «In fact, a very common pattern of observed language change, probably the characteristic pattern, involves precisely such interaction» (1979:176). KAY and MCDANIEL, on re-examination of data from LABOV, find that linguistic constraints on the rules do interact with the constraints of group membership, i.e. LABOV's own observed synchronic data do not live up to the mathematical assumptions made in variable rule analysis. (1979:176ff.) The point is stressed here, because all the p's *(po* as well as *pa* to *pn)* can now be related to the characteristics of the variety in question.

In spite of the fact that variable rules were developed not to differentiate whole language varieties from each other, but to show variation in language at one point and one time only, the probabilities of rule application in a varieties grammar might be calculated of variety specific rules in the same way as in the models proposed by LABOV (1969), CEDERGREN and SANKOFF (1974) and SANKOFF (1975). In a varieties grammar, however, the use of variable rules would never be a clever device for the display of statistical data,[8] but a means to establish a clear-cut tabulation of

8 KAY and MCDANIEL (1979:151f.) suggest that variable rules should not be considered linguistic rules in the usual sense of the term. «Rather the variable

rules. That is why, in a varieties grammar, only the basic idea of variable rules would be used, and not the whole and intricate computing apparatus. Instead of assigning any one rule a probability of application under certain extra- and intra-linguistic conditions, it is more desirable for a varieties grammar to have the rules contained in the overall inventory of rules (the supergrammar) associated with a selection probability according to variety. That is to say, the grammar would indicate whether and to what degree it is probable that a certain rule will be selected from the stock of rules and operate in a given variety. A rule would have a probability of application between 0 and 1 – just as in ordinary variable rule theory; but the varieties grammar would now specify the probabilities according to individual varieties. Accordingly, a rule number 5, e.g., would have various subsets according to the variety specific probabilities of application, so that

R 5:	$p\ (V_1)$	1
	$p\ (V_2)$	0.8
	$p\ (V_3)$	0.6
	$p\ (V_4)$	0.3
	$p\ (V_5)$	0

saying that a (fictitious) rule number 5 operates with a probability of 1 (= always) in variety 1, but only with a probability of 0.8 in variety 2, . . . , and with a probability of 0 (= never) in variety 5.

If the varieties grammar is expected to be fully descriptive, an exact indication of the probabilities is called for. If, however, it is expected to be predictive and prescriptive as for educational purposes like the teaching of second dialects or the teaching of special registers, further abstractions and idealizations are necessary. The question whether speakers actually know the probabilities of application of variable rules has repeatedly been debated – even into

rule methodology provides a family of mathematical models that dictate probabilistic constraints on possible distributions of linguistic variants in a speech community and a statistical method for deriving measures of the relative importance of different determining factors from a matrix of observed linguistic variation. The variable rule method thus provides a battery of related statistical models and accompanying data reduction techniques for the descriptive analysis of a certain kind of linguistic corpus.»

making the whole issue look absurd and ridiculous.[9] Here I certainly do not want to discuss whether native speakers of any language variety can be said to have internalized such probabilities; but I am quite certain that non-native speakers would never be able to cope realistically with a rule of which they know that it can be applied only in x% of all the cases. For prescriptive purposes, therefore, the probabilities attached to the rules in the supergrammar must be rounded to either 0 (meaning that the rule is not selected as part of the variety grammar in question) or 1 (meaning that it *is* selected as part of the variety grammar in question). One might also include probability roundings to 0.5 (saying that you may, but need not, observe that rule in the variety in question). The result being a new set of categorical (probability 1) and optional (probability 0.5) rules produced by a simplified and greatly idealized variable rules mechanism.

4.2.3.3 Variable rules and Typolects

Difficulties encountered by grammarians when working with variable rules have to do with the main flaw of variable rule theory: its fluctuation between a sociological set of reference (the data on which the rules are based) and a psychological one (the theoretical framework of transformational-generative grammar within which the rules are formulated). The data side is responsible for the great number of contextual categories (both extra- and intralinguistic) which may determine probability statements. Since their exact

9 Witness this extract from BICKERTON (1971:461): «. . . since the group figure is the crucial one, and since (within the approved limits) individual scores will vary around it, each individual must – if that group figure is to be maintained – keep track, not merely of his own environments and percentages, but also of those produced by all other members of his group: in other words, speaker B must continually be saying to himself things like: 'Good Lord! A's percentage of contractions in the environment V___ NP has fallen to 77! I'll have to step up mine to – let's see: A's production of his environment-type stands to mine in the ratio 65:35 over the last LL token-occurrences, so I'd better compensate by shooting up to . . . what? About 86%?' And to crown it all, he must not only be able to perform all these highly sophisticated calculations – he must also (since the rules apply to 'single' as well as 'group' styles) somehow continue to do so EVEN IN THE PHYSICAL ABSENCE OF ALL OTHER GROUP-MEMBERS!» (emphasis in original)

number and nature cannot be listed finally, it is unrealistic to expect that probability statements could ever be associated with each rule for each context category. Being aware of this difficulty, LABOV himself was forced to limit his own investigations to clearly defineable cases only. In view of this situation, it appears that a limitation of the variable rule procedure to certain (given) classes of varieties might also be sanctioned. It would not be an intolerable simplification but, indeed, a way out of apparent disorder into a more satisfactory and orderly system.

While BERDAN, in his campaign for a probabilistic grammar, repeatedly maintains that variation is random (e.g. 1971, 1973), it is important for the conception of a varieties grammar of the kind envisaged here to note that variationist investigations made by LABOV (1969, 1972d), FASOLD (1972), WOLFRAM (1969) and CEDERGREN and SANKOFF (1974) indicate that fluctuation between linguistic forms is not completely random or haphazard. LABOV's work, it is true, was concerned above all with 'inherent variability', that is, with variation occurring even while speakers are maintaining the same level of style. It was not aimed at the more obvious type of variation found between stylistic levels, between the speech patterns used by different social classes, by speech patterns observable on a diachronic axis, etc. Yet, LABOV himself and his followers, notably WOLFRAM, extended the concept of variable rules so as to deal exactly with such 'larger' group- or time-specific variables. It will be possible for us, therefore, to link probability statements not only to the notion of a supergrammar or 'potential', but also to that of typolect.

In the variable rule model proposed by CEDERGREN and SANKOFF (1974), the 'extralinguistic' parameters (like class, sex, age, etc.) are incorporated in the input probability; the strictly linguistic parameters (like preceding or following features; grammatical status, etc.) are set at fixed values for the whole community. Nevertheless, illustrative rules are written in terms of individual speakers' grammars, not in terms of group or social grammars; but, as CEDERGREN and SANKOFF say, «these constructs can be attained if desired by appropriate adjustments of input probabilities.» (1974:35) Variable rules are often said to «predict accurately the behavior of each individual» (CEDERGREN and SANKOFF,

1974:3). Yet, the use of variable rules presupposes homogenous and stable linguistic behavior (KAY, 1978:82). This apparent contradiction can be explained by reference to the statistically idealized member of the speech community created by the variationists. There is no doubt that LABOV's peer groups showed internal variation; but LABOV was able to find statistical regularity in the speech behavior of the group. Variable rules do not predict the speech behavior of any real individual in a group; what they formalize is an average based on data culled from a group. Variable rules thus can create intragroup homogeneity. Since they are statistical idealizations of variable data and represent an average, they can be expected to predict the linguistic behavior of any member of the group from which the data was drawn; they reliably mirror typical speech patterns, but, if used predictively, cannot be expected to indicate any individual speech behavior. There is no question, therefore, that variable rules can be used in an account of varieties as typolects.

4.2.3.4 Application of the variable rules model

As early as 1971, Walt WOLFRAM made use of the variable rules model in a greatly simplified form to illustrate some differences between four varieties of English. The result of his attempt can be used to show how a variable rule based varieties grammar might look. WOLFRAM was dealing with black-white speech differences and studied these four varieties of English:

V_1: Standard English
V_2: White Non-Standard Southern
V_3: Black Non-Standard North-Eastern
(LABOV's Black informants in New York City)
V_4: Black Non-Standard Southern
(Mississippi children)

In a table, WOLFRAM presented these varieties as either having a certain rule, as not having it, or having it optionally; i.e. the probabilities or rule application were limited to either 0, 0.5, or 1, as suggested above.

Table 1: Poss. – Z and Poss. Pronoun in Four Varieties of English (WOLFRAM, 1971b:148)

-Z Poss.			Differentiated Poss. Pro.	
V_1	+	/ man's book	+	/ her book
V_2	~	/ man book ~ man's book	+	/ her book
V_3	–	/ man book	+	/ her book
V_4	–	/ man book	~	/ she book ~ her book

Variable rules, it appears, can be related both to a supergrammar and to typolectal varieties. WOLFRAM interpreted his four varieties as group varieties (statistically homogenized) and implicitly derived the rules of their grammars from a supergrammar. The application of the variable rules model made by WOLFRAM illustrates paradigmatically how a simplified version of the Labovian apparatus might be brought to work. At the same time, however, it also demonstrates that the sophistication the variable rule methodology can achieve in dealing with variation in language is lost in the coarser context of a varieties grammar interested in typolects. How the rival method of scalogram analysis is suited to the writing of a varieties grammar is to be discussed next.

4.2.4 Polylectal grammars and implicational scales

4.2.4.1 Introductory

In the framework of a varieties grammar, individual varieties are viewed as having their own grammatical systems; in parts – and often large parts – these systems overlap; the overlapping areas form what was referred to above as the 'common core' or the 'family part'. Every variety is considered as expressing certain social and cultural factors; every variety is expressive only of its own culture; that of another variety can be expressed only by borrowing from it. This view is easily connected with that of a language forming a repertoire of varieties, each part of which is used by speakers only in clearly delimited fields. If one field is left, the corresponding language variety is left, too; and another variety will be used. Such an approach postulates the existence of many grammars, one for each variety in the repertoire. One way of relating these grammars is in terms of generative dialectology (co-existent grammars), a second in terms of variable rules, and a third by ordering them along a continuum and accounting for their areas of overlap and difference in terms of the implicational analysis method.

A theoretical approach toward the accomodation of language varieties within the framework of a unifying model different from variable rules is that based on GUTTMAN's 'Scalogram Analysis'.[10] Whereas the adherents of the variable rule model have their main interest in the quantification of forms occurring in actual speech, the proponents of the scalogram or implicational scales analysis method are interested in determining whatever might be implied regarding the status of one feature or rule from the status of another or others (ORNSTEIN and MURPHY, 1974:151).

4.2.4.2 DE CAMP's implicational relationship

David DE CAMP (who can claim fatherhood for this second method), like LABOV, remains within the framework of transformational-generative grammar. He recognizes that «the generative transformational model is the most hospitable to sociolinguistics of any theory yet known.» (1970:162) Against LABOV he argues that variable rules are an unnecessary and undesirable revision of a basically sound theory. He reproaches LABOV with handling variation only in a performance oriented way; with indexing actual idiosyncratic performance data rather than specifying abstract communal competence; with proceeding in an inductive rather than deductive way; with aiming at description rather than explanation. As a corrective measure, it can be inferred, DE CAMP has in mind a kind of generative theory which should incorporate both idiolectal and communal competence, i.e. a combination of competence in the traditional sense and a new competence of performance; a generative model which would also include situational (i.e. pragmatic) features. Consequently, he suggests to include stylistic and sociolinguistic features as further selectional restric-

10 The GUTTMAN scale was developed in psychology and not devised to handle linguistic variation. Its adaptation to linguistics is due to DE CAMP, its specific use for linguistic variation to BICKERTON.

tions in lexical dictionary entries and to treat these features within the generative mechanism just like phonological or semantic features. By analogy to feature analysis (where one feature may also imply other features, since features are arrayed hierarchically), DE CAMP suggests that language varieties can be ordered along a continuum expressive of an implicational (hierarchical) relationship. Since not all distinguishable styles can be treated as specific stylistic features, a grouping of styles according to a GUTTMAN scale is suggested (implicational scales). In the following table, DE CAMP illustrates his system in which features are related to varieties.

Table 2: Relating features to varieties (Adapted from DE CAMP, 1970)

Features						
F_1	F_2	F_3	F_4	F_5		
1	1	1	1	1	V_1	
1	1	1	1	0	V_2	
1	1	1	0	0	V_3	Varieties
1	1	0	0	0	V_4	
1	0	0	0	0	V_5	
0	0	0	0	0	V_6	

This table shows that if the value of a square (the intersection of features and varieties) is 1, any square above or to its left will also be 1; if 0, any square below or to its right will also be 0. Thus, one can predict that if a speaker uses the variant pronunciation *vahz* for 'vase' he will almost certainly say *It is I* as opposed to *It's me* as well. As will be shown in a later section, this aspect of implicational analysis is directly related to the notion of co-occurrence rules and thus of great importance to the definition of varieties in a varieties grammar.

4.2.4.3 BAILEY's dynamic grammar

Charles-James N. BAILEY (1973), exploring the same research direction as DE CAMP, wants his related model to acknowledge for the speaker-hearer's capacity to understand a wide range of distinct surface grammars and to respond to them appropriately. The rules of the 'dynamic' grammar BAILEY has in mind must account for all the possible varieties in the language. (BAILEY makes use of the term 'lect', which is meant to apply to regional and social as well as stylistic and other varieties). The rules would thus be 'panlectal' or 'polylectal'. And, as in DE CAMP's proposal, their application would be constrained through their ordering in implicational sets (GUTTMAN scales).

BAILEY is more specific with regard to a characterization of the implicational relationships. Implicational relationships are established in terms of markedness and feature weighting. Rules are written in their most weighted, i.e. least general, form. The system is linked to SCHMIDT's (1872) Wave Theory. BAILEY gives an example to illustrate the spread in time of a given feature (1973:68):

Time 0:				0
Time 1:			*a*	0
Time 2:		*b*	*a*	0
Time 3:	*c*	*b*	*a*	0

which is interpreted as meaning that, given a relative time 0 at some focal point in social or regional space, a feature *a* may enter variably at Time 1 and spread to a larger space; later (at Time 2), a more general version of *a,* called *b,* enters at the same point and spreads; even later (at Time 3), an even more general form of the rule enters, so that the ensuing wave can be described as being on an implicational scale, where *c* implies *b,* and *b* implies *a.* It seems to me that a model like this is well devised to account for language change along a continuum as, perhaps, in language development through time[11] or, more, probably, in communities that show a great number of varieties on a continuum as between a creole and a standard language.

4.2.4.4 BICKERTON's panlectal grid

More than DE CAMP and BAILEY, Derek BICKERTON approaches the notion of language varieties from a creolist point of view. He (1973) attempts to find an adequate way of describing a creole con-

11 I am somewhat doubtful about this because I am not convinced that rules necessarily and always move to 1 or 0, although it is highly convenient to assume categorialness and obsoleteness as the only points of reference.

tinuum and also comes to work with a 'dynamic' model incorporating both static, synchronic models of polar dialects as well as all the intermediate varieties. According to BICKERTON, «Language is seen as a dynamic process evolving through space and time (...), a seamless whole.» It follows, «that to speak of 'dialects' or even perhaps 'languages' may be misleading; these terms merely seek to freeze at an arbitrary moment, and to coalesce into an arbitrary whole, phenomena which in nature are ongoing and heterogenous.» (1973:643) Instead of terms like 'dialect' and 'language', BICKERTON suggests the unit of the 'isolect', which he defines as «a possible set of rules such that it will differ from adjacent sets of rules on a panlectal (implicational) grid by only a single rule-conflict or resolution of such conflict.» A 'panlectal grid' is defined as «the totality of possible sets of rules for an (arbitrarily limited) area in space and/or time, which in turn constitutes a selection from the totality of possible sets of rules for human language.» (1973:643) Both terms newly introduced by BICKERTON are purely abstract: «A given isolect may be realized by one or many speakers, or it may not.» (1973:643) The 'panlectal grid' is «based on a totality of determined possibilities, which does not depend on the existence of any particular speaker or speakers.» (1973:667)

4.2.4.5 Implicational scales and typolects

For BICKERTON's purpose of describing a continuum in a creole situation, working with isolects indeed seems to make sense. On a theoretical level we can speculate whether the method developed by BICKERTON could not be used for typolects as well. Although BICKERTON himself sees such a possibility by collapsing sets of contiguous isolects with social groups (1973:667), he would not support it (personal communication). After all, the point of developing his model at all, was to account for very fine types of variation: «It is time for linguists in general to stop looking for static systems which have no objective existence, and accept the fact that language is an ongoing process, not a steady state. Only when they have done this, will they be able to disentangle and account for its real patterns.» (1973:668) Nevertheless, implicational scale analysis allows exploitation for a varieties grammar built on the principle of homogeneity within heterogeneity.

Usually, the notion of a language continuum implies an ordering of varieties between two poles; as such the notion has been applied mainly to creolized speech communities so far. In DE CAMP's post-creole continuum of Jamaican English (1971) there is a kind of Standard English at the one end of the language continuum and an English-based creole at the other. The features of the two poles are used to characterize the intermediate varieties. The closer a variety on the continuum is to Standard English, the more features of Standard English it will have; and the closer a variety is to the creole, the more creole features it will have.

An application of the implicational analysis model outside the creole situation is that by STOLZ and BILLS (1969) in their work on the differentiation of two varieties of Texas English. In Table 3 (p. 184), the two top informants represent Central Texas Rural White Anglo-Saxon Protestant Non-Standard English in its purest form; the four speakers at the bottom that of Standard Central Texan English. The idiolects of the informants that are placed between the two poles can be said to represent intermediate varieties. In BICKERTON's terminology, they can be considered isolects since they differ from each other at least at one point; but they are certainly not typolects. Only if a number of the intermediate isolects would be found to cluster around a certain score figure, could one construct a typolect. Two typolects, however, can be read into the scalogram analysis of STOLZ and BILLS without much difficulty. The one, Central Texas Rural White Anglo-Saxon Protestant Non-Standard English, represented by the top speakers, would be seen as extending almost down to the middle, to speaker LB, to be exact, whereas the second typolect, Standard Central Texan English, represented by the bottem speakers, would be seen as reaching up to speakers MVW or GJ. The three speakers in the middle with scores from 5 to 7 do not warrant, at least not on the basis of this restricted analysis, the postulation of an additional typolect.

It seems to me that implicational scales can be used to demonstrate whether a given variety actually functions as a typolect. If, in sample analysis, relative majorities of informants are found to cluster around some scores, they will be representatives of a typolect, which, much as in variable rule methodology, appears as a

Table 3 Isolects of Texan English (Stolz and Bills, 1969, Table 2)

Informant	Dialect Feature												score	
	ain't	AuxD	p-pp	DN	ing	s/p	have	th → ∅	adj	wadn't	there's	that	max	min
AF	1	1	1	1	1	1	1	1	1	1	1	1	12	12
MJW	1	1	1	1	1	1	1	1	1	1	1	1	12	12
ML	1	1	1	1	1	1	1	1	1	1	1	nd	11	12
JP	1	1	1	1	1	1	1	1	1	1	1	0	11	11
RC	1	1	1	1	1	1	1	1	1	0	1	0	11	11
NC	1	1	1	1	1	1	1	1	1	1	0	1	12	12
GK	1	1	1	1	1	1	1	1	1	1	0	0	10	10
DW	1	1	1	1	1	1	1	1	1	0	0	0	9	9
MW	1	1	1	1	1	1	1	1	1	nd	nd	0	9	11
EW	1	1	1	1	0	1	1	1	1	0	0	0	9	9
WF	1	1	1	1	1	1	1	1	1	0	0	0	9	9
LB	1	1	1	1	0	1	0	1	1	0	0	0	9	9
JM	1	1	1	1	1	1	1	0	0	0	0	0	7	7
KF	1	1	1	1	1	1	1	0	0	0	0	1	7	7
BH	1	1	1	0	1	0	nd*	0	0	0	0	0	5	5
GJ	1	1	1	1	0	0	0	0	0	0	0	0	4	4
MVW	1	1	0	0	0	0	0	0	0	0	0	0	2	2
EH	1	0	0	0	0	0	0	0	0	0	0	0	1	1
ENH	1	0	0	0	0	0	0	0	0	0	0	0	1	1
GF	0	0	0	0	0	0	0	0	nd	0	0	0	0	0
JC	0	0	0	0	0	0	0	0	0	0	0	0	0	0
HM	0	0	0	0	0	0	0	0	0	0	0	0	0	0
JT	0	0	0	0	0	0	0	0	0	0	0	0	0	0
Max Score	19	17	16	16	15	14	14	12	12	7	5	2		
Min Score	19	17	16	16	15	14	14	12	12	9	5	3		

*nd = no data

kind of statistical idealization. HAMILTON's *The People's English* (1975), referred to above as a kind of popular varieties grammar, certainly derives its notion of class languages from statistical observations. It is interesting to note that typolects construed on the basis of sets of contiguous isolects can again be treated like isolects if placed again in a panlectal grid. *The People's English* can thus be considered as presenting the English language on a scale of education (as it were), the bottom represented by the heavily restricted variety of «lower-lower language» and the top by the maximally developed variety of «upper-upper language» (which yields 1 in every square of the grid; see table 4).

Table 4 Educational varieties of English (based on HAMILTON, 1975)
Selected grammatical items on a continuum

	LL	UL	LM	UM	LU	UU
Basic Word Order	1	1	1	1	1	1
Parts of Speech	1	1	1	1	1	1
Sentence Types	1	1	1	1	1	1
Irregular Verb Forms	0	1	1	1	1	1
Tense	0	1	1	1	1	1
Sequences of Tenses	0	1	1	1	1	1
Mood	0	1	1	1	1	1
Voice	0	1	1	1	1	1
Case	0	1	1	1	1	1
Agreement	0	1	1	1	1	1
Pronominal Reference	0	1	1	1	1	1
Comparison	0	0	1	1	1	1
Omission/Ellipsis	0	0	1	1	1	1
Point of View	0	0	1	1	1	1
shall, will	0	0	0	1	1	1
should, would	0	0	0	1	1	1
for	0	0	0	0	1	1
yet	0	0	0	0	1	1
who/which/that	0	0	0	0	0	1
restrictive/nonrestrictive relative clauses	0	0	0	0	0	1

LL: lower lower language
UL: upper lower language
LM: lower middle language
UM: upper middle language
LU: lower upper language
UU: upper upper language

HAMILTON 1975 does not qualify as a source for or storage of reliable data on the stages of language acquisition. The book does not make any such claims at all. But the way HAMILTON attributes knowledge and use of grammatical structures to social varieties of English makes it possible to use the book to illustrate the working of panlectal grids within a varieties grammar. The grid becomes the supergrammar with reference to which the individual varieties can be defined. «Lower lower language» is thus easily identified as a heavily «restricted code», «Upper upper language» as an «elaborated code».

Greater descriptive accuracy can be claimed for the following example. CRYSTAL and FLETCHER (1979:170–171) is a synthesis of the descriptive findings in the English language acquisition literature. CRYSTAL and FLETCHER provide a postulated set of age-related stages of syntactic development in the language acquisition process of children up to ca. 5 years. The seven stages recognized by them can be related to syntactic structures as on a continuum and be presented in a panlectal grid working as a varieties grammar. (Table 5)

Table 5 Varieties of English as stages of language acquisition (based on data from CRYSTAL and FLETCHER, 1979:170–171).
Syntactic features on a continuum

Stages	I	II	III	IV	V	VI	VII
Single-element sentences	1	1	1	1	1	1	1
Two-element clauses	0	1	1	1	1	1	1
Three-element clauses	0	0	1	1	1	1	1
Four (+) element clauses	0	0	0	1	1	1	1
Clause sequence, connectivity ..	0	0	0	0	1	1	1
Completion of gramm. systems .	0	0	0	0	0	1	1
Other structures .... (sentence connectivity using adverbials; emphatic word order variation, e.g.)	0	0	0	0	0	0	1

Ages:
I: 0:9–1:6 II: 1:6–2:0 III: 2:0–2:6
IV: 2:6–3:0 V: 3:0–3:6 VI: 3:6–4:6
VII: 4:6–

As this last examples illustrates again, it is not only idiolectal varieties that can be represented in panlectal grids, but group varieties as well. Scalogram analysis method clearly allows substitution of idiolectal varieties by group varieties, i.e. what appear as isolects in the grid may be interpreted as typolects. In terms of scalogram analysis, varieties represented in panlectal grids are defineable as sets selected from a kind of supergrammar assumed at either one of the polar ends of the grid. The method thus seems to live up to two requirements of a varieties grammar: the link of individual variety grammars to a supergrammar, and the interpretation of these varieties as typolects. Indeed, in an account of linearly representable varieties of English as along the historical axis of language development or in the process of language acquisition, the writing of a varieties grammar based on the implicational analysis model might be possible. The stages in the evolution of English or in the gradual elaboration of an originally restricted educational code can be seen as isolects having the status of typolects. Varieties that cannot be linearly ordered with each other, however, seem to be outside the implicational approach; i.e. a varieties repertoire consisting of, say, Mellowspeak, Berkeley Fraternity Talk and Academic Standard English could not be arranged within a varieties grammar having the form of a panlectal grid. A model built on suggestions made in generative dialectology and variable rules methodology might still work in such a case.

4.2.5 *KLEIN's « Varietätengrammatik»*

4.2.5.1 Supergrammar

The assumption of a supergrammar (cf. 'potential', 4.1.3.1) is made most explicit in KLEIN (1974). KLEIN views the varieties of a language as existing within a space of varieties. This space is created by the dimensions of language along which varieties can be classified (cf. 4.1.2.3). According to KLEIN and DITTMAR (HPD 1978:5), a space of varieties is «an analytic grid sufficient to distinguish all possible speech varieties thought to exist.» Individual varieties can be defined by indicating their position within that space in relation to the dimensions identified. (My interpretation)

The set of varieties and their grammars are interrelated by establishing a supergrammar or reference grammar (HPD 1978:6) valid for them all. According to KLEIN (1974), the supergrammar («Übergrammatik») of a language covers all the varieties of that language and at the same time subdetermines them. The language described in the supergrammar contains all the sentences of the individual varieties in the form of subsets. In HPD (1978:6) it is defined as «consisting of the union of all rule sets of the particular grammars». Like KANNGIESSER's 'potential', KLEIN's reference grammar «describes nothing; it is merely a useful analytic construct» (HPD 1978:6). As a supergrammar it is the point of reference for the description of the individual varieties.

Just as the total language (L) is understood to be an agglomeration of all the varieties (V_1 to V_n), the supergrammar (SG) is to be understood as an agglomeration of all the individual variety grammars (GV_1 to GV_n). Since the varieties and their grammars have areas of intersection (cf. Figure 3, p. 162), agglomeration cannot mean addition. In the following figure, <,> is used instead of <+>:

Figure 6 Correspondence between language varieties and variety grammars, total language and supergrammar.

L:	V_1,	V_2,	V_3,	V_4,	...,	V_n
SG:	GV_1,	GV_2,	GV_3,	GV_4,	...,	GV_n

4.2.5.2 Probabilistic mechanism

The rules contained in the supergrammar are constrained by probabilistic evaluations so that they apply only to certain individual varieties. The probabilistic mechanism attached to the supergrammar creates the grammar of each variety by means of the association to each rule of an appropriate number between 0 and 1. This number is expected to indicate the probability of application of this rule in the variety in question. The underlying idea is that in a set of rules some rules might have alternative forms; each of the alternative rules are now given a probability of application in a specified variety between 0 and 1, the sum of all the probabilities totalling 1. KLEIN and DITTMAR give this example of their essentially Labovian approach (cp. Variable rules, above): «A given rule may be applied in a certain variety with probability .9, which means, – informally speaking – that it is an important rule in that variety. In another variety its probability may be .2, that is, it is less probable that it occurs in the derivation of a sentence. In a third variety, its probability may even be 0, that is, it does not occur at all in that variety. The same grammar then is used for all the varieties in a given space of varieties, and the differences among them are expressed by the differences of rule values.» (HPD 1978:6)

4.2.5.3 Application

Klein had the possibility of trying out his model of a «Varietätengrammatik» in the *Heidelberger Forschungsprojekt «Pidgin-Deutsch» (HPD).* The several stages in the process of acquiring German by foreign migrant workers in the German Federal Republic were presented in terms of this model. Since each stage in the acquisition process is characterized by a set of grammatical rules, the various stages can be viewed as varieties of German, or, more narrowly perhaps, as varieties of German as a foreign language. The grammars of these varieties are seen as closely related to one another. The problem of how to describe the transition from one grammar into the next is solved in set-theoretical and probabilistic terms by following the proposals made in Klein (1974). In HPD (1978:8) a tentative reference grammar is sketched. It includes all the rules applying at least once among the 48 texts (= varieties) identified. The reference grammar contains 101 context-free rules in all, grouped into 15 rule clusters. A rule cluster consists of all the rules sharing the same left-hand symbol, the rules being alternative ways of rewriting this symbol. (HPD 1978:7) (Table 6)
After a further process of simplification it is possible to write a unified grammar for the 48 text varieties. The 48 rows in Table 7 correspond to the 48 varieties, the columns to rules or collapsed rules of the reference grammar. Rules 2.03 and 2.04, e.g., refer back to rule cluster 2 (Table 6). Accordingly

2. PROP → (NC) VC (Neg)

$$1.\ \mathrm{S} \rightarrow \mathrm{(SA)\ PROP}$$

$$2.\ \mathrm{PROP} \rightarrow \mathrm{(NC)\ VC\ (Neg)}$$

$$3.\ \mathrm{VC} \rightarrow \left\{\begin{array}{l}\mathrm{VG}\\ \mathrm{PVL}\end{array}\right\}$$

$$4.\ \mathrm{VG} \rightarrow \mathrm{(Aux)\ (MV)} \left\{\begin{array}{l}\mathrm{VP}\\ \mathrm{PRC}\end{array}\right\}$$

$$5.\ \mathrm{VP} \rightarrow \mathrm{V\ (NC)\ (NC)\ (AC)\ (AC)\ (AC)}$$

$$6.\ \mathrm{PRC} \rightarrow \mathrm{Cop} \left\{\begin{array}{l}\mathrm{NC}\\ \mathrm{AC}\end{array}\right\} \mathrm{(NC)\ (AC)\ (AC)}$$

$$7.\ \mathrm{PVL} \rightarrow \left\{\begin{array}{l}\mathrm{NC}\\ \mathrm{AC}\end{array}\right\} \mathrm{(NC)\ (AC)\ (AC)}$$

$$8.\ \mathrm{NC} \rightarrow \left\{\begin{array}{l}\mathrm{(Prep)} \left\{\begin{array}{l}\mathrm{NP}\\ \mathrm{Pro\ (ATN)}\end{array}\right\}\\ \mathrm{(Quan)\ Adj}\\ \mathrm{Num}\\ \mathrm{S}\end{array}\right\}$$

$$9.\ \mathrm{NP} \rightarrow \mathrm{(ATV)\ (ATN)\ (ATN)\ N}$$

$$10.\ \mathrm{ATV} \rightarrow \mathrm{(Det)} \left(\left\{\begin{array}{l}\mathrm{Quan}\\ \mathrm{Num}\end{array}\right\} \right)$$

$$11.\ \mathrm{ATN} \rightarrow \left\{\begin{array}{l}\mathrm{(Prep)} \left\{\begin{array}{l}\mathrm{N}\\ \mathrm{NP}\\ \mathrm{Pro}\end{array}\right\}\\ \mathrm{Adj}\\ \mathrm{AC}\\ \mathrm{S}\end{array}\right\}$$

$$12.\ \mathrm{AC} \rightarrow \left\{\begin{array}{l}\mathrm{(Prep)} \left\{\begin{array}{l}\mathrm{NP}\\ \mathrm{Pro}\\ \mathrm{Num}\end{array}\right\}\\ \left(\left\{\begin{array}{l}\mathrm{Prep}\\ \mathrm{Quan}\end{array}\right\} \right) \mathrm{Adv}\\ \mathrm{Quan}\\ \mathrm{S}\end{array}\right\}$$

$$13.\ \mathrm{SA} \rightarrow \mathrm{(MOD)\ (TEMP)}$$

$$14.\ \mathrm{MOD} \rightarrow \left\{\begin{array}{l}\mathrm{(Prep)\ NP}\\ \mathrm{Adv_m}\end{array}\right\}$$

$$15.\ \mathrm{TEMP} \rightarrow \left\{\begin{array}{l}\mathrm{(Prep)\ NP}\\ \mathrm{Adv_t}\\ \mathrm{Num}\end{array}\right\}$$

List of Categories Used

AC	adverbial complex	NC	nominal complex
Adj	adjective	NP	noun phrase
Adv	adverb	Num	numeral
Adv_m	modal adverb	PRC	predicate (copula construction)
Adv_t	temporal adverb	Prep	preposition
ATN	attribute (1)	Pro	pronoun
ATV	attribute (2)	PROP	proposition
Aux	auxiliary	PVL	predicate without verb phrase
Con	conjunction	Quan	quantifier
Cop	copula	S	sentence
Det	determiner	SA	sentence adverbial
MOD	modal element	TEMP	temporal element
MV	modal verb	V	verb
N	noun	VC	verbal complex
Neg	negation	VG	verbal group
		VP	verb phrase

Table 6 Sketch of reference grammar. Syntax (HPD 1978:8)

obtains the readings

2.03 PROP → NC VC
2.04 PROP → NC VC Neg

Each cell in the matrix of Table 7 contains a number between 0 and 1 representing the application probability of the rule in the variety in question. (Table 7)

Table 7 Probabilistic values for selected phrase structure rules (HPD 1978:11)

Informant	Rules: 2.03 and 2.04	3.01	4.02 to 4.08	5.02 to 5.12	8.02 and 8.03	9.02 to 9.06	10.01	12.02 to 12.11	Syntactic index
IT-01	1.00	1.00	.83	.84	.61	.79	.88	.99	1.602
SP-11	.95	1.00	.89	.91	.60	.68	.82	.97	1.448
IT-31	.95	1.00	.60	.93	.54	.67	.80	.94	1.243
SP-29	.85	.99	.61	.89	.60	.72	.82	.91	1.234
SP-19	.94	1.00	.57	.83	.55	.82	.75	.92	1.233
IT-22	.84	.95	.42	.90	.64	.71	.69	.80	.961
SP-31	.89	.97	.47	.75	.47	.84	.79	.85	.956
IT-02	.74	.88	.47	.85	.55	.73	.79	.96	.934
SP-24	.85	.98	.47	.85	.70	.62	.46	.90	.831
SP-17	.94	.85	.41	.80	.47	.64	.80	.88	.765
IT-10	.73	.92	.45	.89	.48	.62	.72	.91	.709
IT-06	.82	.96	.51	.77	.53	.57	.55	.83	.527
IT-33	.77	.90	.60	.86	.43	.61	.50	.66	.375
IT-20	.70	.91	.24	.76	.52	.60	.58	.96	.374
SP-06	.61	.87	.38	.82	.51	.57	.58	.84	.291
SP-13	.72	.79	.15	.85	.42	.57	.61	.89	.208
IT-15	.63	.82	.27	.87	.35	.55	.67	.88	.200
SP-01	.62	.67	.40	.70	.51	.60	.68	.79	.135
SP-36	.65	.72	.21	.92	.33	.50	.59	.98	.116
IT-26	.57	.78	.12	.81	.49	.51	.69	.92	.112
IT-05	.73	.71	.17	.87	.40	.52	.69	.71	.059
IT-25	.64	.69	.42	.76	.49	.57	.58	.68	.031
IT-32	.64	.73	.07	.82	.40	.63	.57	.77	-.030
IT-18	.63	.65	.20	.81	.31	.76	.64	.62	-.033
SP-30	.72	.70	.07	.74	.35	.59	.62	.81	-.092
IT-16	.50	.75	.13	.71	.32	.67	.63	.92	-.092
SP-18	.61	.72	.04	.90	.43	.44	.67	.72	-.124
SP-26	.67	.66	.18	.75	.30	.46	.81	.81	-.128
IT-28	.55	.66	.11	.73	.41	.60	.67	.72	-.220
IT-07	.60	.68	.15	.80	.46	.42	.69	.66	-.225
SP-15	.66	.86	.16	.86	.41	.34	.35	.87	-.236
IT-29	.55	.69	.06	.57	.49	.52	.83	.74	-.265
SP-14	.62	.74	.05	.85	.34	.52	.59	.63	-.285
SP-12	.65	.65	.02	.67	.25	.73	.64	.73	-.290

Informant	Rules 2.03 and 2.04	3.01	4.02 to 4.08	5.02 to 5.12	8.02 and 8.03	9.02 to 9.06	10.01	12.02 to 12.11	Syntactic index
IT-12	.56	.51	.18	.76	.45	.53	.50	.80	–.303
SP-09	.58	.76	.00	.76	.48	.58	.32	.68	–.384
IT-13	.65	.46	.02	.61	.35	.42	.71	.79	–.575
IT-09	.68	.43	.05	.82	.40	.41	.41	.66	–.610
SP-04	.55	.57	.00	.82	.26	.45	.57	.62	–.662
IT-23	.53	.41	.08	.69	.38	.60	.46	.56	–.727
IT-24	.52	.45	.13	.78	.24	.45	.59	.57	–.789
IT-08	.53	.21	.00	.95	.10	.52	.53	.64	–.851
SP-08	.45	.61	.15	.83	.33	.36	.26	.64	–.875
SP-02	.56	.42	.05	.70	.37	.48	.47	.33	–.997
SP-21	.42	.36	.00	.72	.23	.70	.52	.31	–1.035
SP-25	.50	.31	.00	.61	.31	.51	.24	.82	–1.064
SP-22	.72	.49	.00	.49	.30	.46	.42	.43	–1.126
SP-35	.29	.16	.00	.33	.15	.33	.05	.43	–2.396
Mean	.67	.71	.24	.78	.42	.57	.60	.76	
Standard Deviation	.15	.22	.23	.12	.13	.12	.17	.17	

It is shown here how KLEIN's proposal for a «Varietätengrammatik» comes to work in the realm of syntax. The grammars of the individual varieties are described in terms of a single super- or reference grammar which assigns probabilistic weights to rules taken from the overall inventory of rules. KLEIN's model can be said to effectively synthesize suggestions made by KANNGIESSER, LABOV and SUPPES (probabilistic grammar). The case to which KLEIN applies his model is one that might also be handled in terms of implicational analysis. Indeed, BICKERTON thinks that he might handle it even more effectively in a panlectal grid (personal communication). Possible rivalry between the Bickertonian and a basically Labovian approach need not worry us here. It is more important to note that a KLEIN grammar is not restricted in application to varieties that can be arranged on a continuum, but allows the inclusion of disparate varieties that might be found in other variety repertoires.

4.2.6 *Evaluation of variationist models*

All the variationist models sketched in the preceding sections are attractive in certain respects; two of them, however, are not suited to the needs of a varieties grammar. Implicational scales are certainly an excellent instrument to account for variation in language, provided such variation is seen as occurring on a continuum. The continuum assumption, however, is too narrow for the purposes of a varieties grammar whose scope should not only accomodate the various stages in processes like language acquisition or language change, but also varieties repertoires made up of rather disparate typolects. I do not see, e.g., how Mellowspeak, Chicano English and Juvenile Speech could all be arranged within one and the same panlectal grid.

While the space of varieties opened up by implicational scales is not large enough for a varieties grammar purporting to house diachronic, diatopic, diastratic and diatypic kinds of varieties, the space of varieties explorable through variable rules methodology is adequate. Like the implicational scales approach, the variable rule approach can be brought in line with the notion of varieties as typolects. But only the supergrammar envisaged by variable rule methodology is wide enough to contain a system of rules for any variety grammar. If variable rules are simplified and applied in a way like that suggested by WOLFRAM (1971), they can adequately indicate differences between varieties both synchronically and diachronically. The same is true of KLEIN's «Varietätengrammatik», which, after all, is a derivative of variable rule methodology synthesized with KANNGIESSER's model of a grammar family. KLEIN has found a convincing way to derive variety specific rules from a supergrammar containing the rule inventory of all the varieties in a given space of varieties.

Whereas KLEIN's model should not be interpreted as allowing the generation of surface forms from a deep structure common to all the varieties, the models developed in generative dialectology require a knowledge about the deep structure of the whole language and its varieties. To what degree such knowledge is obtainable, however, is uncertain. Relying on surface forms only appears to be a much more reliable procedure. KLEIN's reference grammar can be read as a surface grammar in which the individual variety grammars are generated directly by selecting sets of alternative rules.[12]

Although all the models claim some sociolinguistic status, they have not been applied to all the areas of language organization, but only to questions of variation in phonology and syntax. While the requirements of (a) the family embedding of individual varieties grammars and (b) the interpretation of varieties as typolects can be fulfilled by all the models considered, the third requirement of a varieties grammar, that of a holistic description of the varieties in question poses some problem still. Since generative dialectology will have most difficulties in incorporating cultural facts into a deep structure, and since panlectal grids presuppose a one-dimensional space of varieties only, the only models we will come back to in the later discussion of our approach to a holistic varieties grammar are variable rules and the KLEIN grammar. In particular we will have to determine whether the supergrammar should be defined as a data pool containing not only the rules needed for the appropriate phonological and syntactical shape of a given variety, but also the inventory of lexical items, including idioms, of text types and speech genres, of cultural values and orientations, from which the items needed for a particular variety can be selected. This, however, necessitates a link of the purely linguistic approaches presented in this part with more holistically oriented approaches of sociolinguistics discussed in the next part.

4.3 Further Sociolinguistic Approaches

4.3.1 Introductory

In the following sections, some of the areas of a holistic varieties grammar not covered by the variationists will be mentioned. In

12 It may be noted that linguists who work on data of language in use increasingly come to doubt the usefulness of deep structure grammars. FISHMAN, e.g., expresses his scepticism like this: «success in stating rules and predicting use may remain at a 'surface structure' level and may not reach the level at which the predictable regularities are generated.» (personal communication)

particular these are the variety lexicons and ethnographic descriptions of the varieties. It will be seen that if these areas are included in the information pool of a varieties grammar, typolectal descriptions of varieties are possible to a satisfactory degree. As before, the emphasis does not fall on idiolectal speech behavior, but on typolectal patterns. Only if some idealization of features in terms of typolects is made, does it appear reasonable to explore the implications of dictionaries and further cultural characterizations at all.

An important notion in the following sections is that of conceptualization. Given the assumption that differences between language varieties also derive from different conceptualizations of the world, these differences could not be explained in a TG model. There is apparently not a uniform base from which different surface forms are derived, but there are differences already at the outset in the conceptualization of the world by culturally different groups of speakers. Even if the syntax of Black English and Chicano English, e.g., can be derived from the same underlying deep structure, the set of speech genres and discourse conventions typically used in Black English or Chicano English would have to be explained in cultural terms separate from each other. While at this level comparison across cultures is possible, derivation from a common source seems improbable.

4.3.2 Lexicography

4.3.2.1 Lexicon and grammar

In the description of a language or a language variety the lexicon is certainly of central importance. No texts could be written, no syntactic arrangements made without words being available. Nevertheless, the focus of much linguistic investigation has centred on the generation of syntactic strings, not on the description of the lexicon of a language. To Laurence URDANG (1976:60), lexicography appears as «one of the last few links between the linguist's world of Academia and the real world.» He notes as strange that «comment on usage and other practical aspects of language has passed, for the most part, to the non-professional, and we are seeing books by lawyers on British and American English, by consumerists on language in the law, by businessmen on 'effective' English.» It seems, indeed, that the writing of such manuals is the linguist's task just as much as the search for the mental or biological origins of language. URDANG feels that linguists have lost contact with the real world: «Ivory-tower linguists continue to communicate chiefly among themselves and with the few students left to continue the propagation of the species.» (1976:60) I agree with URDANG on the point that linguistics is not merely a cognitive science but also a discipline that should be concerned with the recording and description of language in operation. It seems unacceptable to me that linguists who take note of new items in language, who investigate the way people make use of language, who describe language with reference to units like region, class, or text are considered second-rate linguists, if not denied access to the guild altogether.[13]

The survey of the varieties of English currently in use in the San Francisco Bay Area (chapter 3) contains ample evidence for the importance of the lexicon in the listing of variety characteristics. Varieties like Fraternity Talk, Gaytalk or Juvenile Speech rely very heavily on their lexicons in order to establish a difference to other varieties of English. And a more broadly defineable variety like Black English, which is often characterized by listing the points at which its phonology and syntax differs from Standard English, also has a vocabulary that is structured quite differently from that of Standard English or any other comparable variety. The holistic definition of grammar aims at a description of the total knowledge a fluent speaker has of his language; and that certainly includes the lexicon as a vital component. Accordingly, in a varieties grammar of English, the lexicon cannot be excluded. If grammar is not understood as a formalism merely describing the generation of sentences, but as an account of language also serving

13 CHOMSKY, in his Immanuel Kant Lectures, Stanford University, February 1979, had no doubts that only cognitivists qualify as true linguists. That modern-age linguists have more often been logicians and psychologists than students of language in use, interested more in abstract mental exercises than in primary data, is something CHOMSKY would not deny but qualify, in fact, as the proper job of linguists.

as a directory for appropriate language use and a key to understand language correctly, variety specific dictionaries are essential.[14]

4.3.2.2 Cultural distance between varieties

In chapter three it was repeatedly pointed out that there are whole lists of vocabulary items characteristic of individual varieties. Either these lists are particular to the variety in question or they are used with particular meaning. It would appear that of the various devices language has to code conceptual categories, words are the most important, certainly the most obvious. Other such devices are grammatical units like function words and function morphemes, word formation patterns, intonation features, speech genres and discourse conventions. These are, however, mostly part of closed systems and less adaptable to reflect changes in culture than the open-system items of the vocabulary. MACKEY (1972:136) finds that the «conceptual categories coded in the vocabulary, in the nouns, verbs, adjectives, adverbs and other form-classes, cover everything that man can see, feel, and imagine». The research project reported by him is directly relevant to our discussion here. MACKEY examines the adaptation of a single language to the evolution of two cultures by studying the vocabularies of the two dialects. His example is French, the two varieties are two dialects of Modern French (of France and of Canada). Obviously, the case of the varieties of English examined in chapter three is not comparable in all instances. Neither the Black nor the Chicano population, e.g., can be traced back to England (or the US East Coast, for that matter) as the Acadians of Canada can be traced back to France. On the other hand, however, Mellowspeak, as a special variety of California English, if compared to General American, is surely on the same level as MACKEY's example. Irrespective of whether their present-day speakers can be traced to a common

14 Although in modern definitions of grammar, the lexicon is not usually included, it is not possible to do without it. Even generative grammar cannot see the lexicon in opposition to grammar, but has it integrated into the total grammar – the lexicon containing the lexical units, or formatives, of the language.

place of origin, MACKEY's point is also valid for all the varieties of English: The conceptual categories coded in the vocabularies of language varieties can be examined to detect differences in the cultural environments of the speakers of these varieties. New words may come into use, others may disappear, and yet others may take on new meanings.

Conceptual categories can be used to measure the distances and differences between cultures as conveyed by different varieties of the same language. The differences, MACKEY assumes, would be «reflected in the names used to segment the realities of the environment and the words used most readily – those which come to the minds of most people in the community.» (1972:138) MACKEY uses 'diversity' and 'intensity' as indices to measure the cultural distance between two varieties. In order to measure the degree of diversity in a category present in one culture (expressed in one variety) in comparison with that of the same category in another culture (expressed in another variety), MACKEY establishes seven types of equivalence (1972:139f.):

Table 8 Cultural distance between varieties expressed through variety lexicons MACKEY's seven types of equivalence (1972:139f.)

(1)	X	X	Two cultures may have the same name for the same thing.
(2)	X^x	X^a	The two cultures may have the same name (X) for two different things (x, a).
(3)	X	A	The two cultures may have different words for the same thing.
(4)	X	O	The two cultures may have different things and different names.
(5)	X	A B	A word representing one conceptual category in one culture may be equivalent to several conceptual categories in another.
(6)	X^x	X^x X^a	The same word may cover a larger semantic category in one culture than in another.
(7)	X	X, A	One word referring to one thing in one culture may be equivalent to several words referring to the same thing in another.

In addition to knowing whether a conceptual category exists in one culture and not in another, MACKEY finds that «one must also know how important the conceptual category is in a given culture at a given time,» (1972:140) i.e., its intensity or degree of availability must be measured. In a varieties dictionary, therefore, the entries should bé indexed with respect to the frequency of their use. For, as MACKEY observes, «People are more familiar with objects that form an important part of their culture than with those that do not» and they «tend to name familiar categories more readily than unfamiliar ones.» (1972:140)

4.3.2.3 Marking of lexical items

The main problem to be addressed, then, is the question how vocabularies can be integrated into a varieties grammar. If one turns to existing dictionaries and word lists, one discovers that they do have a system for marking the entries. Dictionaries use markers to flag a given word as, e.g., regional, archaic, non-standard, colloquial, etc. This system of marking appears to be basically useful although to the extent it is applied in existing dictionaries, it is not accurate enough yet for the purposes of a varieties grammar. Words must be given indices that unequivocally associate them with one or several varieties. Apart from single words, idioms and other fixed expressions consisting of more than one word would be dealt with in the same way.

Dissatisfaction with the marking of lexical items in conventional dictionaries is voiced by MAKKAI (1976). His experience with available dictionaries of English is exactly what a varieties grammar of English with a scope including the lexicon would like to remedy. That is why MAKKAI's account is quoted here at some length. (1976:52–53)

> Some years back I looked up once the entry *maverick* in five leading dictionaries. The definitions conformed with what I knew about the term, and one dictionary even gave me the story of how it arose. (. . .) Two of the five dictionaries consulted also gave the marking US which made me think that this term was only used in the United States. Two weeks later I happened to be in London, England, and heard the television newscaster characterize a rebel Member of Parliament thus: *That indomitable old maverick voted against the Prime Minister's program.* 'Aha' – I said to myself, maverick has been borrowed over into British English. And apparently so it has. No dictionary has made that adjustment in its marking of the entry, however, Then I looked up the entry *hominy grits* to see how it was treated. It said in all five diction-

> aries US and some gave descriptions how it was made of what ingredients. I subsequently tried to order it in a Boston restaurant, then in New Haven, Connecticut, and later in Chicago. Most of the time the waiters simply stared me in the face, only one Chicagoan had the nerve to say 'Hey, Mister, you gotta be kiddin', we ain't in the State of Mississippi aroun' here!' And so it goes. Americanisms are not necessarily only Americanisms, and when they are, they are by no means universally understood in the United States. On the other hand, no dictionary that I ever came across, at least so far, indicates if a term is exclusively British either. It is almost as if the British forms were regarded as the 'unmarked' ones which everyone has the duty of recognizing, with the Americanisms somehow marked for regionalism. Consulting the *American Heritage Dictionary* one learns that the term *perambulator* is 'chiefly' British. But what does the term *chiefly* really mean? What is the margin of usage of *perambulator* (or *pram* for short) in the United States? Zero? Limited to the urban intellectual elite of the East Coast? Only Boston? What about Canada? Australia? New Zealand? Have New Zealanders borrowed the Americanism *baby carriage,* or do they walk their infants in British *prams?* Of course one generally believes that Commonwealth countries use the British term predominantly, but as the case of *maverick* clearly shows, that is not necessarily so either. I have asked many Australians about *pram* and *baby carriage* and the vote was amazingly even: Some knew that *baby carriage* was an actually borrowed 'Americanism' but insisted that they used it regularly instead of *perambulator-pram* which some characterized as 'limey'. If, in the *American Heritage Dictionary,* one tries to look up how to say 'commit a social blunder in speech' there is literally no way to find the appropriate expression since neither *social* nor *blunder* is cross-referenced with any such expression. It is merely by chance that one finds *put one's foot in one's mouth* under the entry *foot.* There is no indication whether it is an Americanism, a Commonwealth expression of common currency, or what. It turns out that in England one says *he really dropped a brick, didn't he?* when they mean to say that someone committed a social blunder. (. . .) (S)ome British speakers might say *he put his foot in it* but not *in his mouth.* (. . .) Similarly, I tried *he dropped a brick* on countless Americans only to find that with the exception of an elderly lady living in Boston nobody got the picture. (. . .)

What is lacking in these dictionaries is a marking of lexical items (morphemes, words, phrases) according to varieties. Only if the user of a dictionary knows where, when, and how a certain term applies is he well served at all. Instead of the unsatisfactory dictionaries around, MAKKAI, in his paper, proposes an 'Ecological dictionary of English', in which lexical items would be indexed for national areas, dialect areas within national areas, sociological stratification of speakers within national and dialect areas, stylistic range of terms, etc. If a form in this dictionary is universally recognized and used in all the national areas, MAKKAI would mark it *NAun,* meaning 'universally understood in all the national areas'. If, by contrast, a form is restricted to the United States, MAKKAI would mark it *NA/USexcl.* meaning that it is exclusively used in the United States of America. And if a form has sporadic use in a number of national areas, MAKKAI would mark it, e.g., *X NA/US, AU, NZ,* meaning that it is used in the United States of America, in Australia, and in New Zealand, but not in the other national areas. If a term is restricted to a particular dialect area within a national area, it would be so marked. MAKKAI's example, *hominy grits,* would be marked *USexcl. So,* meaning that it is restricted to the South of the United States. If a certain form is used or recognized by a certain educational, social, or economic class within a given dialect area, it could be marked as such. According to MAKKAI, a given form X could then be listed, e.g., as *Cockney cab driver, London, England.*

MAKKAI's proposal for an 'Ecological dictionary of English' appears to be well conceived to satisfy the needs of a varieties grammar of English. By means of a marking system using the labels of the varieties in question, the dictionary of any variety can be selected from a kind of superlexicon. The procedure can be seen in analogy to that applying to the selection of rules from a supergrammar discussed above. As in variable rule methodology, the entries for variety specific dictionaries should be accompanied by indices giving their frequency of use in a given variety. In this way, one of the errors made by people unfamiliar with dialectological work could be avoided. Word lists established by dialectologists do not want to say that in a given dialect area only or mainly the words marked as characteristic of that dialect are used; all they want to say is that these words are in use in that area, whereas in other areas they are not, or not to the same extent. But there may be less conspicuous entries in the dictionary of that dialect with much higher frequency counts. Therefore, appropriate verbal behavior can be indicated only if frequency counts are attached to the individual terms in the lexicon. Sceptics might point out that such a proposal is utopistic. There is hope, however, that modern computer technology will soon make it possible for a varieties dictionary to become realistic and feasible.

The extension of the varieties grammar to include the lexicon still makes it possible to preserve the notions of a language as a family of varieties, of the family as a whole having a 'potential' from which the items making up individual varieties can be selected and of the 'common core' as that area in which there is overlap between the varieties considered. Since the lexicon is expandable indefinitely, however, this part of the varieties grammar would always be open-ended. It may be said, however, that if typolectal lexicons are noticed to include a conspicuous number of new terms or give new or different meanings to existing terms, the varieties grammar would be so re-organized as to make room for an additional variety. This is one of the reasons that make it advisable to conceive of varieties grammars only as *ad hoc* grammars. (See 4.4.5.3)

4.3.3 Linguistic Ethnography

4.3.3.1 Introductory

In recent years, linguistic ethnographies labelled either 'ethnographies of communication' or 'ethnographies of speaking' have been put forward as conceptual frameworks effecting a re-integration of linguistics, anthropology, and folklore (HYMES, 1962; GUMPERZ and HYMES, 1964; 1972; BAUMAN and SHERZER, 1974; 1975; SHERZER, 1977). SHERZER (1977:44) defines the ethnography of speaking as «a description in cultural terms of the patterned uses of language and speech in a particular group, institution, community, or society.» Often, in research associated with the ethnography of speaking, linguistic patterns have been equated with ritual and ceremonial speech events more than with everyday uses of language. It can be assumed, however, that in the future further speech events and routines will be focussed on. While the ethnography of speaking so far has only studied spoken language, it is also possible to consider set patterns of written (e.g. literary) language. Thus, a varieties grammar of a holistic orientation will be able to detail the routines of the varieties it includes, whether written or spoken.

Especially, it will catalog the speech genres occurring in particular varieties; it will indicate the way in which routines differ from group to group or text type to text type; how routines differ in settings characterized by topic, participants, or channel. While lexicographers can contribute to a varieties grammar by listing the entries for the various variety dictionaries and affixing these with frequency counts, linguistic ethnographers make available the lists and the characterizations of the routines, the typical ways of expression, found in the language of particular varieties. Inclusion of the ethnography of speaking into an approach to a varieties grammar is necessary because it provides that grammar with the cultural matrixes for the various varieties. Recent work by John GUMPERZ (1977, 1978, 1979b), e.g., shows that apparent linguistic ambiguities can be resolved in most cases if the relevant frame is known and the seemingly ambiguous items can be placed within their proper varieties.

4.3.3.2 Communicative competence

Knowledge of «the patterned uses of language and speech in a particular group, institution, community, or society» (SHERZER, 1977:44) is part of 'communicative competence', originally advanced by Dell HYMES (1967). Through the concept of communicative competence language is approached in holistic terms as required by a varieties grammar. Communicative competence can be defined as the knowledge and ability to express oneself linguistically in contextually appropriate ways, i.e. in ways that acknowledge the existence of language varieties. It is, as HYMES has repeatedly pointed out, more than a matter of using correct grammar (in the narrow sense); it also involves the knowledge of strategies of communication, of the norms valid within a community and the proper interpretation of communicative signals. Although a varieties grammar does not aim primarily at a full description of inter-personal communication, it nevertheless integrates essentials of communicative competence. For competence in a varieties grammar is to be clearly distinguished from the definition of competence prevalent in current grammatical theory. HYMES formulated the concept of communicative competence as an extension of CHOMSKY's much narrower notion of linguistic competence. Competence for CHOMSKY and most current grammar theory denotes the speaker-hearer's implicit knowledge of his language; it is separated from and contrasts with the use of language in concrete situations, which CHOMSKY calls performance. Competence, in CHOMSKY's sense, only deals with the speaker's ability to produce, out of a finite set of rules, an infinite number of grammatical sentences. However, a person having only such narrowly defined linguistic competence would not know when, where, and how to apply the sentences he can generate. He would be an 'innocent', unexperienced in the use of language. (FILLMORE, 1979a) Still, there is no urgent need to do away with CHOMSKY's notion of competence, but it has to be subsumed under the broader notion of HYMES' communicative competence, in which there is room not only for syntax and semantics, but also for pragmatics. As MUNBY (1977:232) has put it: «HYMES' formulation, by incorporating grammatical (along with sociocultural, etc.) under communicative competence as one of its parts, emphasizes the all-important relationship, rather than the pedagogically less relevant contrasts, between the grammatical and the sociocultural and psycholinguistic aspects of a person's competence.»

The holistic definition of grammar covers competence in the broad sense of the term. Rules about appropriate verbal behavior state which sentence structures, which lexical items, which narrative and conversational routines, etc. belong to which variety. If discrepancies between variety specific rule systems are considerable, misunderstandings can arise. This is true, obviously, in the case of EFL speakers who have been trained in Textbook English only and therefore often fail to understand texts encoded in other varieties or cannot express themselves appropriately according to varying contexts. It is also true, apparently, in the case of native speakers of English. Since schools generally represent only the system of one language variety, children who do not speak Standard English may not fully understand the rule system operating within their classroom; and teachers may misunderstand the meaning potential of some of their students. To master more than one language variety, to know which is situationally appropriate is important for any speaker, native or foreign-born. GUMPERZ

(1967:4) adduces an example which we may use here to illustrate this point. He quotes a white teacher of a century ago reporting an interchange with southern Negro boys: «I asked a group of boys one day the color of the sky. Nobody could tell me. Presently the father of one of them came by, and I told him their ignorance, repeating my question with the same result as before. He grinned. «Tom, how sky stan'?», «Blue», promptly shouted Tom.»» Since the boys only speak Gullah, the plantation Creole of the Caroline Coast current a century ago, and the teacher only speaks the Standard English of his time, communication is very difficult. It needs the help of an interpreter. Even less radical differences between varieties may bring about a break-down in communication. In cases like those referred to in chapter 3.9 where sentence structure and even lexicon are practically identical, it is only the sociocultural part of competence that can relieve the after-Babel effects of linguistic diversity.

4.3.3.3 Ways of speaking

Within the ethnography of speaking one proposal appears to be especially suited to the needs of a varieties grammar. It is Dell HYMES' suggestion to describe language as various ways of speaking. Exploring language in terms of ways of speaking is HYMES' contribution to mend the «principled schizophrenia» of linguistics, i.e. the compartmentalization of the scientific and social goals of its practitioners. (1973:60)

Ways of speaking can be interpreted as being similar to varieties bundled together in speech repertoires. They «comprise speech styles, on the one hand, and contexts of discourse, on the other, together with the relations of appropriateness obtaining between styles and contexts. Membership in a speech community consists in sharing one or more of its ways of speaking – that is, not in knowledge of a speech style (or any other purely linguistic entity, such as language) alone, but in terms of knowledge of appropriate use as well. There are rules of use without which rules of syntax are useless. Moreover, the linguistic features that enter into speech styles are not only the 'referentially-based' features usually dealt with in linguistics today, but also the stylistic features that are complementary to them and inseparable from them in communication.» (HYMES,

1973:67) The way HYMES speaks of ways of speaking is comparable to the way I speak about varieties. In my account, varieties are to be described holistically combining statements about the internal organization of a variety with statements about the context in which it operates and the cultural load expressed by it. HYMES also mentions members of a speech community «sharing one or more ways of speaking»; this is analogous to my suggestion that people participate in one or more varieties. Since ways of speaking can be shared, they are interpretable as typolects. The main differences between HYMES' approach and mine (as I see it) has to do with HYMES' emphasis on spoken interactive language, while I would also include written language.

If varieties are viewed as ways of speaking, then it is possible to bring 'intralinguistic' and 'extralinguistic' matters together in a unifying approach. In preceding sections I have repeatedly emphasized that differences between varieties of a language like English cannot be described as differences in linguistic structure alone. There is a high probability that such differences reflect different worlds, or help to shape or constitute such worlds. Whatever one's stance with regard to the Sapir/Whorf hypothesis of linguistic relativism, there can hardly be any doubt that «community differences extend to the role of language in naming the worlds they help to shape or constitute» (HYMES, 1973:74). As noted in the section on the lexicon, too, descriptions of language varieties are bound to «reveal basic cultural values and orientations» (HYMES, 1973:75), not only differences in phonology and syntax, but differences in lifestyles as well.

4.3.3.4 Co-occurrence rules

The typolectal approach to a varieties grammar assumes that once a variety is selected by a speaker-hearer it remains the vehicle of communication until new contextual factors make it necessary to select a different variety. The principle of homogeneity within heterogeneity put forward above does not only favor typolects over idiolects but also implies that varieties are to be considered stable entities without internal variation to be accounted for. Although this assumption is part of the idealization process necessary for setting up a varieties grammar, it cannot be denied that the stable use of a variety, i.e. style consistency, is part of linguistic competence. In order to meet the requirements of a typolect in a varieties grammar, style consistency is to be defined in terms of statistical idealization and in terms of co-occurrence rules. We can speak of style-consistency[15] when these co-occurrence rules are observed. «Once a selection has been made (. . .), later occurrences within the same utterance, conversation, or even between the same dyad may be predictable. Whenever there is predictability between two linguistic forms, we can speak of co-occurrence rules.» (ERVIN-TRIPP, 1972, based on GUMPERZ, 1967) In a given variety, co-occurrence rules operate to make lexical items fit sentence structure, pronunciation or spelling, etc. as appropriate. An example of violated co-occurrence rules and of the resulting style inconsistency is quoted in chapter 2 (p. 57). The working of co-occurrence rules is illustrated by GUMPERZ and HERASIMCHUCK (1973:99 ff.). They discuss these three sentences:

(1) They are holding a meeting to discuss the issue.
(2) They are getting together to talk it over.
(3) They're sittin' down to rap about it.

which are referentially equivalent. Nevertheless, they cannot be mixed at will:

(4) They're hav'n' a meet'n' to discuss the issue.
(5) They are sitting down to rap about it.

(4) and (5) are found to be strange or impossible because they violate ordinary stylistic co-occurrence restrictions. The sentences (1) to (3), in my account, belong to different varieties, and therefore their particular linguistic structure (here: morphology, syntax, lexicon) is also associated with meaning. It is this social or cul-

15 Style consistency can be defined in terms of statistical idealization. It would not mean that individual speakers need observe a style consistency of 100 all the time. LABOV (1966) showed that neither upper-middle-class nor lower-class speakers have such total consistency in their use of a variety. Nevertheless, LABOV was able to hypothesize certain styles, against which the performances of individuals could be checked.

tural meaning which exercises the co-occurrence restrictions observable in the examples.

Particulars of co-occurrence rules were also studied by FISHER (1958), NEWMAN (1964) and LABOV (1966) and others. In these studies the following co-occurrence relationships were documented:

- lexicon and sentence structure
- lexicon and morphology
- grammatical morphemes and phonology
- style and phonology
- structural elaboration and culturally valued situation
- degree of abbreviation and in-group communication

The research on co-occurrence rules mentioned here corroborates the claim made throughout this study that the grammar of language varieties must be envisaged in holistic terms. Obviously, the linguistic system of a variety is incomplete if the grammar only formulates rules about the selection of phonological and morphological variants and forms of sentence structure; rules about the appropriate selection of lexical items, about stylistic devices like abbreviation and elaboration, about text organization and discourse conventions, etc., must be specified as well. LAKOFF (1979a), in her program for a 'grammar of style', has extended the notion of co-occurrence rules to include even cultural behavior:

> A person given to pontification on large and abstract issues of great universal and philosophical relevance, most likely, will employ an elaborately Latinate and convoluted vocabulary as well as a rather Germanic syntax wherewith to express these thoughts: there is an expected co-occurrence of lexical, syntactic, and semantic material.
>
> A person given to asking questions where others might use declaratives can be expected also to employ euphemistic modes of speech on any topic that might be embarrassing, and might further engage in a lot of linguistic hedging (I guess; sorta; y'know). Here we find co-occurrence of syntactic and lexical patterns. (LAKOFF, 1979a:55)
>
> Someone who dresses conservatively and very carefully can be expected to use language carefully and equally precisely.
>
> Someone who divides humanity into black and white also, cognitively, divides ideas into right and wrong, with no grey areas in either case. (LAKOFF, 1979a:56)

Similarly, in a varieties grammar, co-occurrence rules indicate that different levels of language organization (like phonology, morphology, syntax, text linguistics) must be appropriately matched not only with lexicons and text types or speech genres, but also with cultural values and orientations as they may be expressed in particular varieties. This is not to say that linguistic grammar is to be subsumed under behavioral grammar (as in LAKOFF's 'grammar of style'), but that the idea of grammar is to be extended to those areas of culture that are perceived to be expressed in language varieties.

4.4 Conclusions

4.4.1 Definition of Variety

In chapter 2.4 language varieties were defined in terms of their possible classification as either local-regional, social-educational, functional-stylistic (all of these labels applying synchronically) or historical (diachronic). All through the study, such varieties were further defined as typolects showing consistency and coherency. By consistency I mean that they are stable entities that may be used by individual speakers or writers, but that are not directly affected by the idiosyncrasies of these users. By coherency I mean that typolects are restricted by co-occurrence expectations across the various layers of language. In these concluding remarks I want to further elucidate my definition of variety within a varieties grammar by bringing it into line with the definition of variety given or implied in some recent work in stylistics: (a) with CRYSTAL and DAVY (1969), (b) with Prague School functional stylistics.

CRYSTAL and DAVY (1969) distinguish eight dimensions of situational constraints on the structuring of language:

A: individuality, dialect, time
B: discourse
C: province, status, modality, singularity

Within these dimensions, further subcategorization is possible, such as:

Province: legal, religious, etc.
Status: formal, informal, etc.

While I do not consider 'individuality' and 'singularity', I can nevertheless agree with most of what CRYSTAL and DAVY have to say. They suggest that «Different dimensions will have different numbers of categories. A switch in the categories at any one dimension (. . .) thus by definition produces a different variety.» (1969:82–83) Accordingly, they define variety as «a unique configuration of linguistic features» displaying «a stable formal-functional correspondence». (1969:82) This is a definition of variety I can subscribe to. It allows CRYSTAL and DAVY to speak of a variety as 'the language of X'; e.g. the language of science, the language of law, the language of civil service, and, on a lower level, the language of legal documents, the language of Catholic mass, etc. All these 'languages of X' are examples of typolects; they display «stable formal-functional correspondences». The listing of their linguistic features characterizes not just one legal document (e.g.), but legal documents generally; further subcategorization would make it possible to isolate the variety of 'British legal documents written after World War II', etc. Stylistic analysis, according to CRYSTAL and DAVY, should lead to the explicit determination of varieties in given samples of the English language. The same goal could be reached by consulting a varieties grammar of English listing the linguistic characteristics of all and any variety of English; checking of the sample text against the labeled inventory of the grammar would lead to the identification of the sample as an example of 'the language of X' or the 'language of Y'.

Prague School functional stylistics investigates «variable factors (contexts), both individual and social, in order to explain the preference of one alternative (A) in context X, of another alternative (B) in context Y, etc.» (DOLEZEL, 1968:144f.) While Prague School functional stylistics also considers the individuality factor (which I do not), supra-individual (objective) styles appear to be much more important in their work. These supra-individual styles are comparable to typolects. «Objective styles reflect the impact of social style-forming factors on human communication. Those factors are independent of individual speakers, being immanent to certain text forms or text functions.» (DOLEZEL, 1968:146) One kind of objective style is 'genre', which DOLEZEL interprets in the fashion of literary criticism, thus stretching 'objective style' to include such varieties as 'the language of the Breton Lai' or 'the language of the Tail-Rhyme Romance' (to adduce two examples of genre from Middle English literature). That typolects may be looked upon as the language varieties typically employed in certain literary genres, is a point I have hinted at in chapters 2 and 4 above.[16]

4.4.2 Definition of Grammar

«A grammar accounts for the knowledge that a fluent speaker of a language possesses», this is a definition of grammar on which a varieties grammar can be built. The knowledge a fluent speaker-hearer has of his language, does not only include rules to produce grammatical sentences, but also to produce grammatical discourse. This knowledge enables him to fit language to contexts of use by selecting the appropriate linguistic items on all the relevant levels of language (from phonology to text typology). In a varieties grammar, the notion of grammaticality also covers that of appropriateness, in so far as it uses the concept of co-occurrence as a criterion to define grammaticality/appropriateness. In sentence grammar, non-grammatical results are achieved, if, e.g., (1) number agreement is violated, (2) if tense agreement is not observed, (3) if semantic categories are juxtaposed contrary to universal meaning constraints.

(1) The girls was there.
(2) I shall write to you yesterday.
(3) Colorless green ideas sleep furiously.

In a varieties grammar such co-occurrence restrictions do not only ensure the proper syntactic-semantic organization of sentences,

16 In DÜRMÜLLER (1974) I dealt with the linguistic characteristics (mainly textual) of one literary genre, the shorter Middle English Tail-Rhyme romances. Material presented there could be used to illustrate a typolectal genre.

but the appropriate selection of a certain variety. A grammatical sentence like

(4) I shall write to you tomorrow

is still ungrammatical (inappropriate) in a variety in which the future is expressed by means of *gonna.* And another grammatical sentence

(5) The girls were there

is still inappropriate if the variety in question would have *chicks* instead of *girls.* Thus, a varieties grammar relates linguistic units to classes of varieties. It can do so by indicating how certain forms of one variety are re-written in another variety, e.g.

Black English	Standard English
Johnny car	→ Johnny's car
her lazy	→ she's lazy
[tɪŋk]	→ [θɪŋk]
[nəfin]	→ [nʌθɪŋ]

but its holistic orientation makes it necessary for a varieties grammar to go beyond the conventional scope of grammar (as illustrated in these examples) and write similar rules (if possible) for higher-order units of language organization, for lexical and text-type selection, for discourse conventions, etc.

While grammars in general attempt to describe objectively and systematically the knowledge that a fluent speaker possesses of his language, a varieties grammar allots linguistic items to variously labeled varieties so that the grammar can reflect the varieties repertoire of a speaker and the knowledge he has of the appropriate use of language according to different varieties.

4.4.3 Code Switching in terms of a Varieties Grammar

In a varieties grammar of English, the characteristics of the various varieties would not simply be listed (as envisaged by CRYSTAL and DAVY, 1969), but compared and related to each other in terms of a unifying theory. Practical considerations limit the scope to a few varieties only. Realistic varieties grammars would be set up *ad hoc*, as it were. (cp. 4.4.6) A simple case of such a limited varieties grammar is that which can be written for what has been called code-switching. Sociolinguists have suggested that speakers can switch from one code or register to another according to certain communicative factors.[17] Within the framework of a varieties grammar, such code-switching can be seen as the change from one variety to another, provided the language from which the varieties are selected is the same in both cases. Indeed, shifting from one variety to another has been attested not only in the case of bilingual speakers (e.g. English–Spanish; cp. Chicano English, chapter 3.4), but also in the case of monolingual speakers, where it is called style or dialect switching.

It has been said that dialects should not be considered codes, since there are no direct translation equivalents among codes as there are between dialects, (HAWKINS, 1977:206f.) the reason being that only dialects can be derived from underlying syntactic structures while codes are strategies derived from underlying speech functions. In a varieties grammar, however, where variety selection depends on contextual factors and appropriateness conditions, every kind of variety can be regarded as code. Thus a varieties grammar of English might be set up to mirror the repertoires of speakers switching from, say, Black Vernacular English to Academic Standard English, or of speakers switching between formal and informal English, or to mirror a repertoire of varieties defineable as literary genres. The switching might be the actual switching of people (e.g. inhabitants of the San Francisco Bay Area, ca. 1980), or it might be the switching done by a reader of different texts when turning from one text type to another. Whether the focus is on speakers or writers, or listeners or readers, the English language provides them all with a set of alternative varieties

17 LABOV does not adopt this view because he sees variation as inherent to the system. It occurs at regular intervals and can be expressed in variable rules. LABOV also opposes the possibility of dialect mixture in codes. However, he would agree that speech situation and other social factors largely determine variation. He sees a problem in the fact that variation might occur in individual speech even in one particular situation. Such idiolectal variation, however, does not show if, instead of individuals, groups are examined.

to choose from. Much research has centered on the development of such alternative systems in the linguistic repertoires of children. ERVIN-TRIPP (1973), e.g., reports a two-year-old's shift according to whether it is speaking to dolls or to infants. SHATZ and GELMAN (1973) document how four-year-olds use more complex sentence structures when addressing adults than when speaking to their peers, and even simpler forms when addressing two-year-olds. They appear to switch between varieties that can be described in terms of graded elaboration in ways similar to those identified by HAMILTON (1975; cp. below 4.2.4.5). LEGUM et al. (1971) show that Black children, too, may switch from one variety to another, selecting different grammatical features according to the age of the persons they are interacting with. All these studies (for further examples see ANDERSEN, 1977) adduce evidence for something obvious: Code switching or variety switching is part of ordinary everyday linguistic behavior right from the initial phase of linguistic acculturation onward. The awareness that language varieties correlate with settings or topics or characteristics of partners in conversation appears to develop quite early in the process of language acquisition. The communicative competence of speakers of English certainly includes the possibility for code-switching. An *ad hoc* varieties grammar of English would reflect the linguistic knowledge of such speakers by listing the rules not only of one variety, but of two, three, four (or more) varieties making up the repertoire in question. It would show which rules remain in operation when speakers switch from variety A to variety B, which rules are altered, which added, which deleted. In accordance with the holistic notion of a varieties grammar, these rules would contain the appropriate information on all the relevant features of language operating to create the significant differences between the varieties considered.

4.4.4 ESP in terms of a Varieties Grammar

While for the native speaker of English the building-up of a repertoire of varieties is part of the natural process of language acquisition, speakers of other languages, if they are trained in English, only learn one variety of English, Textbook English or Standard Academic English. However, speakers of English as a Foreign Language (EFL) are also in need of a variety repertoire, both for better understanding and for more appropriate communication (see chapter 2).

A recent development in English Language Teaching (ELT) attempts to alleviate the unsatisfactory situation so many EFL speakers find themselves in. English for Special Purposes (ESP) aims at the teaching of clearly identified typolectal varieties of English in addition to the standardized Textbook English. Very frequently, in modern schools, ESP becomes EST (English for Science and Technology), providing the students with information about varieties like 'English for Airline Pilots', 'English for Computer Programmers', etc. But ESP may also teach the English of certain literary genres or 'The English of the American Blacks'. In short, as STREVENS says (1972), ESP is an umbrella term that can be made to cover just about every aspect of ELT. What is important to ESP is that the study of English should be made more practical and functional for the learner; that knowledge of the English language should be geared towards the student's specific needs as, e.g., when travelling to English-speaking countries, when studying particular genres of English literature, when preparing himself for a job which necessitates command of a certain register, etc.

It is often said that ESP can be added to the 'common core' of the basic course in Textbook English. The 'common core' referred to by English language teachers, however, is not identical with the 'common core' of a varieties grammar (cp. 4.1.3) Courses in Standard English train students in a specific variety of English, only part of which is made up of the 'common core' also shared by other varieties. Given a varieties repertoire of, say, Standard Textbook English and two ESP varieties, the core part common to the three varieties can be identified. After such rectification of the school notion of 'common core', ESP can easily be handled within the framework of a varieties grammar. The grammar would indicate which items and rules already learnt in the basic course are transferable into the special variety added in the ESP program, which must be altered, which deleted, which added. Considering the broad variety of Scientific English, it becomes clear that a varieties grammar would have to give directions not only about the lexicon, but about what has been summarily called rhetorics, too. Scientific English would be characterized, among other features, by:

- extensive use of the passive voice: depersonalization
- word class shifts, especially between nouns and verbs
- extension of rules for word-formation: fewer restrictions with regard to compounding; lists of modifying prefixes and suffixes, possibly including frequency counts
- additional rules for plural formation of nouns derived from Greek or Latin
- use of tense to express generalization or specifity

As in the case of code-switching, a varieties grammar would be set up *ad hoc* so as to serve the specific needs of students and teachers in ESP and ELT programs. While such varieties grammars are descriptive of certain variety repertoires, they can, in the context of language instruction, also be used prescriptively.

4.4.5 Varieties Grammar and Contrastive Analysis

Although contrastive analysis (CA) has been traditionally applied in the comparison of different languages, the method can also be applied in the comparison of different varieties of the same language. If so, CA is the method whereby the differences between two (or more) varieties are made explicit; identical areas, by implication, are also included. CA is mostly considered part of applied linguistics, being motivated mainly by the need of language teachers to uncover relevant areas of difference between the language or variety taught and the language or variety spoken by the students. The following areas are usually singled out for CA: sound systems, writing systems, vocabulary systems, syntactic structures, cultures; other areas might be added.

A contrastive approach to English language varieties was implied in LABOV's et al., (1968) study of Vernacular Black English in New York City, and, more strongly, in FASOLD and WOLFRAM's (1970) contribution to *Teaching Standard English in the Inner City,* as well as in BARTLEY and POLITZER's (1972) *Standard English for Speakers of Non-Standard Dialects.* Walt WOLFRAM, to my knowledge, was the first scholar to relate CA openly to language varieties, especially sociolects, and variation theory (1978). As a variationist of the Labovian school, WOLFRAM discusses the quantitative dimension in what he calls 'contrastive social lectology' and demonstrates the relevance of variable rule methodology for a unified, though still contrastive, approach to language varieties. CA may thus very well be carried out within the framework of a varieties grammar. If this varieties grammar is defined in terms of the Labovian model, CA is implied from the start. CA, however, need not be bound to any particular approach. As a branch of applied linguistics, it may be carried out in an eclectic way. For the type of varieties grammar envisaged here, CA offers the possibility to deal efficiently with those aspects of language neglected in grammatical theory (including variationist theory). Although, at present, a kind of generative-transformational model is probably the most suitable to CA, CA is also done in purely structuralist, or quite informal terms. If language variation is detected, the procedure of CA is to describe a number of specific varieties and then to extrapolate what is shared (the common core) and what is different (the variety specific features). DI PIETRO (1976a:29–30) shows one possibility to list the steps to be taken in CA:

(1) observe the differences between the surface structures
(2) postulate underlying universals
(3) formulate the deep-to-surface (realizational) rules

Like DINGWALL (1964), DI PIETRO thinks that working with deep and surface levels is extremely useful in CA. His awareness of the limitations of TGG – voiced, e.g., in DI PIETRO, 1976b – makes him complement the final apparatus of conversion rules by a taxonomy of contrasts.

When reviewing models purporting to do justice to language variation (above, 4.2), I pointed out the shortcomings of all these models with regard to their coverage of all the areas relevant for a descriptive characterization of language varieties within a varieties grammar, in particular lexical systems and linguistic units larger than the sentence. These limitations, it appears, can be overcome if taxonomies are accepted in the varieties grammar in order to complement the set of conversion rules covering phonology and syntax; points of difference in other areas could then simply be listed. As in CA, the comparison of language varieties could thus be extended beyond the coverage of grammar in the narrow sense to include features of the cultural systems represented by the varieties in question. This option of CA is taken in 4.4.6.4, where it leads to the 'transformational-additive model'.

4.4.6 *The Scope and Form of a Varieties Grammar*

4.4.6.1 Generalities

A varieties grammar can be read as a grammar of choice. People are viewed as selecting one variety over another because this particular variety is understood to be the appropriate one in a given situation (chapter 2, fig. 5, p. 61). Following HALLIDAY (1978:5) we can say that «the structure of sentences and other units is explained by derivation from their functions» in a wider context.

Although a varieties grammar wants to provide a framework for a unified approach to diverse language varieties, it is basically comparative-contrastive and cross-cultural. A varieties grammar shows how particular groups of speakers, or situations, or literary genres, etc., demand their own linguistic code due to their own specific socio-cultural input. A sketch of varieties as typolects illustrates what is similar and different between varieties – much as in language typology; and by concentrating on the common core shared by different varieties, it can point out the manifestations of the language characteristics of all the varieties – much as in language universals.

A varieties grammar makes use of the concept of the verbal repertoire. It takes for granted that language is heterogenous and consists of a multitude of generic varieties. These varieties, however, due to a process of statistical idealization, are again seen as homogenous (typolects). A varieties grammar reflects the fact that language is not only dynamic and variable, but, in its important social and cultural manifestations, also quite stable, a vehicle of communication made to be used by more than one. It follows

Gumperz' observations on communication (1971:224) as «a two-step process, in which the speaker first takes in stimuli from the outside environment, evaluating and selecting from among them in the light of his own cultural background, personal history and what he knows about his interlocutors, in order to decide on the social norms that apply to the situation at hand. These norms then determine the speaker's selection from among the communicative options available for encoding his intent.» In a varieties grammar these options are seen as culturally standardized in the form of typolects. The selection by a speaker of the communicative options available to him is interpreted as his selection of a particular variety in which he is going to participate (at least for a while); he is going to monitor his verbal behavior (and, if necessary, his general cultural behavior as well) according to supra-individual norms.

4.4.6.2 Coverage

A varieties grammar does not only account for the creation of correct sentences, but sees sentences in the wider context of texts, and texts within cultural frames indentified by the variety label. In addition to particulars of phonology, morphology, and syntax a varieties grammar may list types of texts and speech genres, with frequency counts concerning their occurrence in given varieties, textual characteristics, like statistical regularities concerning, say, mean sentence length; type-token ratios for lexical items; frequency counts of words taken from particular vocabulary fields; characteristic transformations, types of surface organization, ways of distributing background and foregorund information (cp. Fillmore, 1974); discourse routines, rules of address and leavetaking, etc. So far there exists no single grammar model that would include all the levels of language as required by a holistic varieties grammar. While rules concerning phonology, morphology, and syntax can probably be formulated in terms of generative dialectology, variable rule methodology, or a Klein grammar, problems of grammar writing arise in the textual and cultural parts of a varieties grammar. Once one moves outside the conventional areas of grammar, the problems of notation are not solved yet. Formal grammar writing, however, is possible only with the help of an adequate notational system. A typolectal kind of varieties grammar needs a notational system which allows the consistent coverage of all the areas included according to its holistic orientation. Solutions to these problems might come from text grammars, from formalizations developed out of discourse analysis, and from explorations into the possibilities of writing the grammars of literary genres and of styles (cp. WEHRLICH, 1976; CLUYSENAAR, 1977; OHMANN, 1964; TRAUGOTT and PRATT, 1980; LAKOFF, 1979a). In view of the still existing problems in notation and formalization, it might be advisable to abandon the idea of writing a formal grammar and resort to an informal one; i.e. the individual varieties would be described not in terms of an abstract formalism, but in terms of a set of descriptive statements giving direct information about the variety in question. Such an informal procedure would make it quite easy to include even further relevant points, like worldview and lifestyle characteristics of the typical speakers of a particular variety, and the cultural embedding of that variety in general. All this means that, at least for the time being, a varieties grammar of English would have to be approached in an eclectic or simply taxonomic way. As George LAKOFF has put it, «The problem with all current theories is that they are just too weak to deal with most linguistic phenomena.» (1974:XI-35) Taken individually and applied to certain areas of grammar only, such theories might be quite powerful. The point therefore is, not to posit a situation of rivalry between linguistic models, but to use them in combination with each other, each in that area where it has its best possibilities.

4.4.6.3 The Varieties Grammar as an Ad Hoc Grammar

Another problem a varieties grammar has to cope with is the enormous amount of data it is expected to store. To provide all the material needed for a complete varieties grammar of English cannot be the job of any man alone. Modern technology, however, has made it possible to store data in machines. But even with the help of the modern computer at hand, it is still beyond the powers of man to put at our disposal a data bank containing all the information about all the varieties of English. Again, since nobody knows how many varieties of English there are, the job of gathering data would never come to an end.

What is reasonable and what can be done, however, is the storing of variety data according to repertoire clusters. A varieties grammar of English can be written, e.g., for a repertoire of clearly specified English language varieties current in the San Francisco Bay Area ca. 1980 (synchronic), or a repertoire of English educational language varieties through time (diachronic). Further simplification of such *ad hoc* varieties grammars can be achieved if the varieties included are fully comparable in scope. This restriction may need some amplification. The terms 'variety' and 'typolect' have been left open on purpose to cover such disparate kinds of language varieties as dialects, genres, jargons, styles. Obviously, there are differences of scope and dimension. Dialects, e.g., may have subvarieties like jargons and styles, while any of these might not have any subvarieties at all. The simplest type of a varieties grammar would be envisaged for a repertoire of varieties that have comparable scope, e.g.,

(1) British English
American English
Australian English

(2) Standard English
Black English
Chicano English

(3) Aelfredian Old English
Ricardian Middle English
Elizabethan Early Modern English

(4) The English of White Teenagers in Boston
The English of Black Teenagers in Watts
The English of Chinese-American Teenagers in San Francisco

(5) The language of Old English prayers
The language of Middle English prayers
The language of Modern English prayers

(6) The English of lawyers
The English of physicians
The English of educators

'Ad hoc' may also be understood in a different sense. The levels of language included may differ from one type of varieties grammar to another, depending on the kinds of varieties considered. While in (5) there is obviously no need (and no possibility) for a complete listing of speech act realizations – praying being the only one to be considered –, such a list would point out essential differences between the varieties of repertoire (4). Specialized lexicon will be important for (4), (5) and (6); intonation for (1), (2), and (4); speech genres for (4), text types for (3), etc.

There would thus not be one single varieties grammar of English; but there would be several *ad hoc* grammars, each written for two or more varieties. There are two models I can propose for the structure of such grammars: (1) the 'transformational-additive' model, and (2) the 'potential-selection' model.

4.4.6.4 The Transformational-Additive Model

Both terms, 'potential-selection' and 'transformational-additive' reflect the process by which the grammar of a single variety is obtained from the overall varieties grammar. While in the 'potential-selection' model the way is simply to select V_X from the overall inventory of the potential, the 'transformational-additive' model is more complex. Its apparatus reflects the conclusions reached in the preceding sections that none of the existing models can deal with all the aspects of language that seem to be relevant to the codification of a variety in a varieties grammar. Following the suggestions made by Di Pietro for contrastive analysis (see 4.4.5), the transformational-additive model has two parts:

(1) a transformational grammar for phonology, morphology and syntax, and

(2) a catalog of features and general characteristics of individual varieties outside the areas covered in (1)

In part one, the common core of the varieties grammar is interpreted as a kind of deep structure underlying the various surface forms of the individual varieties. The grammar then works along the lines of the models developed for generative dialectology (see 4.2.2). In part two, the transformational grammar is complemented with a taxonomy of contrasts, containing the additional information needed for a particular varieties repertoire, e.g. information on spelling conventions, prosodic features, speech acts, speech and textual genres and their structure, lexicon, cultural values.

The 'transformational-additive' model is openly eclectic and, since it borrows from contrastive analysis, intended to be useful in applied linguistics, especially language (variety) instruction, i.e. in cases like those mentioned in chapters 1 and 2.

4.4.6.5 The Potential-Selection Model

The 'potential-selection model' is based on KANNGIESSER's notion of the 'potential' discussed above (4.1.3.1) and that of KLEIN's 'reference grammar' (4.2.5). Here, the meaning of 'potential' and 'reference grammar' is extended beyond what both KANNGIESSER and KLEIN had envisaged, so as to account for the full knowledge a fluent speaker possesses of his language and the varieties he uses (see 4.4.2). This extended potential is to be thought of as a data pool fed by descriptive surface form data of various varieties (limited according to the specific varieties repertoire for which the grammar is to be set up) and yielding, by means of a speaker-writer's or listener-reader's selection of variety X, not only grammatical sentences, but also appropriate pronunciation habits, the appropriate dictionary, the appropriate discourse routines and conversational strategies, the text types or speech genres needed, even the cultural values and orientations expressed in X. In short, it is supposed to make available the manual requested by FILLMORE's outside god (cp. p. 147f.). With all the information contained in that manual at hand, the speaker-writer or listener-reader could then proceed to encode a text into X or decode another text from X.

The potential must be thought of as consisting of several parts, separating the inventories of graphemes, phonemes, morphemes, words, set phrases, sentence types, text types, conversational routines, cultural values, etc. The 'potential-selection' model presupposes a description of the varieties included in a particular *(ad hoc)* varieties grammar according to a unified organizational plan. The data are to be made available in the format of a unified description[18] listing everything needed for a reliable manual of any of the varieties to be stored. Items in the inventories would be indexed with variety labels so that, in the case of the lexicon, e.g., entries might look like this:

policeman$^{V_{1,4,5}}$
cop $^{V_{2,3}}$
copper ^{V_7}
dick ^{V_6}

In addition, all these entries might be affixed with frequency counts. Rules for phoneme realization, word-formation or sentence formation contained in the potential would be numbered from 1 to x, with indexes for the individual varieties accompanying every entry. Thus, in a given part, the rules might be ordered like this:

${}_1V_{1,2,3,\dots}$
${}_2V_{3,\dots}$
${}_3V_{1,2,\dots}$
${}_4V_{1,2,3,7,\dots}$
${}_5V_{2,3,5,\dots}$
${}_6V_{1,3,5,6,\dots}$
${}_7V_{2,3,6,7,\dots}$ etc.

yielding an output for varieties like this:

V_1: rules 1,3,4,6, . . .
V_2: rules 1,3,4,5,7, . . .
V_3: rules 1,2,4,5,6,7, . . . etc.

The complete set of rules selected from the potential, together with the complete set of units selected from the potential inventory, produce the surface realizations of the language characteris-

18 A model-neutral proposal for a uniform-format grammar was made by BLANDSITT (1976). It is advertised here because it is straightforward, realistic and geared towards a lucid description of grammatical structures.

tic of the variety in question. The 'potential-selection' model ideally mirrors the way a fluent speaker competently selects a segment of language according to the factors perceived as constituting language varieties (cp. chapter two, Figure 5, p. 61). As a model of grammar it is taxonomic. If variety X is selected, all the linguistic items labeled (indexed) X in the potential will be at the speaker-writer's or listener-reader's disposal, so that speech or writing can be encoded or decoded in the variety-specific way; discourse or text will be identifiable as being in variety X.

The 'potential-selection' model may appear to be quite simple. This, in my view, is certainly to its credit. The main objection is therefore probably not directed against its workability, but at its validity as a model for a varieties grammar. After all: Isn't it just that the data of an accurate and complete description of, say, Black English, are stored into a computer, and that, since this computer has been programmed correctly, it will give back the same data if so required? And isn't it true that the same procedure also applies in the case of any other variety that is to be included? What then is the difference between the mechanism of the 'potential-selection' model and the old-fashioned consultation of separate manuals of Black English and other varieties of English? The answer to that kind of objection is to point out that, since the 'potential-selection' model makes use of a unified description and a unified terminology, comparison of the structures of the various varieties is possible without further processing. The features shared by all the varieties are easily obtainable, and equally the features shared only by two (or more) varieties. A printout of the common core (surface manifestation) of any two, or more, or all varieties included can be obtained readily. The indexing of the entries according to varieties also allows a printout of those features particular to any one variety. Although it is removed from the framework of generative grammar KANNGIESSER was working in, the 'potential-selection' model can nevertheless be defined in terms of KANNGIESSER's potential and standard. It still qualifies as a model for a varieties grammar and has clear advantages over the separate consultation of varieties manuals.

References

ABRAHAMS, Roger D. 1962. Playing the Dozens. Journal of American Folklore, 75:209–210.

ABRAHAMS, Roger D. 1964. Deep Down in the Jungle. Hatboro. Pa.: Folklore Associates.

ADAMS, Ramon F. 1936. Cowboy Lingo. Boston.

ADAMS, Ramon F. 1944. Western Words. Norman.

ALLEN, H. B. and UNDERWOOD, G. N. (edd.), 1971. Readings in American Dialectology. New York.

ANDERSEN, Elaine. 1977. Learning to speak with style. A study of the sociolinguistic skills of children. Ph. D. dissertation, Standford University.

BAILEY, Charles-James N. 1973. Variation and Linguistic Theory. Arlington, Va.: Center for Applied Linguistics.

BAILEY, Charles-James N. 1974. Contributions of the Study of Variation to the Framework of New Linguistics. Linguistische Berichte 29:1–10.

BAILEY, Charles-James N. 1978. Native Accent and Learning English as a Foreign Language. IRAL 16:229–240.

BAUMAN, Richard. 1977. Linguistics, Anthropology and Verbal Art: Towards a unified perspective, with a special discussion of children's folklore. GURT 28:13–36.

BARATZ, J. C. 1969. A bi-dialectal task for determining language proficiency in economically disadvantaged Negro children. Child Development 40 (3), 889–901.

BARTH, F. 1969. Ethnic Groups and Boundaries. Introduction. Boston: Little, Brown & Co.

BARTLEY, D. E. and POLITZER, R. L. 1972. Practice-Centered Teacher Training: Standard English for Speakers of Nonstandard Dialects. Philadelphia: Center for Curriculum Development.

BERDAN, Robert. 1971. Polylecial comprehension and the polylectal grammar. In: FASOLD, R. W. and SHUY, R. (eds.), Studies in language variation. Georgetown University Press. Pp. 12–29.

BERDAN, Robert. 1973. The necessity of variable rules. In: FASOLD, R. W. and SHUY, R. (eds.), Analyzing variation in language. Washington, D. C.: Georgetown University Press. Pp. 11–26.

BERDAN, Robert. 1975. On the nature of linguistic variation. Unpubl. Ph. D. dissertation. University of Texas, Austin.

BERDAN, Robert. 1980. Idealizations in the Development of a Sociolinguistic Theory. In: PERRY, Th. A. (ed.), Evidence and Argumentation in Linguistics. Berlin/New York: de Gruyter. Pp. 73–93.

BEREITER, Carl and ENGLEMANN, S. 1966. Teaching disadvantaged children in the preschool. Englewood Cliffs, N. J.: Prentice-Hall.

BERNSTEIN, Basil. 1971. Class, codes and control, 1: theoretical studies towards a sociology of language. London: Routledge and Kegan Paul.

BICKERTON, Derek. 1971. Inherent variability and variable rules. Foundations of language, 7:457–492.
BICKERTON, Derek. 1973. The nature of a creole continuum. Language, 44: 640–669.
BLANDSITT, Ed. L., Jr. 1976. A unified format for grammatical description. LACUS Forum 1975:44–51.
BLOM, J. P. and GUMPERZ, J. J. 1972. Social meaning in linguistic structures: Code switching in Norway. In Gumperz and Hymes, 1972:407–434.
BLOOMFIELD, Leonard. 1933. Language. New York: Holt.
BORST, Arno. 1957–63. Der Turmbau zu Babel: Geschichte der Meinungen über Ursprung und Vielfalt der Sprachen und Völker. Stuttgart.
BRENNEIS, Donald. 1977. 'Turkey', 'Wienie', 'Animal', 'Stud': Intragroup Variation in Folk Speech. Western Folklore 36:235–246.
BRIGHT, Elizabeth S. 1971. A Word Geography of California and Nevada. Berkeley: University of California Publications in Linguistics, 69.
Bureau of the Census. 1970. General Population Characteristics. California. U.S. Dept. of Commerce.
CARDEN, Guy. 1973. Dialect variation and abstract syntax. In: SHUY, R. (ed.), Some new directions in linguistics. Washington, D. C.: Georgetown University Press. Pp. 1–35.
CARRINGTON, L. D. 1976. Deforming Language Education Policy in Carribbean Sociolinguistic Complexes. Linguistics 175:27–43.
CEDERGREN, H. J. and SANKOFF, D. 1974. Variable Rules. Performance as a statistical reflection of competence. Language 50:333–355.
CHIHARA, Tetsuro and OLLER, John W. Jr. 1978. Attitudes and attained proficiency in EFL: A sociolinguistic study of adult Japanese speakers. Language Learning 28 (1): 55–67.
CHOMSKY, Noam. 1957. Syntactic Structures. The Hague: Mouton.
CHOMSKY, Noam. 1965. Aspects of the Theory of Syntax. Cambridge, Mass.: MIT Press.
CHOMSKY, N. and HALLE, M. 1968. The sound pattern of English. New York: Harper and Row.
CLUYSENAAR, Anne. 1976. Introduction to Literary Stylistics. London: Batsford.
Conference of Composition and Communication. 1974. Students' Rights to Their Own Language. College Composition and Communication, special issue.
CORREA-ZOLI, Yole. 1970. Lexical and morphological aspects of Italian in San Francisco. Diss., Stanford University.
CRYSTAL, D. and DAVY, D. 1969. Investigating English Style. London: Longman.
CRYSTAL, D. and FLETCHER, P. 1979. Profile analyses of language disability. In: FILLMORE, Ch. J., KEMPLER, D. and WANG, W. S-Y (eds.), Individual Differences in Language Ability and Language Behavior. New York/San Francisco: Academic Press. Pp. 167–188.
DAVIES, Ossie. 1972. The English Language Is My Enemy. In: SMITH, A. L. (ed.), Language, Communication and Rhetoric in Black America. New York: Harper and Row.

De Camp, David. 1958–1959. The Pronunciation of English in San Francisco. Orbis VII: 372–391; VIII: 54–77.

De Camp, David. 1968. Toward a generative analysis of a post-Creole speech continuum. MS. Rev. version in Hymes, D., 1971, Pidginization and creolization of languages, CUP, pp. 349–370. (= 1971a)

De Camp, David. 1970. Is a sociolinguistic theory possible? GURT 21:157–73.

De Camp, David. 1971a. Toward a generative analysis of a post-creole continuum. In: Hymes, D. (ed.), Pidginization and Creolization of languages. Cambridge University Press. Pp. 349–370.

De Camp, David. 1971b. Implicational scales and sociolinguistic linearity. Linguistics 73:40–43.

Dillard, J. L. 1972. Black English: Its History and Usage in the United States. Random House.

Dingwall, W. 1964. Transformational-generative grammar and contrastive analysis. Language Learning, 14:147–160.

Di Pietro, Robert J. 1976a. Language Structures in Contrast. 2nd edition. Rowley, Mass.: Newbury House.

Di Pietro, Robert J. 1976b. The strategies of Language use. LACUS Forum 1975:462–467.

Dolezel, Lubomir. 1968. Russian and Prague School Functional Stylistics. Style, 2:143–158.

Dubois, Betty Lou. 1976. Societal and Linguistic Correlates in an Investigation of the English Writing of a Selected Group of University Level Chicanos. In: Mackey, W. F. and Ornstein, J. (eds.), Sociolinguistic Factors in Language Contact. Quebec: Laval University.

Dundes, Alan. 1975. Slurs International: Folk Comparisons of Ethnicity and National Character. Southern Folklore Quarterly, 39:15–58.

Durbin, Marshall. 1972. Sociolinguistics: An approach to functional grammar. In: Ghosh, S. K. (ed.), Man, Language, and Society. The Hague: Mouton. Pp. 51–63.

Dürmüller, Urs. 1975. Narrative Possibilities of the Tail-Rime Romance. Swiss Studies in English, 83. Bern: Francke.

Dürmüller, Urs. 1981. What Is a Varieties Grammar. CAL-ERIC ED 208 692.

Edwards, Allison J. and Doviak, M. J. 1975. Linguistic Constraints on Variation in Chicano English. MS. Paper deli vered at Winter SLA, San Francisco.

Englemann, S. 1970. How to construct effective language programs for the poverty child. In: Williams, F. (ed.), Language and Poverty. Chicago: Markham.

Ervin-Tripp, S. 1964. An analysis of the interaction of language, topic, and listener. In: Gumperz and Hymes, 1964.

Ervin-Tripp, S. 1968. Sociolinguistics. Working Paper No 3, Language Behavior Research Laboratory, Univ. of California, Berkeley.

Ervin-Tripp, S. 1972. On Sociolinguistic Rules: Alternation and Co-occurrence. In: Gumperz and Hymes, 1972:213–250.

Ervin-Tripp, S. 1973. Children's sociolinguistic competence and dialect diversity. In her Language acquisition and communicative choice. Stanford University Press. Pp. 262–301.

FALK, Jane and LAKOFF, R. in preparation. Marin English. Dept. of Linguistics, University of California, Berkeley.

FASOLD, Ralph W. 1970. Two modes of socially significant variation. Language 46:551–563.

FASOLD, Ralph W. 1972. Tense Marking in Black English: A linguistic and social analysis. Washington, D. C.: Center for Applied Linguistics.

FASOLD, Ralph W. 1978. Language veriation and linguistic competence. In: SANKOFF, 1978:85–96.

FASOLD, R. W. and WOLFRAM, W. 1970. Some linguistic features of Negro Dialect. In: FASOLD, R. W. and SHUY, R. (eds.), Teaching Standard English in the Inner City. Washington, D. C.: Center for Applied Linguistics.

FERGUSON, Charles. 1977. Linguistics as Anthropology. GURT 28:1–12.

FILLMORE, Charles J. 1972. A grammarian looks to sociolinguistics. GURT 23:273–287.

FILLMORE, Charles J. 1974. Pragmatics and the description of discourse. Berkeley Studies in Syntax and Semantics, I: V.

FILLMORE, Charles J. 1979a. Innocence: A second idealization for linguistics. Proceedings of the Berkeley Linguistics Society, 6:63–76.

FILLMORE, Charles J. 1979b. On Fluency. In: FILLMORE, Ch., KEMPLER, J. D. and WANG, W. S-Y (eds.), Individual differences in language ability and language behavior. New York: Academic Press. Pp. 86–101.

FISHER, J. 1958. Social influence on the choice of a linguistic variant. Word, 14:47–56.

FISHER, J. 1964. Formal lexicon and «-ing». Ellipsis and informal style. In: HYMES, D. (ed.), Language in culture and society. New York.

FISHMAN, Joshua A. 1971. Advances in the sociology of language, 1. The Hague: Mouton.

FISHMAN, Josua A. 1972. The sociology of language. Rowley, Mass.: Newbury House.

FISHMAN, Josua A. 1973. Historical dimensions in the sociology of language. GURT 23:145–155.

FISHMAN, J., COOPER, R. L. and CONARD, A. W. 1977. The Spread of English. The Sociology of English as an Additional Language. Rowley, Mass.: Newbury House.

FOLB, Edith. 1980. runnin' down some lines, the language and culture of black teenagers. Harvard University Press.

GODINEZ, Manuel and LINDAU-WEBB, M. 1980. Reliable phonetic differences between dialects. Chicano and General Californian English. Paper presented to American Dialect Society, summer meeting, July 16–17, University of New Mexico.

GREGORY, M. 1967. Aspects of Varieties Differentiation. Journal of Linguistics 3 (2), 177–198.

GRICE, H. P. 1975. Logic and Conversation. In: COLE, P. and MORGAN, J. L. (eds.), Syntax and Semantics III. New York.

GUDDE, E. G. 1969. California Place Names. Third edition. Berkeley and Los Angeles: University of California Press.

GUMPERZ, John J. 1966. Linguistic repertoires, grammars, and second language instruction. GURT 18:81–90

GUMPERZ, John J. 1967. Sociolinguistics and communication in small groups. Working Paper No 33, Language Behavior Research Laboratory, University of California, Berkeley.

GUMPERZ, John J. 1970. Verbal strategies in multilingual communication. Working Paper No 36, Language Behavior Research Laboratory, University of California, Berkeley. (= 1971a).

GUMPERZ, John J. 1971a. Verbal strategies in multilingual communication. In: GURT 23, Washington, D. C.: Georgetown University Press.

GUMPERZ, John J. 1971b. Language in social groups. Stanford University Press.

GUMPERZ, John J. 1972. Introduction to Directions in Sociolinguistics, edd. J. J. GUMPERZ and D. HYMES, New York: Holt, Rinehart and Winston.

GUMPERZ, John J. 1977. Sociocultural knowledge in conversational inference. GURT 28:191–211.

GUMPERZ, John J. 1978. The conversational analysis of interethnic communication. MS. University of California, Berkeley.

GUMPERZ, John J. 1979a. The role of dialect in an urban community. MS. University of California, Berkeley.

GUMPERZ, John J. 1979b. The sociolinguistic basis of speech act theory. MS. University of California, Berkeley.

GUMPERZ, John J. 1979c. Language and Society. Lectures. University of California, Berkeley.

GUMPERZ, J. J. and HYMES, D. (eds.). 1964. The ethnography of communication. American Anthropologist, 66 (6), Part. 2.

GUMPERZ, J. J. and HYMES, D. (eds.). 1972. Directions in Sociolinguistics. New York: Holt, Rinehart and Winston.

GUMPERZ, J. J. and ROBERTS, C. 1978. Developing Awareness Skills for Interethnic Communication. Southill, Middlesex: National Centre for Industrial Language Training.

GUMPERZ, J., JUPP, T. C. and ROBERTS, C. 1979. Crosstalk. Southall, Middlesex: The National Centre for Industrial Language Training.

GUMPERZ, J. and HERNANDEZ, E. 1971. Bilingualism, Bidialectism and Classroom Interaction. In: CAZDEN, C., JOHN, V. and HYMES, D. (eds.), The Functions of Language in the classroom. New York: Teacher's College Press.

GUMPERZ, J. J. and BENNETT, A. 1979. Language and Society. MS. To be published in: ROSSI, I. (ed.), Man in Culture. New York.

GUMPERZ, J. J. and HERASIMCHUCK, E. 1972. The conversational analysis of social meaning: A study of classroom interaction. GURT 23.

HALLE, M. 1962. Phonology in a generative grammar. Word, 18:54–72.

HALLIDAY, M. A. K. 1978. Language as a Social Semiotic. Baltimore: University Park Press.

HALLIDAY, M. A. K. et al. 1964. The Linguistic Sciences and Language Teaching. London: Longmans.

HAMILTON, James. 1975. The People's English. Dubuque, Iowa: Kendall-Hunt.

HARTMANN, R. K. and STORK, F. C. 1973. Dictionary of Language and Linguistics. Barking.

HAUGEN, Einar. 1973. The Curse of Babel. Deadalus 102:47–57.

HAUSMANN, Robert B. 1975. Underlying representations in dialectology. Lingua, 35:61–71.

HAWKINS, P. R. 1977. Social Class, the Nominal Group, and Verbal Strategies. London: Routledge and Kegan Paul.

Heidelberger Forschungsprojekt «Pdgin-Deutsch» (HPD). 1978. The Acquisition of German Syntax by Foreign Migrant Workers. In Sankoff 1978:1–22.

HERMAN, Simon R. 1961. Explorations in the social psychology of language choice. In: FISHMAN, J. (ed.), Readings in the Sociology of Language. The Hague: Mouton. Pp. 412–511.

HERNANDEZ-CHAVEZ, E., COHEN, A. D. and BELTRAMO, A. F. (eds.). 1975. El lenguaje de los Chicanos. Arlington, Va.: Center for Applied Linguistics.

HESS, Karen. 1973. Dialect and Dialect Learning: Where We're At. English Education 5:26–34.

HOEPPNER, J. E. and ROSENFIELD, E. et al. 1977. Experiences in the American Language, Instructor's Manual. Preliminary edition. University Extension, University of California, Berkeley.

HOCKETT, C. F. 1958. A Course in Modern Linguistics. New York: Macmillan.

HOFFER, Bates. 1975. Towards Implicational Scales for Use in Chicano English Composition. In: DUBOIS, B. and HOFFER, B. (eds.), Papers in Southwest English I: Research Techniques and Prospects. San Antonio: Trinity University Department of English.

HUSTVEDT, S. B. 1948. Spanish Elements in the Style of the Los Angeles *Star*. Western Folklore, VII: 1–20.

HYMES, Dell. 1964. Language in Culture and Society. New York: Harper and Row.

HYMES, Dell. 1962. The ethnography of speaking. In: GRADWIN, T. and STURTEVANT, W. C. (eds.), Anthropology and Human Behavior. Washington, D. C.: Anthropological Society of Washington. Pp. 13–53.

HYMES, Dell. 1967. Models of the interaction of language and social setting. Journal of social issues, 23:8–28.

HYMES, Dell. 1968. On Communicative Competence. In: PRIDE, J. B. and HOLMES, J. (edd.), Sociolinguistics. Harmondsworth.

HYMES, Dell. 1969. Linguistic theory and the functions of speech. MS. Published in Proceedings of International Days of Linguistics, Rome 1969.

HYMES, Dell. 1972. The Contribution of Folklore to Sociolinguistic Research. In: PAREDES, A. and BAUMAN, R. (eds.), Toward New Perspectives in Folklore. University of Texas Press.

HYMES, Dell. 1973. Speech and Language: On the Origins and Foundations of Inequality Among Speakers. Daedalus 102:59–85.

HYMES, Dell. 1974. Foundations in Sociolinguistics. Philadelphia: University of Pennsylvania Press.

JANSEN, Hugh. 1965. The Esoteric-Exoteric Factor in Folklore. In: DUNDES, A. (ed.), The Study of Folklore. New Jersey: Prentice-Hall.

JENSEN, Arthur. 1968. Social Class and Verbal Learning. In: DEUTSCH, M., KATZ, I. and JENSEN, A. R. (eds.), The isadvantaged social class, race, and psychological development. New York: Holt, Rinehard and Winston.

JESPERSEN, Otto. 1925. Mankind, Nation, and Individual from a Linguistic Point of View. Oslo-London 1946.

JOOS, Martin. 1962. The Five Clocks. Bloomington.

JORDAN DE CARO, Rosan. 1972. Language Loyalty and Folklore Studies: The Mexican American. Western Folklore 31:77–86.

KANNGIESSER, Siegfried. 1971. Untersuchungen zum Aufbau einer generativen Linguistik. In: WUNDERLICH, D. (ed.), Probleme und Fortschritte der Transformationsgrammatik. München, Hueber. Pp. 24–46.

KANNGIESSER, Siegfried. 1972. Aspekte der synchronen und diachronen Linguistik. Tübingen: Niemeyer.

KAY, Paul. 1978. Variable Rules, Community Grammar, and Linguistic Change. In: SANKOFF, 1978:71–84.

KAY, Paul and MCDANIEL, C. 1979. On the logic of variable rules. Language in Society, 8:151–187.

KEYSER, S. 1963. Review of KURATH, A. and MCDAVID, R. I. The Pronunciation of English in the Atlantic States. Language 39:303–316.

KLEIN, Wolfgang. 1974. Variation in the Sprache. Ein Verfahren zu ihrer Beschreibung. Kronberg/Ts.: Scriptor.

KLEIN, W. and DITTMAR, N. 1978. = Heidelberger Forschungsprojekt «Pidgin-Deutsch».

KLIMA, E. S. 1964. Relatedness between grammatical systems. Language, 40:1–20.

KOCHMANN, Thomas. 1969. Culture and Communication: Implications for Black English in the Classroom. Florida FL Reporter, 7.

KURATH, Hans. 1949. A Word Geography of the Eastern United States. Ann Arbor.

LABOV, William. 1966. The social stratification of English in New York City. Washington, D. C.: Center for Applied Linguistics.

LABOV, William. 1969. Contraction, deletion, and inherent variability of the English copula. Language, 45:715–762.

LABOV, William. 1970. The logic of nonstandard English. GURT 20:1–44. (= 1972d).

LABOV, William. 1971. Methodology. In: DINGWALL, W. O. (ed.), A Survey of Linguistics Science. University of Maryland Press.

LABOV, William. 1972a. Language in the Inner City. Philadelphia: University of Pennsylvania Press.

LABOV, William. 1972b. Where do grammars stop? GURT 23:43–88.

LABOV, William. 1972c. On the mechanism of linguistic change. In: GUMPERZ and HYMES, 1972: 512–537.

LABOV, William. 1972d. The logic of nonstandard English. In: GIGLIOLI, P. P. (ed.), Language and social context. Harmondsworth. Pp. 179–215.

LABOV, William. 1972e. Sociolinguistic Patterns. Conduct and Communications. 4. Philadelphia.

LABOV, William. 1976. Some principles of linguistic methodology. Language in Society, 1:97–120.

LABOV, William. 1978. Where does the linguistic variable stop? A response to Beatriz Lavandera. Sociolinguistic Working Paper No. 44, Southwest Educational Development Laboratory. Austin. Texas.

LABOV, W., COHEN, P., ROBBINS, C. and LEWIS, J. 1968. A study of the nonstandard English of Negro and Puerto Rican speakers in New York City. Cooperative research report no. 3288 (2 vols.). U.S. Office of Education (ERIC ED 028 423).

LAKOFF, George. 1974. Interview with Herman Parret. Berkeley Studies in Syntax and Semantics, I: XI.

LAKOFF, George. 1980. Image Schemas. Paper delivered to Cognitive Science Seminar. University of California, Berkeley.

LAKOFF, G. and JOHNSON, M. 1979. Toward an experientalist philosophy. The case from literal metaphor. MS. University of California, Berkeley.

LAKOFF, Robin. 1979a. Stylistic Strategics within a Grammar of Style. Annals of the New York Academy of Science: 53.

LAKOFF, Robin. 1979b. «Marin English». Talk delivered to a Charles Fillmore Seminar. Dept. of Linguistics, University of California, Berkeley.

LAVANDERA, Beatriz. 1978. Where does the sociolinguistic variable stop? Language in Society, 7:171–182.

LEGUM, St., PFAFF, C., TINNIE, G. and NICHOLAS, M. 1971. The speech of young black children in Los Angeles. Technical Report no 33. Inglewood, Calif.: Southwest Regional Laboratory.

LEHMANN, W. P. 1972. Historical Linguistics. An Introduction, second ed. New York: Holt, Rinehart & Winston.

LIPPMANN, Walter. 1922. Public Opinion. New York: Harcourt, Brace & Co.

LODGE, David. 1980. Where It's At: California Language. In: MICHAELS, L. and RICKS, Chr. (eds.), The State of the Language. Berkeley: University of California Press.

LOFLIN, Marvin D. 1967. A note on the deep structure of nonstandard English in Washington, D. C. Glossa 1:26–32.

LOFLIN, Marvin D. 1969. Negro Nonstandard and Standard English: same or different deep structure? Orbis, 18:74–91.

LOFLIN, Marvin D. 1970. On the structure of the verb in a dialect of American Negro English. Linguistics, 39:11–28.

LUCKMANN, T. 1969. Soziologie der Sprache. In: KÖNIG, R. (ed.), Handbuch der empirischen Sozialforschung II. Stuttgart. Pp. 1050–1101.

LUDLOW, Lynn. 1979. Youth lingo. San Francisco Chronicle, April 1: A-1 etc.

LURIE, Margaret A. 1978. Black English Vernacular: a comparative description. In: LURIE, M. and CONCLIN, N. (eds.), A pluralistic nation. Rowley, Mass.: Newbury House.

LURIE, M. A. and CONKLIN, N. (eds.). 1978. A pluraliste nation. Rowley, Mass.: Newbury House.

MA, Roxanna and HERASIMCHUCK, E. 1968. Linguistic dimensions of a bilingual neighborhood. In: FISHMAN, J. A. (ed.), Bilingualism in the Barrio. HEW, Dept. of Education.

MACKEY, William F. 1972. Concept Categories. In: GOSH, S. K. (ed.), Man, Language, and Society. The Hague: Mouton. Pp. 134–168.

MAJOR, C. 1970. Dictionary of Afro-American Slang. New York: International Publications.

MAKKAI, Adam. 1976. Toward an Ecological Dictionary of English. LACUS Forum 1975: 52–59.

MARTIN-JONES, M. 1978. Spoken English Usage. Teacher's Notes. Stanford. Mimeo.

MCDAVID, R. I. Jr. 1970. A Theory of Dialect. GURT 22:45–62.

MCDAVID, R. I. Jr. 1975. Review of E.S. Bright, A Word Geography of California and Nevada. American Speech 50:114.

MCDAVID, R. I. Jr. 1979a. Review of LABOV, W. Language in the Inner City, and Sociolinguistic Patterns. American Speech 54:291–304.

MCDAVID, R. I. Jr. 1979b. American English: A bibliographic essay. American Studies International, 17:3–45.

MCFADDEN, Cyra. 1978. The Serial. New York: American Library.

METCALF, Allan A. 1972. Mexican-American English in Southern California. Western Review, 9:13–21.

METCALF, Allan A. 1974. The Study of California Chicano English. Linguistics 128:53–58.

METCALF, Allan A. 1977. Riverside English. Dept. of English, University of California, Riverside.

METCALF, Allan A. 1979. Chicano English. CAL-ERIC.

MITCHELL-KERNAN, Claudia I. 1971. Language Behavior in a Black Urban Community. Monograph No. 3, Language Behavior Research Laboratory, University of California, Berkeley.

MOULTON, W. G. 1960. The short vowel systems of Northern Switzerland: A study in structural dialectology. Word 16:155–182.

MOULTON, W. G. 1976. The Sounds of Black English. In: HARRISON, D. and TRABASSO, T. (eds.), Black English, A Seminar. Hillsdale. N.J.

MUNBY, John. 1977. Applying sociocultural variables in the specification of communicative competence. GURT 28:231–247.

NEWMAN, S. 1964. Vocabulary Levels: Zuni Sacred and Slang Usage. In Hymes 1964:397–406.

NEWTON, Brian. 1972. The generative interpretation of dialect: A study of Modern Greek phonology. Cambridge studies in linguistics, 8. London: Cambridge University Press.

OGAWA, D. N. 1969. Small Group Communication: Stereotypes and actual communicative behavior of Japanese Americans in discussions. UCLA Speech Dissertation.

OHMANN, Richard. 1964. Generative grammars and the concept of literary style. Word 20:423–439.

ORNSTEIN, Jacob and MURPHY, R.F. 1974. Models and approaches in sociolinguistic research in language diversity. Anthropological linguistics, 16: 141–167.

ORNSTEIN, J. and DUBOIS, B. L. 1977. Mexican-American English: Prolegomena to a neglected regional variety. LACUS 1976 Conference Paper.

ORNSTEIN, J. and PENFIELD, J. 1980. Homogeneity of Phonological/Grammatical Variants of Mexican-American English in a 5-State-Area. Paper delivered to ADS Summer Meeting, University of New Mexico.

PEI, Mario. 1967. The Many Hues of English. New York: Knopf.

PENFIELD, Joyce. 1980. Stress and Intonation in Mexican-American (Chicano) English. Paper presented to Summer ADS, July 16–17, University of New Mexico.

QUIRK, R., LEECH, G., GREENBAUM, S. and SVARTVIK, J. 1972. A Grammar of Contemporary English. London: Longman.

QUIRK, R. and GREENBAUM, S. 1973. A University Grammar of English. London: Longman.

REED, Carroll. 1977. Dialects of American English. Amherst, Mass.: University of Massachusetts Press.

REYES, Rogelio. 1973. Bilingualism and Language Switching. MS. Harvard University.

REYNOLDS, Anthony M. 1974. Urban Negro Toasts: A Hustler's View from L. A. Western Folklore 33:267–308.

RODGERS, Bruce. 1979. gaytalk. New York: Paragon Books.

RONA, J. P. 1970. A structural view of sociolinguistics. In: GARVIN, P. L. (ed.), Method and Theory in Linguistics. The Hague: Mouton.

ROUSSEAU, P. and SANKOFF, D. 1978. Advances in variable rule methodology. In: SANKOFF 1978: 57–70.

SANKOFF, David. 1975. VARBRUL, version 2. MS.

SANKOFF, David. 1978 (ed.), Linguistic Variation: Models and Methods. New York, San Francisco, London: Academic Press.

SANKOFF, D., THIBAULT, P. and BERUBE, H. 1978. Semantic Field Variability. In: SANKOFF. 1978: 23–44.

SANKOFF, Gillian. 1974. A quantitative paradigm for studying communicative competence. In: BAUMAN, R. and SHERZER, J. (eds.), The ethnography of speaking. London: Cambridge University Press. Pp. 18–49.

SAPORTA, Sol. 1965. Ordered Rules, Dialect Differences and Historical Processes. Language 41:218–224.

DE SAUSSURE, F. 1916. Course in general linguistics. New York: Philosophical Library, 1959.

SCHLEICHER, August. 1861–1862. Compendium der vergleichenden Grammatik der indogermanischen Sprachen. Weimar: Böhlau.

SCHMIDT, Johannes. 1972. Die Verwandtschaftsverhältnisse der indogermanischen Sprachen. Weimar: Böhlau.

SHARPE, Pamela J. 1977. (compl.) Barron's How To Prepare for the Test of English as a Foreign Language. Woodbury, New York: Barron's Educational Series.

SHATZ, M. and GELMAN, R. 1973. The development of communication skills: Modifications in the speech of young children as a function of listener. Monographs of the Society for Research in Child Development, 38.

SHERZER, Joel. 1977. The ethnography of speaking: A critical appraisal. GURT 28:45–57.

SILVERSTEIN, Michael. 1977. Cultural prerequisites to grammatical analysis. GURT 28:139–151.

SIMONICI, Forrest. 1959. The San Francisco Italian Dialect. Orbis 8:342–354.

SMITHERMAN, Geneva. 1977. Talkin and Testifyin: The language of Black America. Boston: Houghton Mifflin.

SMITHERMAN, Geneva. 1979. Toward Educational Linguistics for the First World. College English, 41:202–211.
SMITHERMAN, Geneva. 1980. White English in Blackface, or Who Do I Be? In: MICHAELS, L. and RICKS, C. (eds.), The State of the Language. University of California Press. Pp. 158–168.
STANLEY, Julia P. 1970. Homosexual Slang. American Speech 45:45–60.
STEINER, George. 1976. After Babel. Oxford University Press. Paperback.
STEWART, William A. 1969. Historical and Structural Bases for the Recognition of Negro Dialect. GURT 22.
STOLZ, W. and BILLS, G. 1969. An investigation of the nonstandard dimension of Central Texan English. ERIC-ED 026–130.
STRANG, B. M. 1970. A history of English. London.
STREVENS, Peter. 1972. British and American English. London: Collier-MacMillan.
STREVENS, Peter. 1973. Technical, Technological, and Scientific English. English Language Teaching, 27:223–234.
SVEJCER, Aleksandr D. 1978. Standard English in the United States and England. The Hague: Mouton.
TAMONY, Peter. 1965. Chinaman's Chance. Western Folklore 24:202–205.
TAMONY, Peter. 1966. Shanghai. Western Folklore 25:41–43.
TAMONY, Peter. 1968a. One-armed bandit. Western Folklore 27:117–124.
TAMONY, Peter. 1968b. Sandlot Baseball. Western Folklore 27:265–269.
TAMONY, Peter. 1969a. Hoodlums and Folk Etymology. Western Folklore 28:44–48.
TAMONY, Peter. 1969b. Beat Generation: Beat: Beatniks. Western Folklore 28:274–277.
TAMONY, Peter. 1970. The Hell's Angels: Their Naming. Western Folklore 29:199–203.
TAMONY, Peter. 1971. 1851 Vigilante Daguerrotypes – Modern Mugging. Western Folklore 30:127–132.
TAMONY, Peter. 1972. Chinatown: The Podil. Western Folklore 31:199–203.
TAMONY, Peter. 1973a. Business Names Incorporate Social Change: Levis, Hard Hats, Cats. Western Folklore 32:39–48.
TAMONY, Peter. 1973b. Sourdough and French Bread. Western Folklore 32:265–270.
TAMONY, Peter. 1974. Malarkey: Tad, and its San Francisco Roots. Western Folklore 35:141–148.
TAMONY, Peter. 1976. Skidroads' Skidway to Inner City. Western Folklore 35:141–148.
TARONE, Elaine E. 1973. Aspects of Intonation in Black English. American Speech 48:29–36.
TAYLOR, Danielle. 1976. Black English in Black Folklore. In: HARRISON, D. and TRABASSO, T. (eds.), Black English, A Seminar. Hillsdale, N. J. Pp. 209–225.
TAYLOR, Quintard. 1977. Blacks in the American West. The Western Journal of Black Studies 1:4–10.
THOMPSON, Roger M. 1975. Mexican-American English: Social Correlates of Regional Pronunication. American Speech 50:18–24.

TRAUGOTT, Elizabeth Closs. 1976. Origins of Vernacular Black English. In: HARRISON, D. and TRABASSO, T. (eds.), Black English, A Seminar. Hillsdale, N. J. Pp. 57–93.

TRAUGOTT, Elizabeth and PRATT, M. 1980. Linguistics for students of literature. New York: Harcourt Brace Jovanovich.

TUCKER, C. Allen. 1978. The Chinese Immigrants' Language Handicap. In: LURIE, M. and CONKLIN, N. (eds.), A Pluralistic Nation. Pp. 51–55.

URDANG, Laurence. 1976. Sociolexicography – a proposal for a real dictionary. LACUS Forum 1975: 60–64.

VONNEGUT, Kurt. 1973. Breakfast of Champions. New York: Delacorte Press.

WÄCHTLER, Kurt. 1977. Geographie und Stratifikation der englischen Sprache. Düsseldorf: Bagel.

WALD, Benji. 1976. The process of unmerger in bilingual phonology: the case of the voiceless palatals in the English of Mexican-Americans in Los Angeles. MS, Dept. of Linguistics, UCLA.

WEINGARTEN, J. 1954. An American Dictionary of Slang and Colloquial Speech. New York.

WEINREICH, Uriel. 1953, Languages in Contact. New York: Linguistic Circle of New York.

WEINREICH, Uriel. 1954. Is a structural dialectology possible? Word 10: 388–400.

WEINREICH, U., LABOV, W. and HERZOG, M. 1968. Empirical foundations for a theory of language change. In: LEHMANN, W. and MALKIEL, Y. (eds.), Directions for historical linguistics. University of Texas Press. Pp. 97–195.

WENTWORTH, H. and FLEXNER, S. 1960. Dictionary of American Slang. New York: Crowell.

WERLICH, Egon. 1976. A Text Grammar of English. Heidelberg: Quelle and Meyer.

WILLIAMS, Ronald. 1976. The Anguish of Definition: Toward a New Concept of Blackness. In: HARRISON, D. S. and TRABASSO, T. (eds.), Black English, A. Seminar. Hillsdale, N. J. Pp. 9–24.

WILLIAMSON, J. V. and BURKE, V. M. (eds.). 1971. A Various Language. Perspective on American Dialects. New York.

WINFORD, Donald. 1976. Teacher Attitudes Towards Language Varieties in a Creole Community. Linguistics 175:45–75.

WOLFRAM, Walter W. 1969. A sociolinguistic description of Detroit Negro Speech. Washington. D. C.: Center for Applied Linguistics.

WOLFRAM, Walter W. 1971a. Social Dialects from a linguistic perspective. In: SHUY, R. (ed.), Sociolinguistics. Washington, D. C.: Center for Applied Linguistics. Pp. 86–135.

WOLFRAM, Walter W. 1971b. Black-White Speech Differences Revisted. In: WOLFRAM, W. and CLARKE, N. H. (eds.), Black-White Speech Relationships. Washington, D. C.: Center for Applied Linguistics. Pp. 139–154.

WOLFRAM, Walter W. 1972. Sociolinguistic premises and the nature of nonstandard dialects. In: SMITH, A. L. (ed.), Language, Communication and Rhetoric in Black America. New York. Pp. 28–40.

WOLFRAM, Walter W. 1974. Sociolinguistic Aspects of Assimilation. Puerto Rican English in New York City. Arlington, Va.: Center for Applied Linguistics.

WOLFRAM, Walter W. 1976. The linguistic study of variation in American English. Unpubl. Manuscript.

WOLFRAM, Walter W. 1978. Contrastive Linguistics and Social Lectology. Language Learning, 28:1–28.

WOLFRAM, W. W. and FASOLD, R. W. 1974. The Study of Social Dialects in American English. Englewood Cliffs, N. J.: Prentice-Hall.

WUNDERLICH, Dieter. 1974. Grundlagen der Linguistik. Reinbeck: Rowohlt.